Evans' admir   book conducts an extraordinary conversation between moder-
nity and over   housand years of God-talk by petitioners and prophets, preachers and sch   , and the devout and the visionary. Also invited to her table are
those who !   ve that a high god is of no earthly use, that a monotheistic religion
creates co   ct not consensus, and that the more accessible deities are all too
human. Be   : A Short History for Today will be required reading for historians of
Western rel   ion, for clergy and theologians, and for all those who think that the
less that's sa about God, the better.

Richard K. Fenn
Maxwell M. Upson Professor of Christianity and Society
Princeton Theological Seminary

G.R. Evans is widely respected especially for her work on patristic and medieval
theology, but she has never been afraid to wrestle too with fundamental theological questions such as evil, or to explore issues of great ecumenical importance.
While deploying the remarkable range of her scholarship, *Belief: A Short History for
Today* offers a very substantial essay in apologetics, exploring the topic with great
imagination and philosophical skill. This is a book that deserves to be read again
and again.

Fergus Kerr, OP
*Regent of Blackfriars, Oxford, and Honorary Senior
Lecturer in Theology & Religious Studies, University of Edinburgh*

BELIEF

A Short History for Today

G. R. Evans

I.B. TAURIS

LONDON · NEW YORK

Published in 2006 by I.B.Tauris & Co. Ltd
6 Salem Road, London W2 4BU
175 Fifth Avenue, New York, NY 10010
www.ibtauris.com

ISBN 10: 1 84511 225 3
ISBN 13: 978 1 84511 225 7

A full CIP record for this book is available from the British Library
A full CIP record for this book is available from the Library of Congress

Library of Congress catalog card: available

Typeset in Goudy Old Style by A. & D. Worthington, Newmarket, Suffolk
Printed and bound in Great Britain by TJ International Ltd, Padstow, Cornwall

Contents

Preface

Attempts to answer great questions about where the world came from and where it is heading have given rise to several world religions and the innumerable private explanations people work out for themselves. Interfaith comparisons and a clear understanding of the way each system of belief works have never been so urgent. This book is mainly concerned with Christian beliefs and the way they have been pummelled into shape in the debates of history and emerged into the modern world.

To get a sense of the authentic original quality of Christianity against which to measure all this, we cannot do better than ask what it was that the early Christians found so attractive in Jesus' teaching. The main thing was that it was liberating. It 'worked' as a way of living. Socially it encouraged gentleness, kindness, making up quarrels and repairing misunderstandings straight away. It turned its back on the pursuit of power and wealth and exploitation of the disadvantaged. Christians gave to the poor and supported the weak and sick and visited those in prison. To the individual believer the freedom offered opened up another dimension of experience, an optimism, something to hope for, a sense of life as moving forward towards a 'perfecting' which was also a completion. It took away anxiety and guilt in a moment and offered a way of living supple and flexible, in which the believer could balance unwelcome moods and events and accept and forgive mistakes and misbehaviours. It gave the believer a place in the universe and a sense of taking part in an infinitely greater 'perfecting' involving everyone else (and everything else) in the universe. We cannot now return to the first generation with its fresh recent sense of what Jesus was like and the way he spoke. Yet all these features of this practical and aspiring way of life and belief, with its attractive simplicity, are to be found in the New Testament account and met in living people today.

Events did not go at all smoothly as this system of belief unfolded over the generations. Within a very short time of the death of Jesus his followers were squabbling and losing sight of the clear lines of what he had taught. They began to lose the 'feel' of what he had said. Christianity was never meant to be complicated. It was never meant to be burdensome. Yet it has divided into competing 'versions', and believers have violently rejected other believers and even killed one another in defence of differences of opinion. Christianity has been the subject of passionate argument throughout its 2,000 years. This poses some awkward questions about the validity of a belief system so fragmented and capable of being so destructive, and it makes it extremely important to try to keep the original vision in view.

What went wrong, and has the profound simplicity of the original idea been compromised, or even lost? Can it be recaptured? That is partly a historical question, and without some pointers to the places, times and debates the modern believer may find it hard know where to 'locate' a number of the awkward questions which occur to him or her, and what to think about them. It is not by reading history that an individual comes to belief, but knowing some of the history of belief is like having a map to show you where you are and allow you to make . an informed choice about where to go next and how to get there.

Some readers may come to this book with a different sort of enquiry in mind, seeking to answer or just to 'place' a number of the questions, part philosophical, part religious, which occur to the reflective and may stand in the way of ready acceptance of a system of explanation of life. Enquirers like this are likely to be wondering about another question, whether there has been any 'progress' through all this history. Does it make sense to dismiss older explanations in favour of more modern ones on the grounds that the modern ones are more likely to be right? One of the lessons of studying belief historically it that there are no guarantees about that. The same questions, or very similar ones, recur in each generation, and it becomes obvious that they have not been dealt with by the preceding answers in any final way.

Belief in the sense of holding a set of attitudes or opinions is not the same thing as belief in the sense of having faith. The devils Jesus cast out are said to have recognized him for what and who he was (Mark 1.34). But it made no difference to their response. It did not commit them to him or even convince them that he had a point and that they might benefit from adjusting their approach to life. That story exemplifies the problem that to hold a set of views does not necessarily lead to behaving in a particular way. But it can transform not only the way things look but the experience of life and the way it is lived.

> There must have been something stronger than the stake, the fire, even the habit of twenty years! There must have been an idea more powerful than any disaster, famine, torture, plague, leprosy, and all that hell which mankind could not have borne without that one binding idea which directed men's minds and fertilized the springs of life (Dostoevsky, 1821-81).[1]

This is offered as a guidebook for those who want to understand that 'idea' in the context of Christian history so as to decide what it may mean as a belief for today.

Acknowledgements

The idea for this book was born in conversations in which the vanities of academic 'expertise' have been put to a hard test. Challenged by the intelligent lay thinker, who has been thinking hard and purposefully within the Christian tradition, and with the freedom of not being much afraid that chasms of heresy may open on either side of a narrow path, the academic learns the limitations of his trade. The natural academic response is to begin by helpfully filling in the detail of who said what to whom in which religious controversy, on each topic which arises, only to find that all that 'expert' knowledge can add is a dimension of interest and the rounding out of the picture. The main acknowledgement to be made here is to the 'changing' potential of such talk. It is to be recommended.

Abbreviations

CCCM	Corpus Christianorum Continuatio Medievalis
CCSL	Corpus Christianorum Series Latina
CSEL	Corpus Scriptorum Ecclesiasticorum Latinorum
PG	Patrologia Graeca
PL	Patrologia Latina
S Anselm	*Opera Omnia*, ed. F.S. Schmitt, (Rome/ Edinburgh, 1938–68), 6 vols
ST	Thomas Aquinas, *Summa theologiae* (Alba, 1962)

English translations of the Bible

NEB	New English Bible
RSV	Revised Standard Version
RV	Revised Version

PART I. BELIEVING

Belief is not the same as knowledge. It is both more and less. A believer takes a risk, makes a commitment, which has something more in it than the certainty of 'knowing' what day it is. But there is less security, for the evidence is not of the same kind. I say it is Tuesday and you say it is Wednesday and all we have to do is look at a newspaper to decide who is right. I say there is a God and you say 'Prove it!'

In this first section the would-be believer can get some bearings in the maze of ideas which have been put forward about the reasonableness of belief, the nature of the evidence for belief, the ways in which it is possible to talk about it, and whether it stands up to the challenge of science. In the end the test is probably whether a particular idea chimes or resonates with what an individual finds acceptable. That is not far from the idea of 'self-evidency', that 'feeling right' we all experience when we hear that two and two make four. But it is more subtle and 'allows in' all sorts of awarenesses and confidences and insights.

This book will use the Bible as interpreters have used it though the ages, taking key words and marrying them with certain background ideas which are really assumptions drawn from contemporary philosophy and science; but here the idea will be to illustrate rather than to seek to 'prove' points of belief.

1

What is reasonable?

If there is a God, why does he leave us guessing? An infant deer gets to its feet and runs without the need for explanations from its mother about how to do it and why it should. Why did God not just 'hard-wire' into human beings a built-in knowledge of the way the universe works and how it came into existence? Then there need not be endless uncertainty about whether God exists at all and what part he plays in the cosmos.

These are good questions, and they were already challenging the first Christians. They had three main answers.

The first was the idea that there are benefits in having to strive for knowledge, to stretch and thus to extend oneself in pursuit of a more complete knowledge of God. With this went the notion that as a good teacher God knew that this was the best way for people to grow in understanding, enabling them to embrace freely for themselves what would be much less valuable if it were merely handed out automatically. If we knew it all we should have nothing to hope for, offers St Paul. 'Now hope that is seen is not hope. For who hopes for what is seen?' (Romans 8.24-5). There was the reassurance that God would be helping. 'We know not how to pray as we ought, but the Spirit himself makes intercessions for us' (Romans 8.26, RV). This energetic and demanding approach is endorsed in much more modern times by the philosopher Immanuel Kant (1724-1804), who says that 'reason should not learn from nature like a schoolchild, who merely regurgitates what the teacher wants, but like an authoritative judge, who compels the witnesses to answer the questions he asks them'.[1]

Or does the problem lie with us? It has, secondly, often been argued that this short-sightedness is an unavoidable creaturely limitation. But, in that case, why did a God who could have made things as he pleased choose to set human limitations where he did? Why make us struggle for understanding when he could just have told us what we needed to know and made us capable of understanding?

That prompted the further and third explanation, that human beings would have known God a great deal better and more fully if they had not set up a screen between themselves and him by their bad behaviour.

Whichever of these three explanations has been favoured, and it has usually been a combination of all three, the conventional Christian belief has been that God, angels and humans all think in basically the same way, because all rational minds understand the same rules of reasoning, although of course God, who invented the system, does it best. The assumption is that whether we are looking at a series of experiments designed to test the behaviour of a new drug in clinical trials or a debate about the existence of God, the essential mechanisms of argument rely on the same deep principles. Modern science takes it for granted that the laws of reasoning are universal, for a scientific journal is not culture-specific. Contributors, in whatever language and from whatever part of the world, send in articles relying on the same laws of inference. They check and challenge one another's conclusions with the aid of the same laws. And just as theologians have had to wrestle with uncertainties about the reliability of the propositions from which they construct their arguments, so scientists have to arrive at a 'rating' of their evidence and its sources and their reliability.

Not everyone would agree that it is so simple, however. Philosophers are only too well aware that there is plenty of room for dispute about what is 'rational':

> As a philosophy post-graduate I have to say that I find the concept of 'the rational' to be very hazy. If by rational Mr. Newell means 'subject to logical analysis' then I feel obliged to point out that the notion of logic is still, in many ways, ill-defined. ... It is entirely unclear whether many aspects of existence, such as beauty or free choice, can be made to submit to any kind of rational or logical analysis. At this stage of the game, knowing as little as we do about rationality, it seems rather irrational to conclude that everything must fall under the heading of a term the meaning of which has not yet been fully decided.[2]

So the modern reader, aware of the complexity of the very idea of 'reasonableness', need not be too readily overwhelmed by the claim that belief is 'irrational'.

Reasonableness

Consistency

Early and medieval Christians borrowed the formal skills they needed to frame and test arguments from Greek and Roman classical works on logic, especially those of Aristotle. Aristotle (384-322BC) took it to be one of the basic laws of reasonableness that contradictory statements cannot both be true.

In theory, Christian thinkers embraced with enthusiasm the confidence that truth is consistent. 'Truths of the Christian faith do not contradict truths arrived at by reasoning,' agreed Thomas Aquinas (c.1225-74).[3] Yet there are apparent contradictions on all sides in the Bible and in Christian theology. Moreover, the Gospels do not agree, giving different accounts of events and different details. Authors from Augustine of Hippo (354-430) in the fourth and fifth centuries to Calvin in the sixteenth have struggled unsuccessfully to 'harmonize' their narratives.

Others have acknowledged that beliefs and ordinary reasoning may involve such utterly different kinds of things as to be incommensurable. This seemed obvious to John Toland (1670-1722), one of the early modern 'Platonists' who studied at Cambridge in the seventeenth century. 'To say, for instance, that a Ball is white and black at once, is to say just nothing; for these Colours are so incompatible ... as to exclude all Possibility of a real positive Idea or Conception'[4] of what such a simultaneously black and white ball would look like.

The modern reader who mistrusts the use of logical devices to 'rescue' unpalatable beliefs is going to be in good company. Toland was discussing the uncomfortable contemporary question whether unbaptized infants may have to go to hell. It had been suggested that they might be able to be in hell without actually suffering. The doctrine that 'Children dying before Baptism are damn'd without Pain, signifies nothing at all,' Toland suggests. If they have understanding their damnation cannot be painless, for 'to be eternally excluded God's Presence, must prove ineffable Torment to them'. If they have no understanding of what is happening to them damnation could not be meaningful for them. Either they 'had no Souls, or were annihilated',[5] he concludes. Many such attempts will be met with as we explore the arguments put forward to 'save' points of belief in which contradictions seemed to arise.

If reason and belief could be relied upon to meet on the same ground, there might have been less argument about Christian beliefs. In reality, Christian opinion has been divided throughout history on almost every point of doctrine, from the moment it was identified as 'doctrine' at all. Thomas Browne (1605–82) exclaimed in his *Religio Medici*:

> Take our opinions together, and from the confusions thereof there will be no such thing as salvation ... for first the Church of Rome condemneth us, we likewise them; the sub-reformists and sectaries sentence the doctrine of our Church as damnable; the Atomist or Familist reprobates all these – and all these them again ... we go to heaven against each others' wills, conceits and opinions.[6]

Christian theology has had to find ways to deal with this seeming contradictoriness, mismatch and incommensurability. A medieval method was to suggest that what looked like contradictions were only 'apparent', that words were being used in different senses and there was no real contradiction at all. It has also been argued that differences are real enough, but are mere diversities, not contradictions. The sixteenth century held a debate about whether there are things which 'do not matter' (*adiaphora*). There was an attempt to distinguish 'essentials' and 'things indifferent', on which believers could be left free to think as they liked. Another idea was that there might be a hierarchy of truths, so that some were more important than others, and the varieties and even apparent contradictions could be tucked away as insignificant. But even to admit variation is a bold step in a world that expects reasonableness to lead to consistency and certainties. The French Jesuit Jacques Bénigne Bossuet (1627–1704) took it to be an axiom that variation in religion is always a sign of error.[7]

Then there is the rich tradition of Christian paradox and inconsistency in which the defiance of reason is taken to be somehow a proof of the truth of Christian teaching, not evidence against it. It heightened amazement. Perceptions intuitively arrived at; glimpses of glory poetically stated, with the mind humbled before the impossibility of saying anything at all adequate; can these be taken to obey these same rules of rationality, and to stand to reason? Even the innumerable Christian paradoxes (the belief that God is three and one, for example) can be stated only within the frame of reference of conventional Aristotelian reasoning. They are paradoxical only because they seem to challenge it.

Different ways of reasoning

The Greek geometer Euclid (325–265BC) worked out a method of proof known as 'demonstrative argument', because it 'demonstrated' the conclusion. This became the envy of everyone with a case to put. It began from self-evident truths and agreed postulates and definitions and proceeded by a valid process of argumentation to arrive at conclusions which could be considered not merely probable but necessary. It worked well for geometry. It enabled Euclid to 'demonstrate' a number of things about plane figures and solid objects which have been taught to children until the twenty-first century. A few Christian theologians tried to apply the same method to the 'demonstration' of the 'truths' of the Christian faith and failed, because they do not turn out to be self-evident or easy to define or to agree. An example is Alan of Lille in the late twelfth century, who began his 'theological rules' confidently with the assertion that God is a Monad, absolutely 'One', but was soon in hopeless difficulties about how to get from there to the doctrine of the sacraments.

In 'syllogistic' arguments, as designed by Aristotle, two propositions or statements, sometimes called 'premises', are put together and an inference drawn. It is perfectly possible for a valid sequence of argumentation to be constructed out of fictional assertions. The conclusion may then be 'valid' but not true. The conclusion is only as secure as the probability of the premises which lead to it. So one of the points at which the would-be reasonable believer had to be vigilant was in inspecting the propositions. For more than 1,500 years it was taken that the 'best' propositions for the purposes of argument would be those every reasonable person would accept (such as $2 + 2 = 4$), propositions of a quality which could be used in demonstrative arguments; and those which were taken from an 'authority' such as the Bible, which might be relied upon for the sake of the author's reputation.

Yet belief sometimes rests on kinds of evidence which do not lend themselves readily to putting into propositions so as to see what conclusions follow. Christians have always been sensitive to the accusation that they believed in things they could not see. The name of Augustine of Hippo is going to appear a good deal in this book because of the sheer scale of his influence on the history of Christian doctrine. He wrote a great deal, addressing key questions, often for first time, and he was widely read for well over 1,000 years by every serious student of Christian belief in the West who could get copies of his writings. Augustine's book *On Faith in Things Unseen* points out that there are many things which are of their nature invisible, because they are abstractions – for example faith itself – but whose existence is not (for him) in dispute.[8] He accepts that there was a recognized sense in which 'knowing God' involved speculating and that speculating involved going beyond what could be evidenced.[9]

Such modes of understanding and persuasion, the poetic, the affective, the spiritual, have their advantages and disadvantages. Intuition, experience, even emotion, can bring someone to belief. By these means things may be glimpsed which cannot be arrived at solely by rational inference and explanation. But they are not so good for reliable communication and clarity.

One way of bringing evidence to bear has been to draw inferences by making comparisons between what we think we know and what we want to know. Such arguments by analogy had great force in earlier centuries and until quite modern times. At the end of the eighteenth century, Joseph Butler (1692–1752) in his influential *The Analogy of Religion* proposed 'analogy' as the main law of the universe from which strong probabilities verging on certainties may be arrived at. Consider the 'therefore' in the following:

> The states of life in which we ourselves existed formerly in the womb and in our infancy, are almost as different from our present in mature age, as it is possible to conceive any two states or degrees of life can be. Therefore that we are to exist hereafter in a state as different (suppose) from our present, as this is from our former, is but according to the analogy of nature.[10]

John Henry Newman (1801–90) was saying something very similar in the mid-nineteenth century in his Oxford University Sermons, when he remarked that 'we are obliged to receive information needful to us through the medium of our existing ideas',[11] and it was still an attractive assumption when Dorothy Sayers (1893–1957) wrote *The Mind of the Maker* a century later.

> It is to the creative artists that we should naturally turn for an exposition of what is meant by those credal formulae which deal with the nature of the Creative Mind'. ... The expressions 'God the Father' and 'God the Creator' are thus seen to belong to the same category – that is, of analogies based on human experience, and limited or extended by a similar mental process in either case.[12]

In the late Roman world where Christianity began there was a well-established tradition of 'rhetorical' argument, in which reasoning was couched in language calculated to move and persuade as well as convince. In ancient Rome in its heyday, all educated people were taught these skills because they needed them in public office and so as to participate in the general duties of citizenship. Early Christian writers were extremely conscious of this, and Augustine had to make a decision in his book *On Christian Doctrine* about the desirability of Christians making use of such skills (if they had them), what preachers were to make of the comparatively simple, plain and unsophisticated language in which the Bible was written, and how they were to win respect for it among the sophisticated who were inclined to sneer (as Augustine himself had done when he was a professional teacher of rhetoric).

Such devices of persuasion are still familiar to the modern world as instruments of 'thought control' and political propaganda. President Bush's State of the Union address, published in the *New York Times* on 29 January 2003, contained examples of rhetorical 'reasoning'. Saddam Hussein was said to be 'assembling the world's most dangerous weapons [in order to] dominate, intimidate, or attack'. '[He] has already used them ... if this is not evil, then evil has no meaning.'[13] The devices used here include shocking the audience, evoking righteous indignation, and thus making religious language seem appropriate and the shock somehow salutary, the enemy God's enemy, a demon with almost supernatural and magical powers, and attack upon him in truth merely defence of all that people hold sacred. The United States' own collection of 'the world's most dangerous weapons' in this attack is 'marketed' so as to appear a crusade and not 'evil' at all. During the presidential election campaign which followed a year later George W. Bush and, briefly putting in an appearance for the Democrats, ex-President Clinton, could be seen cultivating a relaxed charm as they strolled on to a stage, deprecatingly accepting the easy adulation of the crowd, its whoops and screams.

With the exception of the modern use of the mass media, these are essentially examples of orator's skills the early Christian world knew well. Jesus' educated Roman contemporaries knew perfectly well how to move a large crowd and conduct a meeting which would generate evangelical fervour and bring forth converts. So it has been well understood throughout Christian history that reasoning has uses in persuasion, and that when it is employed so as to evoke emotion things may seem to 'stand to reason' which they would certainly not do by the strict rules of logic. This is rather the sense in which Tony Blair, as Prime Minister and leader of the British Labour Party, said, 'I only know what I believe' at the Labour Party's annual conference in September 2004.

There have been different schools of thought on the question whether all human capacities for feeling and sense should enter into 'belief' in the way rhetorical argument and these other semi-rational and non-rational processes seem to make possible. On one view clear thought prepares the ground, adjusts expectations, determines what will seem 'reasonable', keeping its eye on clarity and a lack of clutter.[14] Emotion may be a distorting influence. An attitude of mind, a preparedness is something else, and a number of writers have approved of that. 'When Men are arrived at thinking of their very Dissolution with Pleasure, how few Things there are that can be terrible to them? ... The religious Pleasure of a well disposed Mind moves gently and therefore constantly. ... The Pleasure of the religious Man is an easie and portable Pleasure, such an one as he carries about in his Bosom, without alarming either the Eye or Envy of the World,' said *The Tatler* in 1710.[15]

So the first lesson of a history of Christian belief is that being reasonable is not as simple as it looks. These considerations were worked out more fully for Christianity than for any other world religion because for over 1,000 years the educational system which emerged in the Latin-speaking world during and after the collapse of the Roman Empire was extremely interested in such questions. 'What can a reasonable person believe' is a question full of unexpected turnings and hidden places where unforeseen forms of 'reasonableness' have been 'discovered'. This need not make the modern enquirer nervous; but it should make him or her resistant to being persuaded that belief is somehow unworthy or old-fashioned or unscientific because it is 'unreasonable'.

The nature of the evidence: revelation and science

Revelation

'All that may be known of God by men lies plain before their eyes; indeed God himself has disclosed it to them. His invisible attributes, that is to say his everlasting power and deity, have been visible, ever since the world began, to the eye of reason, in the things he has made' (Romans 1.19–20, NEB). This became the definitive statement for Christians of the idea that God explained himself by revealing what he was like in the world he had made. There is much more to be said about this in Chapter 3. But it confronts the would-be believer at the outset with one of the great central questions about the place of science. Can science contribute anything in matters of belief? Some scientists staunchly deny the possibility. Others think it can.

> As a scientist ... the conclusion the evidence brings me to is that the world is designed, that evolution is fine on a micro-scale but highly questionable when extrapolated to the macro scale, and that belief in a creator God makes perfect sense.[16]

Like 'reasonable', 'scientific' has not always meant the same thing. The root of the English word is the Latin *scientia*, which originally meant 'knowledge'. Its modern sense is comparatively recent. The definition of science today has two aspects which are important here. It is 'a branch of study which is concerned either with a connected body of demonstrated truths or with observed facts systematically classified'. It 'includes trustworthy methods for the discovery of new truth within its own domain' (*Oxford English Dictionary*). The important question is where this 'domain' ends and how far it is possible to draw conclusions beyond that domain, as the letter just quoted tries to do by 'extrapolating' from the demonstrated truths and the observed facts.

Broadly speaking, the modern sciences concern themselves with those things in the universe which can be measured and made the subject of experimental verification. They do not include the discussion of the 'super'-natural. Ancient science, because it was treated as a part of philosophy, thought differently. It recognized the existence of a boundary between the natural world, containing such measurable things, and a supernatural world, but it did not consider that the two worlds necessarily had to be discussed according to different methodological assumptions. There was a sense of the essential unity of a cosmos in which powers operating in the supernatural world also reached into the natural one and many of the laws governing the two were the same. For example, the sixth-century Christian philosopher Boethius (c.480–c.534), author of the book On the Consolation of Philosophy which he wrote while under sentence of death, used the word theologia; he meant it to embrace all those aspects of belief which can be reasoned about. He included such topics as the existence and nature of God and the created world, along with the natural laws of the physical world. These were all subjects not peculiar to Christianity, and the earlier Greek and Roman philosophers Boethius had read had had plenty to say about them.

The Christian tradition was seen to move into its own territory only in its story of the birth and death of Jesus and the resurrection. Those events could not be inferred by pure reasoning from the observable facts of the state of the universe. They were historical and had to be described by a reliable source or 'witness' such as the accounts to be found in the Bible. This difference has been recognized and allowed for century by century. For example, in the middle of the twelfth century, Hugh of St Victor (c.1096–1141) made exactly this distinction between matters which could be worked out by reasoning and those which required the imparting of additional information because they were historical events. 'There are two "works" in which are contained everything which was done. The first is the "work of creation"; the second is the "work of restoration".'[17] The thinking was that the first 'work' can be discussed by any reasonable person on the basis of observations. The second could not be known about at all if there was no reference book to give the necessary information to form a basis for discussion. The same idea is repeated by others, for example the early Oxford academic and later Bishop of Lincoln Robert Grosseteste (c.1170–1253). 'Things believable are of two kinds. Some things are believable because of the likelihood of the things themselves; others, because of the authority of the one who speaks.'[18] In the eighteenth century Joseph Butler pointed out that even the most confident believer in 'our whole system of natural philosophy and natural religion' could not fail to be

> sensible, that it was but a very small part of the natural and moral system of the universe that he was acquainted with. He could not but be sensi-

ble, that there must be innumerable things, in the dispensations of providence past, in the invisible government over the world at present carrying on, and in what is to come, of which he was wholly ignorant, and which could not be discovered without revelation.[19]

A shift of perspective made possible the beginning of modern science. It concerns experimental verification of hypotheses and the question what reliance is to be placed upon them. In the first Christian centuries the important thing about an explanation or hypothesis was its beauty and elegance and how well it matched generally with the existing 'picture of things'. The same system of explanation took it for granted that all particular exemplifications of things in the physical world, the things which could be made use of in experiments or observed, were inherently inferior to these ideal-ideas. They were capable of corruption and decay. So a series of experiments which seemed to prove the hypothesis wrong could not possibly have greater probative force than the inherent attractiveness of the idea which was being tested. The evidence base could never be sufficiently solid. Only when it became possible to move away from that expectation could the routine work of conducting a set of experiments test a hypothesis or establish an answer at all. Galileo stubbornly insisted, on the basis of observation, that the earth goes round the sun, until contemporary orthodoxy was obliged to agree with him.

In the second half of the twentieth century, Thomas Kuhn helped to bring about a rethinking with talk of 'paradigm shifts'.[20] Until then, modern science had tended to see itself as steadily and progressively filling out a picture whose outlines, that is its theoretical underpinnings, had been pretty much settled from at least Isaac Newton (1642–1727) onwards. Kuhn suggested a broad division. On the one hand would lie the routine work of conducting a set of experiments to establish the answer to a detailed question already known or predicted to arise within this framework. This was problem solving with a good chance of success within its limited parameters. The other possibility was to question the very framework, even at the level of the great mysteries of the universe. A Christian belief for today must take account of the possibility that such grand shifts in the way scientists 'see' the world may affect their 'idea' of God too, if the world is his 'doing'.

How does the would-be scientific enquirer begin? Whether we ask that question about ancient or about modern science the answer does not seem to be any tidier here than it was in the case of finding out what is 'reasonable'. In reality the process involves a conflation or interaction of rigorous scientific method with accidents and half-recognized assumptions. 'It wasn't intuition and it wasn't common sense. It began with a logical inference, was all but wrecked by prejudice, and then saved by system,'[21] about sums it up. But it is not much different in Aristotle, hard though he tried to be methodical and rigorous. In the *Physics* (I.1.184a) Aristotle suggests that it is a good idea to begin with what we know by way of the concrete and particular and move from there to the abstract and general, and in that way we shall get the general principles right. His methodological intentions are of the highest. But the edges blur in practice. In his *Meteorologica* (II. vii.365a) Aristotle assembles the various views of earlier authors on earthquakes. The earlier Greek philosopher Anaxagoras (he thinks) must be wrong in suggesting that earthquakes are a form of upward explosion of pockets of air trapped underground, because it is foolish to talk of 'up' and 'down' in that way. Aristotle tries to be systematic but he can be seen to make assumptions. Writing before the discovery of gravity, he points out that heavy bodies fall to earth from all directions and light ones (such as fires) rise up from the earth, but he seems to be assuming that 'rising upwards' is a single phenomenon which is somehow the converse of 'falling downwards'. Modern science would question that, though, on the face of it, it is a perfectly 'reasonable' hypothesis. In considering in his 'Problems' (I.xiii.861a) why 'change' should be 'unhealthy' he mixes observation and assumption again, in trying to explain why (a scientific observation of its day?) a change of water should apparently foster the growth of lice on the heads of those who already have them. His answer is that the brain is moist. This can be seen from the fact that the most luxurious growth of hair is on the head. Lice flourish in dampness. QED. The modern reader smiles, but similar unnoticed assumptions can clutter the best efforts of modern scientific argument to be perfectly rational. 'Respectable' science has always made assumptions it was not always aware of, and proceeded to conclusions other generations have smiled at. The whole business has been, historically, fraught with complications, and we stand in the same danger today if we try to be too rigid about what 'scientific' means and how it differs from 'theological' or 'philosophical'.

So in dealing with the notion of the scientific we are left with the same requirement not to over simplify and expect to find a consistent set of answers, as we were with 'reasoning'. Again, the modern enquirer can afford to be robustly open minded in approaching the scientific aspects of questions of 'belief'.

The nature of the evidence: the Bible and consensus

> There's a world of difference between finding that there's some very powerful, intelligent being in the background and finding that what you've discovered is the God of Abraham, Isaac and Israel.[22]

The Bible

What kind of 'evidence' is provided by the Bible? In the last five centuries there have been communities of Christians such as the Lutherans, who were prepared to say in the context of the debates of the Reformation that belief should rest on 'Scripture alone' (sola scriptura). Christians in the Evangelical tradition still place 'Bible truth' before everything else.

The book of Genesis tells a story of the creation and the subsequent 'Fall' of Adam and Eve which was taken literally for many centuries. It was sometimes asked what were Moses' sources as the alleged author of the first books of the Bible.[23] For how could he have known how God separated light from darkness and proceeded with the six days of creation up to the point where the first humans who could have reported the matter were made? No one was there.

The strong underlying confidence that the human authors of the Bible were deriving their authority from God himself got round this difficulty nicely. The Old Testament was taken to be the inspired Word of God from the very beginning of the Christian tradition. The risen Jesus himself is described as explaining to his disciples 'that all things needs must be fulfilled which are written in the Law of Moses and the prophets and the psalms, concerning me' (Luke 24.44, RV; see also II Timothy 3.15 and Hebrews 1.1). David is often called the 'author' of the Psalms in the Middle Ages and Paul the 'author' of his New Testament Epistles, but that is on the understanding that they wrote what God told them. The four Evangelists are often shown in medieval pictures with the Holy Spirit in the form of a dove with its beak in each Gospel writer's ear telling him what to say as he writes.

These are not merely amusing medieval curiosities. They reflect assumptions about the divine authorship and authority of the Bible which have continued to be of enormous importance, but which do not necessarily marry tidily with the historical evidence about the way the Bible came into being. Jesus' 'sayings' were being interpreted before they were recorded and certainly before the records in the present versions of the Gospels were generally accepted as authentic or authoritative. The letters of Paul and others which have become the Epistles of the New Testament were already relying on things Jesus had taught without being able to quote a written text. Centuries elapsed while the Church made up its mind which of the accounts available to it it was going to approve. The list was still being debated during the lifetime of Augustine's correspondent and contemporary Jerome (c.342–420). The 'canon' of the four Gospels, a history of the 'acts' of the Apostles, a selection of epistles, together with the books of the Old Testament were drawn from a much wider selection in circulation in the early centuries as candidates for inclusion in an agreed 'sacred text' or 'canon'.[24]

A group of 'apocryphal' writings is still printed between the Old Testament and the New Testament in some modern editions and is accepted by some but not all communities of Christians. An example is the Wisdom of Solomon, which seems to date from the second century BC. Origen (c.185–c.254) and Jerome knew this was not by Solomon, and in fact it is probably the work of a Hellenized Jew who was anxious to bring Greek philosophical thought into harmony with Judaism. His leading ideas about wisdom united notions which fore-shadow both the Logos-talk we shall come to in a moment and the Christian theology of the Holy Spirit:

> For in wisdom there is a spirit intelligent and holy, unique in its kind yet made up of many parts, subtle, free-moving, lucid, spotless, clear, invulner-able, loving what is good, eager, unhindered. Beneficent, kindly towards men, steadfast, unerring. Untouched by care, all-powerful, all-surveying, and permeating all intelligent, pure and delicate spirits (Wisdom 7.23, NEB).[25]

Other texts still were eventually excluded altogether but remained popular and influential, though acknowledged to be 'outside' the Bible. The 'Gospel' of Nicodemus, for example, provided a supple-ment to the accounts in the four canonical Gospels of the trial, death and resurrection of Jesus. It was probably written in the fourth century and by the fifth century it had acquired a second part, dealing with

Christ's descent to 'Hades' and 'his harrowing of hell'. This was still being read and quoted as an authority in the thirteenth century.[26]

The New Testament texts were in Greek, the Old Testament in Hebrew. There was an ancient Greek version, the Septuagint, traditionally compiled by 70 translators, from which this version got its name, and completed by about 130BC. But half the Roman world spoke Latin. Latin versions began to emerge, causing a good deal of confusion, for there was no standard translation. In the late fourth century, Jerome set about creating a translation which could fulfil that need. This became known as the Vulgate (the 'common' version). Although Jerome himself stated clearly that he did not feel himself to have been 'inspired' as a translator, in practice readers and commentators treated his Latin words with as much reverence as though they too had been directly dictated by the Holy Spirit, analysing minutely the exact words he had chosen. Yet when a text is translated its meaning is inevitably subtly altered, however competent the translator.

In the sixteenth century, as a result of the work of reformers who were going back to the 'sources' (*fontes*) and checking the text against the Greek and Hebrew, it became apparent that Jerome's Latin Vulgate translation of the Bible contained many flaws and inaccuracies. Several new Latin and Greek versions were produced and there was acrimonious correspondence about which new readings, even paraphrases and comments, were truly the Bible and which were not.

The sixteenth-century reformers pressed for a return to the original languages and for translations into the vernacular to be made, so that ordinary people who were not educated enough to read the Bible in Latin (let alone Greek or Hebrew) could read the Scriptures themselves or understand them when they heard them read. It was argued by the Roman Catholic Church's 'counter-reformers' at the Council of Trent (1545-63) that it was not to be believed that God could have left his Church, and the faithful who were its members, to read and expound a faulty text for so many generations. The message was that, despite the new evidence, in some deep sense the Vulgate was still the true text. There could be no return to the Greek and Hebrew original languages, and certainly no substitution of vernacular translations for Jerome's Latin. The Roman Catholic Church went on relying on the Vulgate until the Second Vatican Council in the middle of the twentieth century, when it was accepted that translations into modern languages could be used.

So the text of Scripture has been conveyed in a variety of natural languages and cultures, in ways unavoidably coloured by context, as translation and exegesis made this text a living and growing thing. A strict 'fundamentalist' approach which wants to take the Bible as the 'only' source a believer can trust, and even insists that every word in the Bible must be taken literally, might seem to require the study of the text in its original languages, but that is not usually insisted upon.

In any case, it has always been the subject of debate what the literal meaning is and whether a passage can be taken out of context without distortion of its meaning. For example, the Bible says that the Church is the body of Christ and Christ is its head. But the passage in which this is asserted (Ephesians 5.23) has a rather different immediate concern. Paul is writing about family relationships. He says that just as the Church is subject to Christ, so also wives ought to be subject in everything to their husbands. The husbands, for their part, are exhorted to a sacrificial and caring love for their wives. These ideas are part of a cluster, including recommendations for bringing up children so that they do not become rebellious, and a set of rules for slaves and masters. To the modern eye some of these ideas seem to be of lasting value, some 'of their time'. In few modern societies are rules for treating your slaves a daily practical necessity. The 'family' Paul envisages is the Roman *familia*, an enormous household, and not the modern nuclear or extended family. Without an awareness of this layering and blending, Old Testament sacrifices might still be routine requirements of a believer's life, and whether to tithe mint and other herbs would remain a regular preoccupation of the faithful (Matthew 23.23; Luke 11.42).

'Official guides'

There is another dimension to Christian thinking about 'revelation' which has gone somewhat out of fashion but was of serious importance for many centuries. Already among the classical authors, Seneca considered that one needs, and should not venture without, a knowledgeable guide when setting off into the cosmic unknown.[27] The modern enquirer may find this sort of discussion refreshing as a fleshing out of the struggles with abstract principles we have just been looking at.

In this category for Christians fell the angels of the Bible, whose name is derived from the Greek for 'messenger'. They pose an important question about the possibility of rational beings being able to move backwards and forwards between heaven and earth. The Book of Job opens with the angels coming into the court of heaven. But were they not there already, enquired Gregory the Great (c.540–604)? Jesus himself said the angels 'always' behold the face of the Father who is in heaven (Matthew 18.10). On the other hand, Paul describes them as 'sent' to minister (Hebrews 1.14). Perhaps they can be in both places at once? If we consider how subtle is the angelic nature, Gregory suggests, it becomes possible to envisage that perhaps even if they go out from the divine presence it is not in such a manner as to deprive them of its joys. It is not as it is with us, for whom out of sight is out of mind. The angels can be gazing on God while they are going about doing good.[28] John Donne (1571/2–1631) was still thinking about this problem in the seventeenth century. He saw this Janus-like 'facing both ways by angels' as raising an important question about the scope of the operations of rational beings, within the framework of seventeenth-century Renaissance science. 'This image of God, even in the angels, being Reason ... it is that which the angels are naturally inclined to doe, to be always present for the assistance of man.'[29]

Human messengers have been reported too. The God of the Old Testament is described as sending messages through the 'prophets', though prophets did not apparently enjoy the same freedoms to come and go as the angels. Traditionally a prophet is a mere mouthpiece. He utters what he is told to utter and more than he understands. Ezekiel threw himself down in worship, but God asked him to stand so that he could talk with him and tell him what he was sending him to do. Ezekiel was to bear witness to the rebellious Israelites. Ezekiel heard the still small voice, in which God accommodated his enormous and overwhelming majesty to Ezekiel's capacities, by turning its volume down.

There is a repeating theme of direct verbal inspiration in the Old Testament accounts of the commissioning of the prophets. Isaiah was 'sent' on his prophetic mission, his lips touched by a coal of fire, much as we read of Ezekiel 'eating' God's words (Isaiah 6.6). God gave Ezekiel a scroll containing laments and words of woe and Ezekiel was instructed to eat it, so as to have God's words ready in his mouth to speak to the people (Ezekiel 1-2). Daniel 'understood the word' which was revealed to him as a shining figure appeared and spoke to him.

Linked with this 'verbal' commissioning is a pattern of 'revelations' of what heaven is like, in powerful and sometimes unexpected images, opaque with mystery and crying out temptingly for interpretation. The prophet Ezekiel's vision (1.1) was of an 'opening of the heavens'. Ezekiel saw a wind coming from the north, a great cloud full of fire and light. He saw within the cloud the four beasts, with four human faces. Beside the four beasts, he saw four wheels. He saw a great vault of heaven over them, and beneath it their wings spread out, touching one another. Above appeared a sapphire throne, and upon the throne a shining being in human form. Thus appeared the 'glory of the Lord'. The prophet Daniel had visions of heaven, too, which came to him in his sleep. Daniel (7.1) also describes how he too saw four beasts, though the associated symbolism is different. There was war in heaven. Daniel strove to understand what he was seeing (8.15). In another vision (10.1-4) the prophet Zacharias saw Satan standing in the presence of God and he was shown a stone in which were seven eyes, the eyes of the Lord ranging over all the earth. Eager Bible students from the early Christian centuries burrowed in these accounts and drew from them images and interpretations.

A few in subsequent centuries have believed themselves to be prophets, or have been treated as prophets by admiring disciples looking for 'guides'. A notable example, who still has his following in Calabria (where his 'return' is expected like that of King Arthur in parts of Britain), is Joachim of Fiore, who died at the beginning of the thirteenth century. He prophesied the end of the world, uttering fierce warnings about the declining times which heralded it.[30]

Andrew Marvell (1621-78) was prepared to rate Milton a prophet, if a blind one:

> Where couldst thou words of such a compass find?
> Whence furnish such a vast expanse of mind?
> Just Heav'n thee like Tiresias to requite
> Rewards with prophecy thy loss of sight.[31]

Not all prophecy by any means has looked solely heavenward. Biblical prophecy was often 'the voice of honest indignation' about the state of things on earth. In the late eighteenth century, another poet, William Blake (1757-1827), describes an imaginary dinner-party conversation he had with two Old Testament prophets which strikes a nice balance between the concern with the eternal and the indignation about the present, which seems to have given many a prophet his fire. 'The prophets Isaiah and Ezekiel dined with me,' he says in *The Marriage of Heaven and Hell*, 'and I asked them how they dared so roundly to assert that God spoke to them. ... Isaiah answered: "I saw no God, nor heard any, in a finite organical perception; but my senses discovered the infinite in every thing, and as I was then perswaded, and remain confirm'd, that the voice of honest indignation is the voice of God, I cared not for consequences, but wrote." '[32]

The fulfilment of the Old Testament prophecies was looked for in the New Testament accounts. Although the last of the prophets, John the Baptist, appears in the Gospel account of the life of Jesus, and the Book of Revelation was itself dramatically prophetic, the New Testament points towards eternity in a different way. The first generation of Christians expected the end to come very soon, in their lifetimes. Jesus had hinted as much (Matthew 25.33-4). A tension was created by a sense of the imminence of the unravelling of the mystery. Matthew's Gospel includes dire warnings of the awfulness of the last days. These last times were expected to be violent. Jesus' apocalyptic discourse in Matthew 24 foretold a time of battle and famine and earthquake which would presage the end and the second coming of Jesus himself. The Gospel account has a conscious Old Testament reference. The prophet Daniel spoke of the 'abomination of desolation' and when he sees this the believer should flee (Daniel 9.27, 11.31, 12.11 and Matthew 24.15). It was to be a time of persecution of the faithful, a time when many who believed would fall away and love would grow cold and some would be deceived (Matthew 24.4-5 and 9-12: 'many will come in my name and lead you astray'). These were to be testing times. The believer must persevere to the end if he is to be saved (Matthew 24.13). II Thessalonians 2.1-12 contains Paul's warning of the nearness of the end, in which he insists that that day cannot come before the last rebellion against God, when wickedness will be revealed in human form.

The tension created in the Gospels is maintained in the Acts of the Apostles by a series of episodes where there are visits and other interventions from heaven. In Acts 12.7-10 Peter is rescued from prison by a visiting angel. Acts 10-13 and 11.7-16 describe his vision of clean and unclean beasts and the way he was shown that Christians are free to eat as they choose and no foods are ritually unclean to them. In Acts 18.9–10 Paul has a vision in which the Lord tells him that he will be safe and should continue to preach without fear. Over all these events hung the eschatological expectation that the end was near.

Subsequent Christian literature is full of 'guides' engaged in this cosmic postal service, some of whom will be met in the pages which follow. They accompany various writers and their characters on their own exploratory fictional journeyings into heaven, and the many stories of this kind have helped to colour conventional ideas of heaven. In the *Divina Commedia* of the Italian poet and political commentator Dante Alighieri (1265–1321), Beatrice is described as bringing Dante to paradise 'in his mind' (Canto XXVIII).

The modern reader has to try to make sense of all this. One theory embraced by such medieval thinkers as the early twelfth-century Rupert of Deutz and Anselm of Havelberg was that where Old Testament and New Testament were clearly joined by a line pointing forward from one to the other, that line could logically be produced further and truths lying along it could be relied on. But that depended on the conviction that the Bible was literally 'inspired' and that God had made it like a crossword puzzle, full of clues which merely had to be solved for the reader to be able to see into the future.

Our questioning has to be rather different, shaping but not defining expectations, provisional but hopeful, rather in the spirit of T.S. Eliot's challenge:

> To have bitten off the matter with a smile,
> To have squeezed the universe into a ball
> To roll it towards some overwhelming question,
> To say: 'I am Lazarus, come from the dead,
> Come back to tell you all, I shall tell you all.'[33]

Authoritativeness beyond the Bible

The Bible is not a textbook of 'systematic theology'. Some beliefs not set out there but eventually becoming central to the thinking of different groups of Christians emerged only gradually during the first Christian centuries and some later still, as a result of the asking of awkward questions. The Creeds (from *credo*, 'I believe') are intended to be short statements of basic beliefs, containing the essential clarifications of some of the points which had been raised. They have been effective in commanding the consent of most Christians until the present day, as twentieth-century ecumenical consultations held by the World Council of Churches discovered.

The notion that the Bible and Church are somehow 'rival' authorities is a relatively recent idea, dating mainly from the sixteenth century in the West. It makes some unhistorical assumptions about the way the text of the Bible was written, agreed and accepted. It also imputes to 'the Church' an institutional sophistication and a degree of control it did not have until late in the Middle Ages, when its claims became so extreme that they prompted resentment and radical attempts at reform. The historical reality has been that the Church as the community of believers has 'accepted' Bible and beliefs alike, by means of various devices, some formal, some not.

The Nicene Creed was 'agreed' by a council of bishops held at Nicaea in 325. This came to be regarded as a 'universal' or Ecumenical Council, whose decisions would be binding on the whole Church, though most of the bishops who were present came from the Greek-speaking Eastern half of the Roman Empire. The purpose of this creed was to settle a controversy, to establish an orthodox position on the much debated question of recent generations, whether Jesus had both a human and a divine nature and whether he was one person or two. The creed was slightly revised at the Council of Constantinople in 381. Its clauses speak eloquently of the struggles which went into their framing and the process of getting agreement to put things this way.

They reflect more than one of the concerns of the day. An example is the insistence that God made matter (the 'visible' earth), which was a rebuttal of the teaching of the Gnostic dualists we shall meet later.

Here, for reference, is the text:

I believe in one God the Father Almighty, Maker of heaven and earth, and of all things visible and invisible:
And in one Lord Jesus Christ, the only-begotten Son of God, Begotten of his Father before all worlds, God of God, Light of Light, Very God of very God, Begotten not made,
Being of one substance with the Father,
By whom all things were made;
Who for us men and for our salvation came down from heaven;
And was incarnate by the Holy Ghost of the Virgin Mary,
And was made man;
And was crucified also for us under Pontius Pilate.

He suffered and was buried,
And the third day he rose again according to the Scriptures,
And ascended into heaven,
And sits on the right hand of the Father.
And he shall come again with glory to judge both the quick and the
dead:
Whose kingdom shall have no end.
And I believe in the Holy Ghost,
The Lord and giver of life,
Who proceeds from the Father and the Son,
Who with the Father and the Son together is worshipped and glorified,
Who spoke by the prophets.
And I believe in one catholic and apostolic Church.
I acknowledge one baptism for the remissions of sins.
And I look for the resurrection of the dead and the life of the world to
come.

Despite its careful articulation of a position on themes of current
or previous controversy, the Nicene Creed was not really comprehensive. It did not touch on a number of matters which were going to
become controversial later. There is nothing in it about 'justification
by faith', for example. So the Nicene Creed did not prove to be an
'always adequate' statement, however well it has lasted in the form it
took.

When someone was baptized the declaration of faith was central
and there had been a need from an early stage for a plain statement
which could be used to affirm belief. The story was that the Apostles'
Creed derived its authority from the Apostles themselves. It was said
that they had met for a meal and each contributed a clause. The text
now known by that name is probably derived from the earliest statements of faith used in worship in the West, but took its final form
some centuries later than the Nicene Creed, by usage, not by the decision of any Council. It is accepted as authoritative only in the Western
churches.[34] Again the text is given here for reference:

I believe in one God, the Father Almighty, Maker of heaven and earth
And in one Lord Jesus Christ,
Only-begotten Son
Conceived by the Holy Ghost
Born of the Virgin Mary
Suffered under Pontius Pilate
Was crucified, dead and buried

He descended into Hell
The third day he rose again from the dead
He ascended into heaven
And sitteth on the right hand of God the Father
From thence he shall come again to judge the quick and the dead
I believe in the Holy Ghost,
The Holy Catholic Church
The Communion of saints
The remission of sins
The resurrection of the body
And the life everlasting.

But even this credal formulation which emerged naturally in the development of a framework of worship did not cover everything that was going to be a subject of debate in Christian belief.

The creeds, like the Bible, do not provide authoritative points of reference on the matters which were to lead to division many centuries later, for example in 1054 when Eastern and Western Churches fell into schism. Bitter religious wars have been fought between Christian communities before, during and since the Reformation of the sixteenth century which divided Western Christendom. Divided communities sometimes made their own 'confessional statements', such as the Augsburg Confession of Lutherans and the Thirty-Nine Articles of the Anglicans, both of which date from as late as the sixteenth century.

'Always, everywhere, by everyone'?

Vincent of Lérins (before 450) set out a useful threefold test to be applied to decide whether a matter of faith was right or not. He asked whether it had been accepted *always, everywhere,* and *by everyone?*[35]

The meaning of 'always' must be affected by the fact that 'historical consciousness' as an awareness of the changes of assumption which can alter the complexion of events is relatively recent, a product of the nineteenth century. The first 'general councils' of the leaders of the contemporary worldwide Church (European and African) which were held in the fourth and fifth centuries saw it more simply. They regularly began by declaring their members to be of one mind not only with one another but also with the members of each previous general council. The idea of continuity has been central to Christian theology from a very early date, and consistency in the maintenance of the apostolic faith has also been held to be of its essence. The Orthodox

Churches which grew up in the Greek-speaking Eastern half of the old Roman Empire, have remained firm that there can be nothing new to say. Their position is that a 'deposit' was given at the beginning and any departure from it is bound to lead to error, that councils state the mind of the Church. They do not have authority to add to the 'deposit'.

That was where 'always' began, with the idea that there was something special about apostolic times, and being faithful to 'always' meant not departing from what was thought then. The Apostles were accorded a special respect because, it was reasoned, they had actually heard Jesus teach and had known him, or had spoken to people who had, and they were therefore bound to have a clearer idea what to believe than later generations. Traditionally the list of 'Apostles' was allowed to include Paul, the author of many of the letters to newly founded churches eventually included in the New Testament.

There was a belief, too, that God had provided an umbrella of special protection over the early Christian period. It was an age when miracles happened and God was being especially vigilant to ensure that the faith was correctly understood. 'Back to the sources' (*ad fontes*), was the cry of sixteenth-century reformers, who were eager to return to these 'apostolic' certainties and abandon what they suspected to be centuries of 'human inventions' during the Middle Ages which had taken the faith down the wrong paths of development. 'God gave his revelation once for all ... the apostles alone knew his mind. They alone knew Christ's teaching and how he wanted to perpetuate his message.'[36]

This assumption did not last. In the nineteenth century, prompted partly by John Henry Newman's *Essay on the Development of Christian Doctrine* (1845), some were ready to argue that an understanding of the faith has emerged over the centuries which was in some sense an advance on what was able to be stated at the beginning. Some modern theologians have gone further and argued that the modern world is different in kind, its apologists entitled to declare themselves more advanced, grown-up enough to leave the old ideas behind and press forward on their own terms. That has led to collapses and reductions to absurdities, but also to the advancing of bold and innovative ideas.

A further kind of challenge to the 'always' test of the soundness of belief arises not from a theory of 'progress' but from the historians' recognition that expectations and requirements are subject to cultural change. What seems an unacceptable challenge in one era may quietly become acceptable and indeed a norm in another, as happened with the early modern translations of the Bible into a range of native languages.

Thirdly, historical 'interruption' to continuity and consistency has occurred as a result of schisms and the breaking away of dissident groups which have claimed that they alone were the True Church. For instance, during the Reformation period in the West, much was made on all sides of the inadequacies of the theology of ministry of other groups. The Roman Catholic Church insisted that an 'apostolic succession' of the laying on of hands from Christ's personal commissioning of his disciples onwards was essential to the validity of ordinations. At the end of the nineteenth century Anglican orders were declared 'null and void' on the basis of an alleged break in this succession in the sixteenth century.[37]

So the 'always' test of the authority of a particular belief, the idea that it depends on its acceptance by Christians in every age, is not straightforward. Christianity has proved astonishingly good at adapting itself throughout the world and century after century. The modern 'technical term' for this is 'inculturation'. In principle it excludes any form of merging in which the distinctive identity of one religion is lost, as happens in 'syncretism'. But what is non-negotiable, and considered to be of the essence of Christian belief, has not always been the same. At one time a Christian would simply point to the book of Genesis. But there are many practising Christians today who do not believe that the story of creation told there can be taken literally. Charles Darwin (1809–82) caused a stir with his On the Origin of Species in the nineteenth century, but the theory of evolution is now hardly controversial. Questions present themselves now which could not have been conceived of even a hundred years ago with anything like their full modern implications. Is a cloned sheep God's creature or man's? Are there built-in limits to what human inventiveness can do to change nature? Is it possible for human activity to bring about ecological disaster in a world with a God in charge?

The challenge of changing times is matched by a challenge from the changing of 'places', Vincent of Lérins' 'everywhere'. As Christianity has spread across the world it has had to adapt itself to local language and custom. It was a proud stance in the period of the Roman Empire that Christianity, like Judaism, was different because it would not accept any form of syncretism. Where pagans philosophically allowed their local gods to be identified with gods already worshipped in the imperial pantheon (the Greek Zeus could be relabelled Jupiter since he was king of the gods), Christians were regularly persecuted because they refused to put Christ into any such melting pot, or to worship the Emperor in even a token manner themselves. But the Christian missions of the nineteenth century took contemporary imperialism with them, imposing the cultural norms of the West in ways which have since caused lingering resentment.

The standard of debate was likely to have been quite sophisticated as belief in Jesus' teaching spread through the Roman Empire. In such circumstances the formation of what came to be known as the 'consensus of the faithful', Vincent of Lérins' 'by everyone', is naturally somewhat blurry. The first believers did not have the formal machinery to arrive at 'agreed statements', though Acts 15 describes an attempt to create a mechanism which could ensure that things were decided by agreement. This involved some exercise of formal leadership to organize the debate and ask the community. It also assumed that God was in some way 'present' and guiding the discussion, in the person of the Holy Spirit whose coming Jesus had promised (John 14.16).

These elements in decision making were strengthened and consolidated in succeeding centuries. An uneasy balance of authority emerged between the formal decision making of councils of the leaders of local communities (who gradually emerged as 'bishops') and the acceptance of decisions by believers in general. Even long afterwards when there was a highly complex institutional Church structure with very firm ideas about what constituted a binding 'decision', it could take centuries for consensus to make itself clear. A case in point is our example of the slow emergence of a changed 'consensus' during the four centuries it took from the Council of Trent in the sixteenth century (which maintained that worship had to be in Latin and the Bible had to be read in Latin) to the Second Vatican Council in the twentieth century (which decided that it was all right for the Bible to be translated into peoples' native languages and that they could worship in the vernacular too). The Roman Catholic Church had taken four centuries to accept a change of 'consensus' on this point.

Besides, the idea that consensus is important raises issues of its own, for it places the individual believer in a community whose members all think alike. The early Christians certainly thought that was important (Philippians 1.27, 2.2, 4.2; I Peter 3.8). The centrality of an ideal of 'one faith' needs justifying in the modern West, where individuality of opinion and freedom of thought and speech are highly valued.

In the early centuries an official statement of an 'orthodox' position often came to be needed only because someone had raised a question the Church's authorities could not answer, and the debate which followed was becoming persistent and threatened to be divisive. The driving force then was the need to preserve unity of faith. In the later Middle Ages and beyond, this threat to unity was still important, but the questioners themselves tended to be driven not by the kind of natural curiosity about an important aspect of belief which lies behind the eventual attempt to settle the matter in the Nicene Creed, but by resentment that, as they saw it, the faithful were being misled or burdened with unnecessary requirements by powerful institutional figures in the Church.

One of the questions posed at the Reformation was whether there was an alternative to this emphasis on universality and consistency in belief, which had come to be associated at least in the West with the administrative oversight of the Church. The same insistence was there in the East, where the Churches had evolved into big autocephalous areas, each with its Primate, which were strongly defensive of their independence in everything but matters of faith. There it was unanimously agreed among them that nothing must be changed. There was one faith, the same faith, established for ever. The reformers in the West turned to the Bible for the authority they were now inclined to deny to the Church, but without the Church to interpret it authoritatively they were left with the problem that private individuals reading for themselves might (and did) come to conclusions which were at variance with the 'official' teachings of the Church. One solution was to suggest that these matters lay between the individual and God, and that the believing reader of Scripture would be correctly guided by the Holy Spirit.

So in this most sensitive area of the study of the Bible and the question of the authoritativeness of teachings about the Christian faith, the modern enquirer is presented once more with a resource of historical effort to address exactly the questions which arise now, together with others which were once just as pressing and are capable of becoming so again.

The trouble with words

Why was talking about God in plain generally understood terms so difficult? It was a central Christian belief from a very early stage that Jesus was the Word of God made human. The New Testament uses a good deal of Word-of-God language about him: 'In the beginning was the Word' (John 1.1), 'And the Word became flesh' (John 1.14), 'The Word of Life' (I John 1.1), 'His name is called the Word of God' (Revelation 19.13).

The Greek term *Logos* was being used in such passages in a way already familiar in ancient Greek philosophical thought and in the Judaic tradition, but which is not necessarily a natural way of thinking to modern minds. To call Christ the Logos included the idea that he was the 'Reason-for-Things' as well as their 'Mode-of-Expression'. This, too, was an assumption which had been borrowed from Greek philosophy. Heraclitus (c.500BC) thought that the world is run by a universal Reason. The idea attracted Stoic philosophers, and the Jews of the Hellenistic period developed it further. Philo of Alexandria (c.20BC–c.50AD), who was a Jewish not a Christian thinker, had already combined the references in the Old Testament to God 'saying' things with this Greek philosophical line of thought. So Word-talk was current when the first Christians began to rationalize their position.

But this divine 'Wordhood' self-evidently does not endow words in human language with a higher capacity for exactitude or automatically make them adequate for discussing the divine. The attempt to talk about God merely seems to overextend such words and the grammar they usually obey, resulting in apparent contradictions and anomalies. Gregory the Great pointed out at the end of the sixth century that it was not to be expected that the sort of thing the Holy Spirit said in the Bible could be confined within the rules of ordinary grammar.[38] He meant that ordinary human language is simply not 'big' enough to allow accurate talk about God, its grammar is not flexible enough, the vocabulary not sufficiently extensive.

He also recognized that language is slippery and can mislead. The early belief was that the obvious unclarities in the language of the Bible were actually rather helpful to human beings. They allowed God to hint at things beyond their capacity to grasp for themselves. Above all, they accommodated in a most helpful way the effect of human sinfulness, which had made every human being muddle-headed and inclined to understand things in perverse ways. By coming round from behind in this way, the Word of God could meet people where they were in their understanding and teach them better.[39]

In any case, what is meant by 'stood for'? The ancient, early Christian and medieval idea was that words function as signs of the things they stand for. Using verbal 'signs' enables people to discuss 'things' without actually bringing them along to point to. They make it unnecessary to assemble elephants in the room in order to be able to hold a conversation about them. But for that to work, it is helpful to be able to go and see or touch or at least to agree about what the things 'stood for' if there turns out to be any argument as to whether elephants have yellow fur coats and manes, or grey skins, tusks and trunks.

When Adam 'gave names to all cattle, to the birds of heaven, and to every wild animal' (Genesis 2.20), was this just an exercise in free-hand labelling? Plainly the actual sounds of words can vary; for the word for 'elephant' is different in different languages. But the idea of an elephant seems to be much the same in the minds of the speakers of all languages. When we learn a new language, lists of 'vocabulary' enable us to equate the familiar sounds of words we know with the unfamiliar sounds of words in the new language by matching them against a common reference point, the 'idea' of an elephant.

The hard question is whether this 'idea' is innate or learned by experience. Two schools of thought emerged about this in early and medieval Christianity. Those later labelled 'Nominalists' said that we associate the words we use with both the ideas or concepts of the things they signify and the actual things they signify, as a result of learning. Others, the 'Realists', favoured the Platonist way of thinking and considered that the apparently universal human capacity to know a cat when you see one, accurately reflects reality. That is not to suggest that 'chat' in French or 'cat' in English are eternal words but that there is something universal about the idea of a cat. This second approach held that the conceptual labels to which names are given in actual languages, and the things they refer to, represent eternal absolutes or 'Ideas' in the mind of God, and are not merely made up by human beings.

Actual human languages are not static. The meanings of words change over time and with the changing cultures in which they are used, as well as varying between languages. Peter Abelard (1079–1142/3) realized as much in the twelfth century.[40] For pagan thinkers of early Christian times 'incarnation' connoted the entrapment of spirit in a material body.[41] It became a 'positive' rather than a 'negative' term only after centuries of usage by Christians and the emergence of the fully fledged doctrine of the incarnation of the Son of God in Jesus which we shall come to in a later chapter. *Ekstasis* in its first Greek sense had a broad range of usage beyond the meaning of ecstatic mystical union with God. It could cover change of mind, amazement, awe, madness, possession.[42] Modern 'convenience' has a subtly different set of connotations from the *convenientia* ('appropriateness' or 'fittingness') of the twelfth century. It was only slowly realized that a word which one language derives from another does not necessarily have an equivalent meaning once it has been adopted.

A modern education is unlikely to spend time on such matters. Yet the conventional explanations of these and other phenomena of language and the way it functions to convey understanding had 1,500 years of history before it ceased to be fashionable to discuss them in this way, and the basic options remain much the same. Is there an idea of God in my mind because he put it there or is the idea of God something I have picked up from experience and reading and conversation and put together in an arbitrary way? Could it change if I did some more reading and talking? Are the words I use capable of conveying the idea of God accurately and fully or are they mere hints? If they cannot do the job properly how do I know what I know about God and whether it is 'right'?

For the 'definition' of words about God is still recognized to pose special difficulties. God cannot be produced in the same way as an elephant can, to settle a point in dispute about what he is like. All talk of God is approximate, hypothetical and challenging to anyone who wants to look behind what it appears to mean. This problem was noted by the fifth-century thinker who was known as Ps-Dionysius (because he was rumoured for a time to be the first-century Dionysius the Areopagite, whose conversion by St Paul is recorded in Acts 17.34). In his book on *The Divine Names* Ps-Dionysius discusses the problem of finding any words adequate to speak of God as he really is. Words fail again and again to give an *adequate* description of belief and believing, as well as of the God believed in. It is common experience that believing is not solely verbal. It involves perceptions and sensations and mysteries and hints and shadings and purposes which do not readily lend themselves to exact verbal expression.

When Jesus said, 'There shall not be left here one stone upon another that shall not be thrown down' (Matthew 24.2), his disciples thought at first that he meant it literally and as a straightforward clue about what was going to happen. They asked him for dates and historical indications of the occurrence of a real event. 'Tell us,' they begged, 'when shall these things be and what shall be the sign of thy coming and of the end of the world?' (Matthew 24.3). They had to be encouraged step by step to understand that the real signification of the words lay somewhere to one side of or behind or beneath the literal meaning (Matthew 24.4-25.46) and that this apparently simple statement contained a huge and complex prophecy, full of potential for misunderstandings. Jesus did a good deal of teaching himself, using human language for the purpose. That teaching appeared to be simple and direct, but because it used stories and images, Jesus could easily seem to readers of later generations to be doing just what Gregory the Great describes, and coming at what he really meant to say by circuitous routes.

Jesus used metaphorical language a good deal. When he said 'I am the Good Shepherd' (John 10.1-16), he did not mean it to be understood that he was herding actual sheep, but rather that he was the 'pastor' of humans whose relationship to him was like that of sheep to their shepherd. It was the nature of the relationship, not the particular example of such a relationship, that mattered. In the parable of the sower (Matthew 13.18-23) the point of the story is arrived at only by asking what the falling of the seed on different kinds of soil stands for, for the story is not about seeds but about the spreading of the Gospel. The parable of the wheat and the weeds (Matthew 13.24-30) is not really about seeds and plants either. It is about the mixed community of the real world and it suggests an answer to the question why a good and powerful God should allow the bad behaviour of some to go apparently unpunished. Nor is the parable of the mustard seed and the Kingdom of Heaven (Matthew 13.31-2) making a botanical point. The mustard seed is small but it makes a sizeable tree. These images all involve taking familiar things whose relations will readily be understood as a way of drawing attention to an underlying relationship or structure of things which represents a general or even a cosmic truth.

Other metaphorical expressions involved taking a word with a familiar this-worldly meaning, and using it to point to something 'beyond' this world. If I call you a 'lion among men' I probably do not mean that you are a roaring yellow beast in a group of human beings. I mean that compared with other human beings you are noble and kingly and have in a general way the characteristics which make lions respected. If you say modestly in reply that you do not think you deserve to be 'lionized', we have stretched the signification of 'lion' further still.

One of the features of the Bible's language is exactly its use of anthropomorphic and other creaturely words for God and his behaviour when it describes him as 'angry', 'loving', 'forgiving', and so on. One question clarified in the Middle Ages was whether we should read these as limited attempts to describe divine attributes which cannot really be fully 'reached' in understanding in that way, or whether when we use the same words for our own anger, love, forgiveness we are merely transferring to creaturely use words whose 'proper' reference is to God.[43] At the Transfiguration of Christ there was a bright 'cloud' and from within it God's 'voice' proclaimed his Son (Matthew 17.5, 6; Mark 9.7; Luke 9.34). The words 'voice' and 'cloud' must be approximations, the nearest comparison human language affords.

This way of using language takes us into the realm of analogy where we have already found ourselves in thinking about reasonableness. Argument by analogy was popular not only because of its vividness and directness. It seemed to most medieval minds to have enormous *force*, an *appropriateness* which goes far beyond the modern sense of 'fittingness'. This is not merely a medieval question. It is still important how comparisons between God and created things 'work'. It may be possible to make comparisons, up to a point, but making comparisons between God and created things can be misleading, said Dorothy Sayers:

> The idea of the Fatherhood of God is not meant to be pressed too far. We are not meant to understand that he can be a cruel, careless or injudicious father such as we may see from time to time in daily life; still less, that all the activities of a human father may be attributed to God, such

as earning money for the support of the family, or demanding first use of the bathroom in the morning. Our own common sense assures us that the metaphor is intended to be drawn from the best kind of father acting with a certain limited sphere of behaviour, and is to be applied only to a well-defined number of the divine attributes.[44]

So the system of talking about God by moving words sideways was not restricted to the early and medieval centuries. We still do it. For instance, a computer mouse gets its name by transference from the small rodent, because it looks like a little animal with a long tail. But it is self-evidently not at all the same kind of thing as the animal in any other respect.

This way of using language still forms part of a consistent system of explanation which has evolved over many generations and is still a useful and natural way of approaching the problem that talking 'straight' about God is not a practical possibility. But it has its dangers. It beauty is seductive and distracting:

> Ink and catgut and paint were necessary down there, but they are also dangerous stimulants. Every poet and musician and artist, but for Grace, is drawn away from love of the thing he tells, to love of the telling till, down in Deep Hell, they cannot be interested in God at all but only in what they say about him.[45]

Once more, as with 'reasonableness' and 'science' and the question of 'evidence', the modern enquirer is presented by these centuries of reflection about the way language works, with a rich and varied apparatus for his or her own use, and the reassurance that there are plenty of approaches to choose from. Perhaps there is, once more, some comfort in the evidence that everyone has always found this difficult.

PART II. MAKING AND BREAKING

All that may be known of God by men lies plain before their eyes; indeed God himself has disclosed it to them. His invisible attributes, that is to say his everlasting power and deity, have been visible, ever since the world began, to the eye of reason, in the things he has made (Romans 1.19–20, NEB).

This passage takes us from the question of the reasonableness of believing at all, where we first met it, into the first two big questions for the believer. What is he or she going to 'believe in' – is there a God? What is the universe – where did it come from and is anyone in charge? These questions had been matters of keen general interest in the Graeco-Roman world for centuries. As a result there is a heavy stamp of classical philosophy upon the way the questions were framed by the first Christians to think about them and the way the answers emerged. Are these ideas still helpful as a way of expressing the underlying assumptions of belief? Are today's assumptions different?

2

Godness

Is God obvious?

Is there a God? The answer is not self-evident. There were extreme sceptics in the ancient world as there are today, who take the only certainty to be the impossibility of being certain about anything,[1] including the existence of God. Cicero (106–43BC), writing *On the Nature of the Gods* (I.i.2), remarks that most people think the gods or a God exists, though Cicero can list some who do not. The modern reader of the horoscope in a magazine is investing 'belief' in the operation of influences which reach from a 'more-than-natural' or 'supernatural' world, into the world where modern science measures things and seeks to account for them.

It is difficult to be sure whether something exists if it is not even clear what it is, and there is no agreed definition of what a God would be (or even what *sort* of thing a God would be, what God would be 'like'). One famous argument is unique in trying to tackle the question at this key point and show that anyone who understands what God is will both recognize that he exists and know what he is like. This 'ontological argument' was the 'discovery' of Anselm of Bec (1033–1109), later Archbishop of Canterbury, which he made at the end of the eleventh century. Anselm pointed out that even non-believers have in their minds the concept of 'that-than-which-nothing-greater-can-be-thought'. But if that idea was only in their minds it would not be what it says it is, for a 'that-than-which-nothing-greater-can-be-thought-which-exists-in-reality-as-well-as-in-thought' would be greater than something which did not also exist in reality. Anselm's 'therefore' makes the leap from thought to reality and says that this must prove the existence of such a being. The twentieth-century mathematician and philosopher Bertrand Russell is said to have walked into a lamp post, so preoccupied was he by the challenge of working out what was wrong with

Anselm's argument, for he was not himself convinced by it but could not say why.

Russell's problem perhaps was that this argument depends for its success on the assumption that thoughts and words operate at a high level of 'reality' and are in fact more 'real' that solid objects. If you show me an image of an elephant on a computer screen and I ask whether this is a 'real' elephant, I probably mean, 'is this a picture of a particular living elephant or has it been edited and put together on a computer as a mere "virtual" elephant?' Until the present generation a modern observer would be likely to consider the actual elephant the 'real' one. But that 'virtual' elephant has taken a step back towards the Platonic idea of a higher reality which inheres in the 'form' or 'essence' or first principle of something and from which all other elephants and elephantnesses derive. From the virtual elephant someone with the right software can derive any number of particular elephant pictures, in different sizes and colours and poses and even make herds of elephants. Anselm's argument works, if it works at all, by thinking of God's 'existing in reality' in something of this way. He himself was quite clear that it would not be possible to prove in a similar manner that the best possible island (or ice cream) one can think of must exist 'in reality' as well as in one's imagination. There is something special about God.

This way of approaching the matter still 'works' for those for whom the internal conviction is clear and vibrates inwardly in sympathy with the idea that God exists. It is partly a matter of intellectual tempera-ment; the world still seems to be divided into those who are Platonists at heart and those who are closer to Aristotle in their habits of mind. The Roman Catholic philosopher René Descartes (1596–1650) began, somewhat like Anselm, from the idea of God he found within him. He began by taking his own thoughts to be the bedrock. 'I think, therefore I am' seemed to him to be the first certainty. He too was able to get from there to a certainty that God exists. But even for those who do not tingle when they read Plato – or the ideas adumbrated in the cluster of philosophical systems to which Platonism contributed in the early Christian centuries – their importance to understanding the foundation ideas of Christianity is inescapable.

The study of late antique philosophy encouraged a taste for an abstract and remote deity. Some Platonist philosophers considered that 'the Supreme' must be above Being altogether, for 'To Be' seemed to them much too particular. 'The Good itself is not Being [*ousia*] but transcends being in dignity and power,' says Plato.[2] It appeared to lower God from that level of utter abstraction which they liked to think must separate the Highest and Best from all that is concrete or individual. The late Platonist Plotinus (*c.*205-270) was such an absolutist on this point that he thought not even existence can be attributed to God. In a tradition which derived from this way of think-ing, there were some attempts to adapt the Latin word *esse* ('to be') in the Middle Ages to allow it to express fine shades of being. It was asked, for example, whether God's existence (*existentia*) was more of an 'essence' (*essentia*).

Such ultimate superiority could no more be said to 'live' in any ordinary sense than it could be said to 'be'. Yet Judaism could cite the Old Testament on the question of God's existence. God said, 'I am that I am' (Exodus 3.2). He said it to Moses, who was left in no doubt that he existed in a way that involved 'living', though the exact import of that pregnant statement has been the subject of a great deal of debate. God is described in the New Testament as the 'living' Father and the 'living bread' (John 6.51 and 57), so the early Christians also believed that God 'lives'.

'Does God have to be a living being at all?' had long been a contro-versial question among philosophers. Cicero, surveying what he knows of the discussions of ancient philosophers, knows that there is much disagreement on this point.[3] Cicero feels quite confident that he knows how the gods live. Nothing could, by definition, be a happier or more blessed way of life; all good things surround deity and deity is not obliged to do any work; deity simply sits and delights in its own wisdom and virtue (or 'power'; the word *virtus* means both). He knows this is not the Stoic view, but he considers the Stoic God distinctly overworked, whirling eternally round the axis of the heavens.[4] So a great deal depends what is meant by 'living' when it is used of a deity.

Aristotle's *Categories* left another legacy both helpful and confus-ing to Christians trying to fix what existence could mean in the case of God. Aristotle focused attention on the kind of 'stuff' God would be 'made of', together with the question what would be its features or properties. Aristotle taught that there are different sorts of substances of different kinds of things (human, angelic, vegetable, for example).

Each of these has different qualities or 'accidents', which can alter without the underlying substance ceasing to be what it is. One's cheerful mood may lapse but the consequent temporary diminution of happiness does not make one a different person. A young oak tree gradually becomes an older and larger oak tree and eventually dies and decays but all the time its substance is that of an oak tree. Aristotle identified ten 'categories': substance, relation, quality, quantity, time, place, action, passion, condition, situation, of which nine were attributes of the first (substance) and could be variable.

God-stuff was described in Latin by Augustine as *substantia* or *natura* or *essentia* (using the words interchangeably). The divine 'attributes', such as goodness and mercy, were understood to be more than mere accidental 'qualities' which can change. God is not just 'good' but 'goodness'. Boethius helped to communicate this set of ideas to the Latin West in his short book *On the Trinity*. 'For when we say God is just, [we refer to] a quality but not to an accident [something which can alter], but the same thing is a substance'; the kind-of-thing God is is 'what-God-is', and it is a super-substance, 'more than a substance'.[5] God is the very Life by which he lives, echoes Anselm in the late eleventh century.[6] Alan of Lille, in his ambitious *Regulae Theologiae* ('Theological Rules') of the late twelfth century, makes it a starting point of what he intends to be a highly coordinated system of demonstrative or 'necessary' proofs that when we say that the Father and the Son and the Holy Spirit are 'just' or 'powerful' that is to be 'taken substantively'.[7] This novel approach reached new levels of technical subtlety in the later Middle Ages, as theologians refined the Aristotelian principles.[8] Christians said that in the case of God, there were not ten categories but only two, substance and relation. For in God there was Father and Son, and there was also the question of the relationship of the Holy Spirit to Father and to Son. Jesus promised that the Holy Spirit would be 'sent' as a comforter, and a great deal of debate ensued about the implications of that 'sending'.

These explanations involve ideas which have slipped out of common usage but are still there in the historical and philosophical foundations of Christianity. And they are actually very helpful in keeping things simple. For the 'Christian philosopher' of the early Christian period is in effect saying that they, God's qualities, are what God is and God is what he is like. 'Does God exist and if so what is he like?' became a single compound question.

Anselm says in the Preface to the *Proslogion*, in which he set out his 'ontological' argument, that the proof of the existence of God he had been looking for would be one which would also show what God is like.[9] For many centuries it was taken to be self-evident that a cause must colour with its own characteristics the things it causes, that there will be a likeness between Maker and made. 'By their fruits you shall know them' (Matthew 7.16 and 20). The same idea lies behind the statement that the sayings which come out of a man's mouth show what he is like (Matthew 15.18). 'Being' and 'being-like-this' seemed especially closely related in the case of God.

Thinking of God within this Christian-Platonist framework encouraged the development of a particular view of 'where' God stands in relation to the known universe. Anselm of Canterbury began his *Monologion* by contemplating the good things of life and encouraging his pupils and readers to begin from there and ascend in their imaginations until they begin to understand higher and finer ideas of what 'Good' means, and, in the end, are able to glimpse Goodness itself. Anselm illustrates simply and clearly how such individually 'good' things fit together in (and only in) the Highest Good. If someone says that a horse is strong and speedy and therefore good, he will point to a robber who is also strong and speedy, but bad. The horse's strength and speed are good because they benefit the horse, so they are 'good' with reference to their fitness for their purpose. It all depends on the integration and harmoniousness and a fitness which is also a fitting together (*convenientia*). He leads the reader on from there to the idea that the Highest Good must be that in which and through which all good things are good.[10] Our good is good by participation in the Good.

The 'ladder-climbing' method was not new to the Middle Ages. It too is a borrowed and adapted 'Platonic' methodology. It works on the principle that all particular exemplifications of things in the world can be referred back or up to an eternal Idea from which they derive and which is also their 'ideal' state. Plato uses it in his *Symposium* to explain how human understanding may rise from the contemplation of the beauty of one beloved human being, to an understanding of the nature of Beauty itself. Anselm's ontological argument for the existence of God depends on exactly this assumption, that to get an idea of what God 'really is' involves the climbing of a conceptual ladder of this sort from a known good to a better, then the Best. Anselm's pupil Gilbert Crispin, who became Abbot of Westminster, took the idea that God is that than which nothing 'better' (*melius*) can be thought as the basis for his own version of Anselm's ontological argument for the very existence of God. In the thirteenth century Bonaventure (c. 1217–74) tried something similar in his 'journey of the soul to God' (*Itinerarium mentis ad deum*).

Christianity carried forward this Platonic insistence that in God the attributes are not only substantive but somehow become one, though carefully excluding what is not God from this equation. There is, for instance, an Idea of a mouse and an Idea of an elephant, but elephants and mice do not form a unity in which mouse is elephant and elephant is mouse. It is the higher, abstract Ideas which tend to become one Idea at the summit of the pyramid of Ideas.

The 'list' of these highest Ideas in Christianity drew together hints in the Bible and added to them so that the result closely matched the Platonic list. Psalm 27.4 speaks of the beauty of the Lord. Beauty was one of the 'substantive attributes' classical philosophers thought were certain to be found in God, just as he must be One. And he must be Omnipotent and Eternal. He must be Changeless and Unmoved. He must be Good and Just and Merciful. This was a way of thinking much approved of by Augustine and, under his influence, by the West for a millennium and a half. Augustine invokes a God of Neoplatonic attributes, a God utterly beautiful, a God of good and truth and light and wisdom.[11] He assures his readers (*The City of God*, VIII) that Plato came closest to understanding the truths Christians can now fully grasp. As Anselm put it several hundred years later, God is Life, Wisdom, Truth, Goodness, Beauty, Eternity and every true Good all at once.[12] This Idealization of God has 'felt natural' to many generations of Christian believers, even in the modern world.

Even George Berkeley (1685–1753), resistant to the very idea that matter exists at all, took comfort from the 'steadiness, order, and coherence' he found in the ideas excited by sense impressions, 'the admirable connection whereof sufficiently testifies the wisdom and benevolence of its Author'.[13]

The poet John Keats (1795–1821) was expressing essentially Platonic assumptions when he wrote the line 'Beauty is truth, truth beauty'. What is ultimately 'one' in God is also somehow 'the same' in him. All the supreme ideas are so profoundly in harmony that when it comes to God they cannot be separated. All the best Ideas we can grasp point in the direction in which God could be thought to 'be' if Being were not beneath him; and in some unimaginable way, and with the same proviso, they collectively 'are' what he is, and end up as the same.

A contradictory God?

Nevertheless, it was found early on that all is not plain sailing with the 'Platonic' divine attributes which were taken over so comprehensively by early Christians and their successors. There turned out to be various contradictions and anomalies to be explained away.

The philosophers of the ancient world respected distance in their gods. The Christian Platonist's assumption was that the supreme divinity could not change or be disturbed in mood, that he always 'felt' the same and could not get upset. Stoic philosophers, who also had a great deal of influence on early Christian thinking, developed this theory further still. Tranquillity became an ideal for intelligent human beings to aspire to, just as they expected to find it in any God worthy of their respect (and also among the good angels Dorothy Sayers put into her play *The Zeal of Thy House*). Sayers gave the following instructions to the actors playing the good angels in her play "'You've got to imagine," said I, "that you are beings who have never known passion, grief, remorse, rebellion, irritability, doubt, hesitation, pain, sickness, fatigue, poverty, anxiety or any of the ills flesh is heir to; you may show a divine anger, but you mustn't sound cross; you may be tender, but on no account emotional; you may be joyful but not excitable."'[14]

But, asks the modern reader indignantly, how can a God who cannot be disturbed or upset feel compassion? What can it mean to call him merciful, for mercy surely involves fellow-*feeling* with someone who is suffering? That objection was raised in earlier centuries too. Anselm of Canterbury included a chapter in his *Proslogion* in which he puts forward the solution that God is incapable of suffering (*impassibilis*) with reference to himself (*quoad se*), but that we humans feel the effect of his compassion with reference to ourselves (*quoad nos*).[15] Yet a belief that God 'cares' was very important to the early Christian belief that God became man, felt all human pain and died a genuinely agonizing death.

The Old Testament speaks frequently of divine wrath. God punishes those who have offended him, because he is angry. 'See, the day of the Lord comes, cruel, with wrath and fierce anger, to make the earth a desolation, and to destroy its sinners from it' (Isaiah 13.9, RSV). 'And if in spite of this you will not obey me, I will continue to punish you sevenfold for your sins ... if in spite of these punishments you have not turned back to me, but continue hostile to me, then I too will continue hostile to you' (Leviticus 26.18 and 23–4, RSV). God's anger and the ensuing punishments have conventionally been seen to be perfectly just. 'His work is perfect and all his ways are just' (Deuteronomy 32.4, RSV). God knows what is right because he made it right; he told his creatures how they were to behave; his creatures have chosen to disobey. It is just and right that God should punish them. 'It is the man of God who disobeyed the word of the Lord; therefore the Lord has given him to the lion, which has torn him and killed him according to the word that the Lord spoke to him' (I Kings 13.26, RSV).

In both Old Testament and New God is always merciful as he is always just, but there are indications that the mercy is in tension with the justice and both in different ways present a challenge to the talk of anger. 'Has God ... in anger shut up his compassion?' asks the Psalm (Psalm 77.9, RSV). 'All the ways of the Lord are mercy and truth,' says Psalm 24.10, though another Psalm says that 'The Lord is just in all his ways' (Psalm 144.17). Justice and mercy, as Anselm points out in the *Proslogion*, appear to be incompatible if they are to be treated as absolutes in the divine nature. If God is wholly just he must punish all sinners as they deserve. If he is wholly merciful he must forgive them all. Anselm is a little nonplussed by this, and has to concede that it is something the believer may just have to accept, for the divine Goodness is also involved, and that too interacts with his justice and his mercy. God's 'immense goodness' is unimaginably generous. From the depth of his goodness flows God's mercy.[16]

The idea that God is 'almighty' is to be found very widely in the Old Testament (Genesis 17.1, 28.3, 35.11; Exodus 15.3; and II Corinthians 6.18 citing Old Testament themes). Revelation 1.8 calls the God who is Alpha and Omega 'Almighty'. Revelation 4.8 has the living creatures full of eyes who surround the heavenly throne crying 'Holy, Holy, Holy, Lord God Almighty' in an echo of Isaiah 6.3. This had a strong appeal especially in the Greek-speaking Eastern half of the old Roman Empire. The emphasis of the early centuries was on the omnipotence of the Pantocrator, the All-Powerful, who gazes down with darkly hooded Byzantine eyes from the apses of churches.

But this power of God's to do anything he liked was not quite what it seemed. For how can God be omnipotent when there are many things he cannot do?, asks Anselm of Canterbury, taking the bull of potential contradiction by the horns once more (*Proslogion*, 7). He cannot be corrupted or lie or make what is true false. God cannot do what it would not be like him to do. Anselm deals with this problem cleverly by suggesting that to be able to do such perverse acts would actually be an 'impotence', not a power, for it would go against the way things are.[17] Questions of this sort were very commonly asked in the Middle Ages, where the conflicting requirements of power and constraining necessity were of great interest.[18]

The Platonists also thought that God knows everything, but the Christians saw problems of consistency here too. Historically their particular area of concern was not so much whether God 'knows everything', but whether he 'knows everything in advance'. For if he does, it seems that none of us can be free to decide or choose anything, because he already knows what we shall opt for, and he is bound to be right. The Bible discusses God's foreknowledge a good deal, in both Old and New Testaments. 'God knew in advance what they would do' (Wisdom 19.1). 'This man, handed over to you according to the definite plan and foreknowledge of God, you crucified' (Acts 2.23, RSV). 'Those whom he foreknew he also predestined to be conformed to the image of his Son' (Romans 8.29, RSV). 'God has not rejected his people whom he foreknew' (Romans 11.2, RSV).

But if an omniscient and omnipotent God foresees what will happen, his foreknowledge looks very like predestination, for he cannot be wrong about what is going to happen and it appears that it must be determined: 'Foreknowledge of all things in nature is really nothing but predestination and predestination the same as foreknowledge,' said John Scotus Eriugena (c.810-77).[19] Anselm presents the problem crisply. 'What God foreknows will necessarily take place; and what is done by free choice [of a rational creature] will not necessarily take place.' But God can also foresee what the creature freely chooses, and he cannot be wrong, so it begins to look as though the creature's choice is not free at all, but predetermined. Even if he changes his mind, God's foreknowledge will be waiting for him down the newly chosen road, for God will have known in advance about the change of mind too. (We shall come back to this problem later.) Anselm's way round this difficulty that divine foreknowledge looks very like predestination, is to argue that if one freely chooses to do what God wills one will meet no obstacles.[20] But saying no when God means yes does not appear to be an option.

The challenge here was to preserve a sense of the profound simplicity of God, the oneness which is of the essence of his substance, when to the eye of reason he has so many attributes, not all of them obviously consistent with one another. The modern challenge is to accommodate different priorities and concerns, for different things now seem to require an explanation – the existence and nature of the God who apparently strikes people down for no reason at all, inflicting hereditary diseases on helpless infants; the intolerance of a God who, some fundamentalists claim, will condemn people eternally for unorthodox opinions or unorthodox sexual practices; the inadequacy of a small cosy God who can remain a comfort figure to the person who wants to remain childishly dependent. Such a list – and the reader will be able to add to it – reflects modern preoccupations with things which are hard to reconcile with respect or with worship, which do not seem to make a God worth bothering with or a God at all.

An unknowable God?

There is one well-trodden way round this centuries-old difficulty of making a description of God 'add up'. Ideas of 'what God is not' were as widely accepted in the formative centuries of Christianity as ideas of 'what God is'. This supposes a God who reveals himself so far and no further, who leaves his creatures tantalizingly in the dark about those things about himself they most desire to know. 'I sought him whom my soul loves; I sought him but found him not; I called him but he gave no answer' (Song of Songs 3.1). Here God is 'known' by the absence of anything positive to say. Lactantius (c.250–c.325), one of the first systematic apologists for the Christian faith who sought to win over a sceptical and highly educated pagan intelligentsia by appealing to the authority of the philosophers, rehearses a number of sources for this idea in his 'On Anger' (De ira).[21] Among them he points to Plato, who says in the Timaeus that the majesty of God is such that the mind cannot grasp it nor language express it.

That God is infinite is a perhaps surprising example. Yet to call God 'infinite' is really to say something negative, that God has no known boundaries. The ancient philosophers' assumption was that the divine is light and definition and clarity, and not formless or boundless at all. Divine infinity was a surprisingly late arrival in the 'set' of things which have added up to the traditional Christian picture of what God is like and not like. The bold idea that God might be infinite seems to appear only with Philo of Alexandria, a Jewish philosopher of the first century AD.[22] The Greek conception up to then was that there was an infinite quantity of original 'stuff', to which limits were set by imposing 'forms' upon it, thus literally 'defining' things by giving them edges. In that scheme of things, God would have extremely sharp edges.

Ps-Dionysius 'the Areopagite', a fifth-century Christian author writing in the Greek language, was probably the first to point out more generally that the only things which can be known with confidence about God are the things we do not know. We say that he is 'infinite' as much because we do not know where his boundaries are or whether he has any as because we positively think he is limitless. One result is that we see God in a paradoxical way. The light which God emits is so bright that it dazzles us and we cannot see. Already in the New Testament it was described as an 'inaccessible light' (I Timothy 6.16).

To say such things is really only to say that God is 'beyond us', and how far beyond we simply do not know. Ps-Dionysius envisages the possibility of union with God in a similar 'light-which-is-darkness'; his idea is that 'we are united to God as to one unknown',[23] as though the greatest intimacy of human existence lies in a final self-loss in the divine.[24]

The modern attraction of this may lie in its apparent open-endedness about what God is like, though it will become increasingly evident that it was not without its hidden agenda.

So what is a God?

In The City of God (VI.v) Christian Augustine suggests that there are three 'kinds' of religion. His theory would have made sense throughout the early centuries of Christianity and it forms a useful background to today's notions of what religion is 'for' in modern society and the ways in which it relates to life and living.

The first sort of 'religion' in Augustine's list is found in fables or myths about 'little' gods. This takes us straight into the modern arena of the cult of unworthy objectives, and the placing of reliance upon things which cannot bear the weight. For practical assistance with life's small difficulties, some being with greater than average human powers (an agony aunt, a social worker?) comes in useful and provides something for the individual to lean on in the expectation that it will 'know best'. In the early Christian world, even a little god was believed to be able to do things human beings cannot, and by methods unavailable to humanity, and to be, in this sense, 'super'-natural. But its level of operations was restricted to such minor activities as mending broken legs and assisting with revenge against a personal enemy. The cult of such gods resembled the 'celebrity' cult of the modern world, in the 'Big Brother' displays of pettiness and bad temper among the gods as they squabbled, in the stories told about them.

In the ancient world most people found it easy and convenient to accept that there were supernatural powers of this sort, and their childish tantrums were not found to diminish a nervous respect for what they could do if you offended them and for what they might be bribed to do if you pleased them. The polytheistic pagan religions of European antiquity identified gods in things which could be pointed to and touched, statues, even natural objects believed to be holy, such as particular rocks or mountains or streams. Sometimes spirits were thought to dwell in these objects (animism); sometimes the objects themselves were thought to be 'gods' compounded of the visible thing and the invisible animating spirit. These small gods were believed to have modest and often very local powers.

Classical philosophers tended to be disparaging about the little gods. They reached for something 'bigger'. But they were relatively relaxed about accepting the reality of such small supernatural powers alongside a kind of Godness which seemed to them more worthy of the reverence of an intelligent and idealistic person. The history of the expansion of the Roman Empire is one of syncretistic absorption of the gods of conquered peoples into the Roman pantheon. Greek Zeus was identified with Roman Jupiter, Hera with Juno, and so on. The conquered Greeks did not need to object to this because it did not compromise the status or identity of their gods.

The Roman world took it to be a duty of citizenship to show respect (*pietas*) to the civil authorities. (The third in Augustine's list is this 'civil' religion.) The 'required respect' could be hard to distinguish from 'worship of the Emperor as though he were a god'. It was the conviction that that was going too far for a human ruler that made Christians refuse, and got them persecuted and sometimes martyred. The nearest modern equivalent is perhaps the moral courage of a Nelson Mandela who is prepared to suffer rather than accept the policies of an unjust state. This is 'belief' which requires life to be lived in a way which is consistent with it, belief to die for.

In early Christianity the little gods of antiquity were not entirely abandoned. Christians sometimes confused the saints with the more benevolent sort of little gods, as Augustine's own mother Monica seems to have done in her enthusiasm for visiting their shrines with gifts. Unlike the little pagan gods, the Christian saints did not expect to be paid, but this 'popular' religion still tended to involve a transaction. The saints were powerful because they had surplus goodness to lend and were believed to be able to make miraculous interventions. They responded to prayer. Little spiritual elevation or intellectual stretching was involved on the part of the pious applicant for their help.

Augustine places second in his list 'natural' religion, the kind which is the subject of philosophical speculation about the physics and metaphysics of the universe. This is the counterpart of modern scientific debates. This is where the deep questions about what 'God' may 'be' really bite, but it is also the area where the possibility of 'relationship' between such a God and human beings with the little daily worries and mid-life crises of one-half of humanity and the Third World famines of the other is least easily envisaged.

One big God?

The 'Jealous God' of the Old Testament would permit no rivals. The Jews stood firm on their ancient monotheism against the invasive tendencies of simple polytheism. 'You shall have no other god to set against me. You shall not make a carved image for yourself' (Exodus 20.3-4, NEB). 'You shall not prostrate yourselves to any other god. For the Lord's name is the Jealous God and a jealous God he is' (Exodus 34.14, NEB).

The insistence on belief in 'one' God did not prove to be a force for unity among the great monotheistic religions, however, despite the fact that they seem to have agreed that their 'one God' was the same

God. Early in its history Christianity took the decision to separate itself from Judaism. The Acts of the Apostles record how it was agreed not to 'require' Christians to continue with Jewish 'observances'.[25] Christian authors consciously relied on the philosophical backing of secular thought. 'There is one God, the beginning and origin of things,' states Lactantius. 'Plato says so in the *Timaeus*.' He adds a confirmation from Cicero.[26] In the twelfth century we find Alan of Lille, who liked to show off his knowledge of ancient philosophy, making it the first of his Theological Rules that 'God is not only said to be One, but a Monad, that is, Unity.'[27]

Islam, from its founding by the Prophet Mohammed (c.570–632), also made the oneness of God its central tenet, sharing the concerns of Judaism, as well as those of Christianity, on this key point. The Koran is insistent on the oneness of God: 'There is no God but him, the Creator of all things. Therefore serve him. Of all things, he is the Guardian.'[28] It reproves those who 'regard the jinn as God's equals, though he himself created them'.[29] But at no point has there been any serious notion that Islam and Christianity might join forces as monotheistic religions with a good deal in common, for Christian monotheism was as distinct from that of Islam as from that of Judaism.

Hinduism and Buddhism are exceptions to the 'rule' that monotheism is central in the great world religions. The relative independence of the evolution of Christian thinking from these Eastern traditions is probably a result of the fact that informed contact with them came relatively late in the Christian story. Hinduism has its supreme God, but it also accepts the existence of thousands of lesser gods, who may be aspects or expressions of the One. Buddhism perceives an interconnectedness of things in every aspect and it identifies no supersubstantial 'supreme being' who is more-of-everything-that-is than anything else, and correspondingly powerful.[30] There were Christians in China and India from an early date, but there was limited contact, certainly little which could be described as 'interfaith dialogue', until the Western trade expansion of the late fifteenth century and the Jesuit missions which began in the sixteenth century. In the 1870s Nisikânta Chattopâdhâya gave a few lectures in German in Leipzig. The second, entitled 'Buddhism and Christianity', was published in an English translation in London in 1882 by the Freethought Publishing Company. Buddhism, it is noted, originally passed over 'in silence the dogmas of a supernatural God and a supernatural immortality'. This caused shock waves of disapproval in the nineteenth century and attracted only a radical publisher for an English translation of these daring lectures. Nevertheless, the juxtaposition of the Christian and Buddhist frames of reference was a great shaker-up of suppositions. It provided a corrective to a number of 'static' presumptions built into the traditional Christian cosmos.

In modern 'multicultural' societies these questions of interfaith comparison have become urgent once more. The modern believer has a choice to make among several mature world religions, some of which begin from the same or a similar insistence on the oneness of God.

One God or three?

The Christian understanding of divine 'oneness' is not identical with that of Judaism or Islam because in Christianity God is also 'three'. Where did this idea come from? No account of the doctrine of the Trinity appears in the Bible. The 'Persons' of the Trinity are mentioned separately. Jesus often spoke of his Father, and he himself is quite frequently called the 'Son of God' (for example in John 3.13-19). Jesus made his disciples a promise that when he had left them, the Father would send a supporter, advocate, 'comforter', to be with them, who would teach them and bring back to their minds the things he himself had said (John 14.26). The nearest hint of an insistence that they are somehow all one God is in Matthew's Gospel (28.19), which mentions the three Persons, Father, Son and Holy Spirit, in connection with baptism.

'Threeness' was not itself a new idea. In order to accommodate the Supremacy which is perhaps even above being - so that God cannot even be described as the 'Supreme Being' without demeaning him - some classical philosophers postulated a 'coming out from' that conceptually unreachable unity. It could be put thus. From the One proceeds the Divine Mind (*Nous* or *Logos*), and from *Nous* the Soul (World-Soul or Spirit of God). In this way God 'emerges into our sight' and is able to have some truck with the physical world without the ultimate heights really having to come down to the depths.

But this descending 'trinity' of classical philosophy could only roughly be equated with the Christian Trinity of Father, Son and Holy Spirit, because its members are not equal but stand in a relation of hierarchical subordination. The Christian contribution was to insist on the equality and co-eternity of these divine entities. The Nicene credal formula says that Christ was 'Begotten of his Father before all worlds', but, as Augustine explains, this did not make him in any way 'subsequent to' his Father. There was never a state of things – the word 'time' must be meaningless here – when God the Father did not have a Son. The Creed also says that Christ was 'of one substance with the Father', to emphasize that he was not of some less divine 'stuff' but shared the divine nature.

Even if it can be agreed that God is 'three' in some way which does not interfere with his also being 'one', there remains the question 'three what'? At the time of the Christological controversies of the fourth and fifth centuries, one of the problems was to explain what the 'three' of the Trinity are. What manner of thing is the Father? The Son? The Holy Spirit? How were they 'different' within the Godhead? Why and how was only the Son 'made man' in Jesus? After some debate, the Greeks settled on the term *hypostasis*; the Latins chose the word *persona*. The meaning of the Greek term tended more towards the idea of a 'face', so that Father, Son and Holy Spirit could be seen as aspects of one God. The Latin *persona* had hitherto been used for a masked character in a drama, which allowed people to think of the Father, Son and Holy Spirit as 'masks' of the one God. Both terms had the drawback of implying a mere presentation or 'front', when orthodoxy increasingly insisted that whatever God is as three 'Persons' is no mere matter of presentation or dressing up, but a profound reality of the divine nature.

The idea of a 'three-in-one' God raises many problems, not least how to use words in discussing him. An example is the question whether to use a singular or a plural verb when talking about the Trinity. In the twelfth century Peter Lombard (c.1100–60) asked which is correct, to say that Father, Son and Spirit 'is holy' or to say that Father, Son and Spirit 'are holy'? 'There are some who say that although you can say that the three persons "are" one God, you cannot say that the divine substance "is" three persons.'[31] The implications go far beyond getting the grammar right.

Various images attempted to depict the Trinity or provide a basis of comparison in the natural world to help people grasp the idea. Was the Trinity like the sun, whose light and heat are different to our perceptions, but it is hard to say how they can be separated from the

sun and from each other? Was the Trinity like a river, with a spring
(the Father) running into a watercourse (the Son) and eventually into
the sea (the Holy Spirit), although it is the same water throughout
and no one can say where one leaves off and another begins? These
analogies quickly break down, for they give only the merest hint of
the incomprehensible reality, and as soon as any weight was put upon
them, for example by seeking to define the relationship of the Spirit to
the Son, controversies began. The most notable of these was the divisive disagreement between Eastern and Western Christians about the
'Filioque' ('and the Son') clause which had been added to the Nicene
Creed by the West in Carolingian times to the great indignation of
the Eastern Churches. They said that this was unacceptable because it
was an innovation and had not been agreed by the whole Church and
also because, in their view, it was wrong. To say that the Holy Spirit
proceeded from the Father and the Son was to say that there were two
First Principles, not one, against all the canons of a Platonist monotheism.

In his *Soliloquies* Augustine holds an experimental conversation
with himself, in which he is paired with his own reason, 'asking and
replying to myself when I was alone, as though we were two, my reason
and I'.[32] He thus assiduously turned over 'with himself' many different matters over a period of some days.[33] This notion of a division of
self for purposes of interior dialogue was worked out more fully in
Augustine's book *On the Trinity*. It seemed to Augustine that a human
being may be an image of the Trinity in some sense. Augustine and
Anselm see God, Father, Son and Holy Spirit, as being in an eternal
relationship. So when memory, understanding and love interact with
one another in a human individual, that individual is behaving 'like'
the divine trinity-in-unity.[34] The theme often reappears in Augustine's
later imitators. Hugh of St Victor, taking Augustine's idea forward in
the twelfth century, defines 'soliloquy' as the solitary conversation of
an individual not only with himself but about himself.[35]

Once it was accepted that God is Father, Son and Holy Spirit,
people began to ask whether all the substantive divine attributes were
common to all three or whether some belonged especially to one or
other of the individual 'Persons' of the Trinity. For example, is God
omnipotent or is only the Father omnipotent? The controversial
Paris lecturer Peter Abelard got into considerable difficulties with

the ecclesiastical authorities in the early twelfth century, when it was suggested that he had been seeking to partition the divine attributes in this way, yet he was in reality merely continuing an ongoing debate on this point.

There is a lot at stake here. It is not only to interfaith dialogue that the insistence on the threeness of the one God has presented a stumbling block and made it difficult for Jews or Muslims to accept Christian belief. The sixteenth-century uncle and nephew both known as Socinus (uncle 1525–62, and nephew 1539–1604) had reopened the doctrine of the Trinity to question in the sixteenth century. Another radical challenge, which tried to return to the simple belief in one God, appeared in England in the writings of John Biddle (1615–62) who popularized his ideas by holding 'conventicles' in London in the 1650s. It was not for another century that a Unitarian denomination was founded by Theophilus Lindsey in 1773–74, and a similarly minded congregation was begun in the USA, in Boston in 1785.

Christian believers still have to grapple with the question of 'threeness' and form an opinion on the ideas of 'Fatherhood' and 'Sonship' and the role of the Holy Spirit.

The Godness and humanity of Jesus

The problems do not end there, for it is a central part of traditional Christian belief that Jesus of Nazareth was the Son of God, become human and yet remaining fully God. The love of this Christ, a loyalty to this 'person', has formed the passionate heart of belief imaginatively, emotionally, intellectually, generation after generation. In the letters of Paul to the young Churches which became part of the New Testament this personal loyalty is repeatedly emphasized. 'Surely you recognise that Jesus Christ is among you?' asks Paul (II Corinthians 13.5), reminding the Christians in Corinth that this is the test that they are living the life of faith.

Why God should have 'become man' is a question for the chapters which follow. Our concern here is with 'how'. On the basis of the foundations which had been laid in the early centuries and all the effort which had been put into explaining how the three Persons were also one God, it was reasonable to ask how Jesus could cry, 'My God, my God, why have you forsaken me? (Matthew 27.46; Mark 15.34 and cf. Psalm 22.1), if God is 'all of a piece' in his substantive attributes, and Jesus was the Son of God 'incarnate'. Only the Son became man, not the Father or the Holy Spirit, and only the Son let out that cry of agony, says the tradition, but what does that say about his divinity?

The main problem has always been to strike a balance and ensure that whatever explanation is proposed insists that Jesus was fully human as well as fully divine. In the first centuries, under the influence of Platonic philosophy, there was some nervousness about accepting his full humanity because that made it look as though God was demeaning himself. In more modern times it has been comparatively easy to think of Jesus as a very good man and an example to all human beings of the way to lead a good human life, but harder for people to accept that he was God.

Defining 'incarnation' and explaining the way it could have happened was a task which occupied the best minds of the first Christian centuries and caused endless strife. A sequence of ecumenical councils from the Council of Nicaea in 325 wrestled with these questions. Almost every variation was tried: two natures and two persons, one nature and one person, and one person and two natures; for the intellectual pressures were those of a world where to be divine implied one thing and to be a creature other things, some of them incompatible with divinity. After the Council of Chalcedon of 451 had called a temporary halt to Christological debate by agreeing that the incarnate Christ was one Person in two 'Natures', divine and human, the non-Chalcedonian or 'Monophysite' Churches, which would not adopt this view, remained a thorn in the flesh of the Emperors and Patriarchs of Constantinople. A new tide of industrious attempts to make things fit together produced a theory that perhaps there was, if not a single nature, a single will or energy in Christ, and the hares were off again, breaking away in many directions in search of explanations, and having to be recaptured.[36]

The concerns of these early generations with the mechanics, the sheer difficulty of understanding how God could come down from his heights to be truly human without hopelessly compromising himself, prompted some extreme contrivances. This would be a God prepared to go some way to meet his creatures and to try to help them, to humble himself to their level, not only to become one of them but to suffer, to die; this was apparently a God capable of vulnerabilities. The idea was shocking to educated minds of the early Christian centuries with their philosophical heritage of high expectations of a Being (or a

Beyond-Being) worthy of the respect of rational minds and certainly incapable of suffering or making himself ridiculous. This was on the assumption that a God worth worshipping could not be vulnerable.

So at one extreme stands an incarnate God so strong and unchange-able that 'becoming man' in this way was indeed an act of power; a God who remained omnipotent and omniscient in Jesus; a God who truly suffered and truly died but rose again, victorious. At the other extreme of the continuum of possible explanations stands a God open to change, perhaps working with and through a creation with which he is somehow joined in a common endeavour with the struggling creatures he has 'become one of':

> But God's nature and action entail that God is not an item in the world, battling for advantage. The religious life, on this account, would be taking on the task of ensuring a habitation for God, a God who does not guaran-tee for himself a place in the created world, a place alongside other agents, and so is visible only when a human life gives place, offers hospitality to God, so that this place, this identity, becomes a testimony.[37]

Centuries of wrestling with these paradoxes created an accept-ance that it was somehow possible for the Son-as-God to remain unchanged, while the Son-as-Man died and was resurrected. This was an uneasy reconciliation of incompatibles, always liable to slippage in one direction or the other. Medieval theologians, accepting the fact of the incarnation as defined by the ecumenical councils, still raised various intricate mechanical questions, such as: Why did the Son take flesh and not the Father or the Holy Spirit? Could the Father or the Holy Spirit have been incarnate? If only the Son was incarnate, did he do something the Father and Spirit did not do?[38] It was asked which human defects Christ assumed. The answer was that he had a capacity to suffer, both bodily ills such as hunger and thirst and ills of the soul such as sadness and fear – in short, everything except sin.[39] This prob-lem of sin was going to become central, as we shall see in Chapter 5, in looking at the question why God would choose to become incarnate.

Was there something special about the Christian belief about Jesus? Among the ancient religions of the Near and Middle East are themes of descent to the underworld and cyclical re-emergence of a 'saviour' god or goddess who has put winter and darkness to flight and brought back spring and hope. The Greek legend of Persephone is based on the same idea. But it was being claimed that something had happened in the death and resurrection of Jesus which was quite different in its cosmic implications.

It has remained open to question whether the resurrected and ascended Jesus is 'still' human, and the Son of God now possessed of more than a (presumably perfect and contemporaneous) recollection of what it feels like to be a human. I Timothy 3.16 explores the resurrection, but still without any clarity about the continuity of the humanity of the Son of God once he was 'ascended', that is, returned to his original divine companionship with the Father in the Godhead. Jesus' ascent into heaven is described in Luke 24.51 in the most laconic terms. He left the disciples and was carried 'up' into heaven. Mark gives a little more detail (16.19; cf. Matthew 22.44), saying that he ascended to heaven and sat at the right hand of God. This additional information made the depiction of Christ in Majesty seem natural in the first centuries. Acts 1.9-11 provides two figures who appear after Jesus has gone up into heaven, and they explain that he will come again in the same way. This promise of return became associated with the end of the world and the Last Judgement, which was - at first - expected to happen very soon, in the lifetimes of those then living. All this must wait for later chapters, for the question of the creation of the world comes first.

3

God's in his heaven; all's right with the world?

Why create anything?

A God who is what he is (and everything he needs to be) is by definition complete. So why would God create anything 'else', anything other than himself? Genesis is economical about God's motives for making the world. It merely says that he did it. 'In the beginning God created the heaven and the earth' (Genesis 1.1) by a series of purposeful 'speakings' which brought them into being in all their detail. It is reported that 'God said' and it was so (Genesis 1.3, 6, 9). Day by day he said things and there the things were. The same confidence is found in the Psalms. 'By the Word of the Lord the heavens were made and all their host by the breath of his mouth' (Psalm 33.6, RSV).

The 'speaking' was to become theologically significant. We noted earlier that the Gospel of John begins with the idea that Christ is the Word of God. This suggested – to contemporary readers with a smattering of philosophy – even more than that he was the starting point of 'Language' and 'Reason', a divine Vehicle of Expression, and a divine Rationale. The Word of God 'made' things by uttering them. The Word was a creative 'Saying', by which things 'were' as God 'said'. Early Christians thus had a literal belief in the power of language.

The 'Christianized' theory of the 'forms' or Platonic Ideas suggests that God thinks the kind of thoughts a God like him *would* think. These become the 'forms' or patterns for things in the created world. There was also a theory that all our ideas come from God anyway, and we cannot ourselves think of anything entirely novel, merely freshly perceived aspects of things God has already 'thought' of. In a computer age this might be described as 'pre-installed software'.

So as rational creatures, we have built-in 'Ideas' (which are also 'Ideals') of various such absolutes or patterns of things: justice, beauty and goodness, which are not things we have ever perceived with the senses. We just 'know' about them. The 'forms' or patterns or ideas exist independently of the embodiment in the material things in which we 'see' them. We did not learn about them by that route, though we are able to recognize their presence in things we can perceive, by making some sort of internal reference. We see a flower and 'know' it to be beautiful, instantly, and we do not arrive at that conclusion by rational analysis.[1]

The favourite idea among Platonists was that the created world is a natural outflow of divine goodness. God wished to share himself, and so he made a universe which was other than himself (though *like* himself) out of sheer generosity, so that it could enjoy him. Christians could accept that, because it did not imply that God was needy in any way and 'had' to make the world. Tertullian (c.160-c.225) asks exactly this question whether God made the world because he had to (*ex necessitate*) or because he wanted to. But the same questions were still pressing a millennium and a half later, in the era when Joseph Addison (1672-1719) was asking searching questions about the *Evidences* of Christian religion:

> If the universe be the creature of an intelligent Mind, this Mind could have no immediate regard to himself in producing it. He needed not to make trial of his omnipotence, to be informed what effects were within its reach: ... in the immense abyss of his essence are contained far brighter scenes than will be ever set forth to view.[2]

This talk of overflowing takes us to important themes in the early Christian explanations of the way the universe is related to God as its creator. The first is the idea that he is 'up' in heaven and the world is 'down' below him.

'Up' and 'down'

There is a general expectation in Christian literature that the place to look for heaven is 'up'.[3] Here Christianity parted company with a good deal of classical expectation, though the late antique philosopher Plotinus describes spirits descending through the heavenly spheres in order to go creating.[4] Classical mythology characteristically envisaged a world 'beyond' this world where the dead lived, which was also in every sense 'below' it. In this world only some shadowy lingering was allowed to the dead – in a place not necessarily painful or punishing, rather just dull, gloomy and melancholy. It is said that when Daedalus flew he hovered above Cumae before he came to earth, took off his wings and set up a temple. In the rock on which it stands, hollowed out, is the cavern of the Sibyl, and behind her, running deep into the rock, are innumerable passages from which call out the voices in which she speaks when she is consulted as the oracle. Thus Virgil begins Book VI of the *Aeneid*, in which Aeneas approaches the gateway between here and the 'there', beyond and below.

Aeneas asks to be allowed to enter Hades and see his dead father. He is accompanied by the Sibyl, who explains to him (and to the reader) the significance of what he sees. 'The descent to hell is easy. The door to dismal Hades stands open day and night.'[5] When it is explained to Aeneas what is involved in going down to Hades, he goes off very thoughtfully, considering within himself the dark matters before him (VI.157–8). It is grey and frustrating on the other side of the grave. These nether realms are above all 'empty'.[6] He finds himself in a dark and desolate place, full of disease and death and dull labour and war and the dubious pleasures of perversion, the furies and discord raving. There are deformed and monstrous beasts. The very landscape boils and belches slime. The dead but unburied crowd the shore, unable to go to their grim end until their bones are laid to rest. The misery of the unburied, the lingerers on the shore in Virgil's underworld, lies in their very restlessness.

Christian beliefs about the resurrection required a radical reconceptualization of the classical Hades.[7] There was a tradition that Christ had descended to the underworld to rescue Adam and Eve, and perhaps others from before the time of Christ.[8] In the East depictions of the *anastasis* (resurrection) show Christ marching into hell to seize and bring out the first man and woman.

The Biblical texts are quite literal-minded in the way they speak of 'up' and 'down'. The Latin encourages this, for the word for heaven is the word for the sky (*caelum*). Jerome and the English monastic writer Bede (c.673–735) were aware that *caelum* is also the Latin for *cosmos* in Greek.[9] In the Old Testament, Jacob's ladder has angels ascending and descending upon it, and God leans upon the top of the ladder (Genesis 28.12–13). In Exodus 19.18–20 God comes down to Moses on Mount Sinai. The New Testament continues the theme of a heaven 'up there'. John the Baptist bore witness that he saw the Holy Spirit 'descending like a dove from heaven' and resting upon Jesus (John 1.32). John's Gospel is full of references to the ascent to heaven. No one ascends to heaven unless he has come down from heaven. The Son of Man is in heaven (John 3.13). Jesus, echoing Exodus 16.8 and the story of the manna which came down from heaven, speaks of the Bread of God descending from heaven and giving life to the world (John 6.33). Jesus raises his eyes to heaven in prayer (Mark 6.41 and John 17.1). In Luke's Gospel, Jesus in agonized prayer, facing crucifixion, is comforted by 'an angel from the sky' (Luke 22.43).

The ascension of Christ took him 'up' into the heavens (II Corinthians 12.2–4), where he reigns with the Father above all heavens (Ephesians 4.10). Luke, writing in Acts, describes a sudden sound from heaven which fills the whole house where the followers of Jesus are sitting (Acts 2.2). Paul on his journey to Damascus is suddenly surrounded by light from heaven above (Acts 9.3), and he falls on his face and hears a voice calling to him (Acts 9.4). Romans records the divine anger falling from heaven on the irreligious and unjust. (Romans 1.18). The theme of divine intervention from a heaven above 'recurs' in Acts 22.6 and 13. At the end of history Christ is to 'descend' and believers are to be 'raised' to meet him (I Thessalonians 4.15–17).

Under the influence of this remarkably consistent description of ups and downs, the idea of a hierarchical universe came to be almost universally accepted in Christendom. When Bernard of Clairvaux (1090–1153), the outstanding figure of the new Cistercian monastic order, designed his book *On Consideration* for the better instruction of Pope Eugenius III, he organized it round the conceptions of up and down. The Pope was to ask himself what was below him, what was on his level and what was above him (I.ii.5).[10] In Dante's *Divina Commedia* and Milton's *Paradise Lost* we have ambitious attempts, of epic proportions, to enter (in imagination now) the world beyond the present one, and to set out a geography in which the organizing principle is this hierarchical arrangement of a 'heaven above'. Both map a heaven 'up' and a hell 'down', so as to provide a hierarchical structure for the cosmos.

Dante travels 'up' through the whole universe in a series of dialogues with his guides – first Virgil, because of his known familiarity with the realms of Hades, who takes him to the borders of heaven, and then Beatrice, a Christian soul in bliss, who is able to assist him in understanding the Christian heaven where she now dwells.

The seventeenth-century Puritan poet John Milton (1608–74) climbed the hill to heaven in a conscious companionship with Dante:

> How shall a man know to do himselfe this right, how to performe this honourable duty of estimation and respect towards his own soul and body? Which way will leade him best to this hill top of sanctity and good-ness [*Paradiso* XXVI–XXVII and *Purgatorio* XXVII.125] above which there is no higher ascent but to the love of God which from this self-pious regard cannot be asunder?[11]

Milton does not offer his own fully worked-out version of the struc-ture of the entire cosmos as Dante does. But he takes for granted and polishes the imagery of a hierarchical universe in which heaven is 'up there'. He describes how, at the end of the six days of creation, God 'desisted, though unwearied' (*Paradise Lost*, VII.552) and ascended:

> Up to the Heav'n of Heav'ns his high abode (VII.553),

to gaze upon his creation and see it beautiful and

> Answering his great Idea (VII.557).

As he ascended the angelic choirs followed him with their acclama-tions (VII.165).

Milton's Satan set himself up as God's rival, 'raised impious war in heaven' (I.43), and that is why he finds himself cast out of heaven and 'down' with his followers, 'fallen' angels, for their 'fall' is downwards.

Is this simple vertical polarity still a useful metaphor for a reality we can now believe in?

Going downhill?

Greek philosophers thought that the separation of the creature from the creator must involve a departure from the best, a diminution of likeness to the creator. They understood this in terms which can be expressed mathematically. If one is multiplied by one it is still only one. God the Trinity is readily understood like that, for he remains one God. If one is added to one the result is two, the beginning of plurality. Creatures are like that because they are other than God.

This 'otherness' was envisaged as a sort of distance, which is more easily understood through the geometrical counterpart of this arithmetical idea. Any number of geometrical points may be superimposed upon one another and there will still be only a single point. But the moment there is another dimension to move into, the series of points becomes a line. Early Christians, under the influence of the philosophical ideas they were absorbing into their world view, took it for granted that the diversity and plurality of 'created' things automatically involved a dropping away from that absolute One Best Thing. The Pythagorean mathematics still in use up to the Renaissance of the sixteenth century and beyond saw it as a philosophical law that the resulting plurality or multiplicity departs from the unity which is the best state of things, and that the multiple and diverse are less good than the One.

Linked with this idea was the assumption that the further a creature is from God in the 'chain of being' the more it is 'bodily'. Angels are pure spirit. Human beings are spirits with bodies. Animals are bodily creatures with movement and life but without spirits or souls. Vegetables are bodily creatures without movement and with life but also without souls. Rocks and stones are bodily creatures with mere existence, for they do not even have life. This theory reached perhaps its most graphic form in the 'hermetic' tradition of the second, third and fourth centuries. Augustine, who knew of these theories, takes up the theme of 'uprightness' of spirit in one of his *Ennarrationes in Psalmos*. The sinner bends his spirit 'downwards' by sinning. But when he gets up from his prone position on the ground and looks upward his spirit is straightened.[12] Medieval writers suggested that it was open to human beings to behave 'spiritually' like gods, or in a bodily way like animals. Those who become 'very different' from God (*longe dissimiles*) grow like beasts and they descend to the 'place of death'.[13] To go away from God is thus to be altered in one's very self.

Alan of Lille was particularly fond of this cluster of ideas.[14] He writes in the language of 'standing up straight'. *Thesis* ('standing') is the *proprius status hominis*, the proper normal human condition, the 'position' in which a person is when he makes rational decisions to do the right thing. Sometimes he falls away from this into vice. Alan of Lille describes this outcome vividly by depicting the beastly human being on all fours, gazing down at the ground like a cow or a horse and no longer able to look up to heaven at all. Sometimes the spiritually ambitious human being exceeds his normal status, moving into a state of ecstasy and becoming godlike.[15]

Creatureliness appears in all this in its relationship with the creator, coming from him, being less than him, but defined with reference to him. The heavenly hierarchy or 'chain of being' forms an important element in the logic of this understanding of the deep structure of things, and with it certain assumptions about the nature of universal order and the manner in which it can be disrupted. As Shakespeare puts it in *The Merchant of Venice*:

> Take but degree away, untune that string,
> And hark what discord follows

Even though the simpler 'up' and 'down' pictures of the past now look like mere images, this basic framework assumption, of One giving rise to many and the Unitary generating the multiple and diverse, has been surprisingly persistent. There seems to be a lingering idea that simple is best. A modern scientist writes: 'The simplicity of nature is not to be measured by that of our conceptions. Infinitely varied in its effects, nature is simple only in its causes, and its economy consists in producing a great number of phenomena, often very complicated, by means of a small number of general laws'. So it is as much a natural defence of the human mind today as 2,000 years ago, to try to find a pattern in the enormously complicated which will make it possible to deal with it a bit at a time and see how it all 'works'.

> When scientists are confronted by complexity, their instinctive reaction is to try to understand it by looking at the appropriate simpler components and the way they interact with one another. Then they hope to find a simple law (or laws) which applies to the system they are studying. If all goes well, it will turn out that this law also applies to a wider sample of complex systems (as with the atomic model of chemistry ...), and that they have discovered a deep truth about the way the world works.[16]

'In' and 'out'

Before we leave these questions of the possible 'location' of God in his relation to creation, there is one further set of difficulties to be looked at, and those concern whether God is 'inside' or 'outside' his creation. Is he part of the world he has made, and if so how, or is he looking on like a carpenter who has made a piece of furniture, giving it an extra polish perhaps, replacing a door handle, but not taking up residence in it in any way? The New Testament gives him an active role in the perfecting of a universe damaged by human bad behaviour (II Corinthians 13.5 and 14), but that is a question for a later chapter.

The Holy Spirit had a recognized place in the creative process, though not an uncontroversial one. Some ancient philosophers spoke of a 'World Soul', a divine presence interfused in the world and working to make and sustain it. Thus God could be involved with the world without demeaning his Highestness by contact with matter, though that would require the World Soul to be lower in the hierarchy than the Supreme (Being). According to the Christian doctrine of the Trinity, any such Soul or Spirit must be true God, eternal, equal with, and of the same 'substance' as the Father, so the maintenance of the world could not involve being part of it. This was one of the most important insistences of Augustine in his influential book *On the Trinity*, in which he put this principle into Latin.

The possibility that the created world might not be outside God at all is challenging to the Christian understanding of things. 'The heaven of heavens cannot contain God,' insisted the Old Testament (I Kings 8.27). If God could be involved with the universe so intimately that he was not presiding above it and directing it, he would be in danger of getting his hands dirty in the way the most refined ancient philosophy found utterly unacceptable.

The 'heavens' might be taken to be the parts of the physical and temporal universe which lie beyond the earth. Or they might be understood to be the supernatural heaven, God's dwelling place or environment, which is not temporal or spatial. We then have a new difficulty. God is not in time or place, for all things are 'in' him, so what can 'in' signify?, asked Anselm (*Proslogion*, 13), thinking like a Christian philosopher. For if being in heaven is 'being in God', a whole new crop of boundary disputes suggests itself. Plato in the *Timaeus* sees the whole universe as a living creature with a soul and a capacity for reason. For him, God and the universe are a single entity, a great organism. This notion hinted at another idea Christians found dangerous, that God the Holy Spirit is really the soul of the universe, giving it life.

Yet it makes quite a difference whether the universe is thought of as consisting *only* of a 'natural world' made of matter which can arguably tell us something about the God who made it, or whether it is taken to *include its own creator*. The universe could then truly be called 'universal' as well as 'eternal', for it would include everything that is (if we are going to decide to let God 'be'), but it would be harder to see what could be inferred from the material creation about the remainder of the universe, for the relationship of the two would be different.

St Paul describes the human individual as the Temple of the Holy Spirit. The conceit is developed by the poet John Donne into a depiction of a human self which can be itself only when indwelt by the Holy Spirit:

> I am thy sonne, made with thy selfe to shine,
> Thy servant, whose paines thou hast still repaid,
> Thy sheepe. Thine Image, and till I betray's
> My selfe, a temple of thy Spirit divine.[17]

An idea closer to the ancient philosophers' 'world soul' seems to have been in the English poet William Wordsworth's mind nearly two centuries later:

> I believe
> That there are spirits, which, when they would form
> A favoured being, from his very dawn
> Of infancy do open out the clouds
> As at the touch of lightning, seeking him,
> With gentle visitation; quiet Powers!
> ... They guided me.[18]

These numinous assistants in the development of the Wordsworth are not his only guides. The landscape itself is teacher:

> ... the huge cliff
> Rose up between me and the stars, and still
> With measured motion, like a living thing,
> Strode after me ...
> ... and after I had seen
> That spectacle, for many days my brain
> Worked with a dim and undetermined sense
> Of unknown modes of being ...
> ... Huge and mighty forms, that do not live like living men, moved slowly through my mind.[19]

> I have felt
> A presence that disturbs me with the joy
> Of elevated thoughts; a sense sublime

Of something far more deeply interfused,
Whose dwelling is the light of setting suns,
And the round ocean and the living air,
And the blue sky, and in the mind of man;
A motion and a spirit, that impels
All thinking things, all objects of all thought,
And rolls through all things.[20]

Wordsworth had a strong personal sense of an 'interaction' with the divine somehow bodied forth in the physical universe, as something which had had a hand in teaching and forming his very self. Critics have called him a 'pantheist'. Wordsworth felt himself to be 'taught' by mysterious powers moving in nature, but it is hard to say whether he thought these powers were God, or 'from' God. Yet there is a lingering aftermath of the ancient notion of a Spirit 'dwelling' in the world, working in it and moving it, which caused the early Christians such uncertainty if it seemed to veer towards the notion that the Spirit of the World might be God at some lower level.

There is still talk among Evangelicals today of the indwelling of the Spirit in the souls of the saved. The important question for the modern believer is whether he remains separate.

This last question takes us into the next part of the history of the debate, which is concerned with the question how far the world tells us that God designed it:

Sir, I think it shows considerable disrespect for God to suggest that he is anything other than a good manager. The concept of intelligent design has all the hallmarks of the deplorable micro-management so loved by new Labour.[21]

God the Maker: like begets like and 'natural theology'

Alongside the idea that 'God is what he is like' stands the belief that when it comes to creation, 'like makes like'. In other words, a God will create things which resemble him. Some civilizations have worshipped the sun. The sun's 'existence' on one level, the level of sense perceptions, is obvious. And some of the things which make it awesome are also plain to see and feel. A Sun-God is hot and bright, yet comforting. He can burn and dazzle, but he also creates a climate in which plants grow and animals and cats stretch out in contented sleep. It is a corollary of the idea that the very proofs of the existence of God furnish strong indications of the kind of God he must be, that to understand the universe you must first understand God.

Cicero says that the most important questions about the gods are whether they take an active interest in running the world and whether they have the power to do so.[22] Christian belief has been in no doubt on either point. 'For what can be known about God is perfectly plain to them since God himself has made it plain' (Romans 1.19, Jerusalem Bible). If God is actively at work in the world any natural–supernatural boundary which may exist must be able to be crossed, and the material world can be acted upon by immaterial or 'spiritual' forces.

This crossing of the natural–supernatural boundary in this way required the believer to accept a pattern of cause and effect as something fundamental to the universal order. Aristotle remained a significant influence here. In the *Metaphysics* (I.iii.1.983a) he lists the four Aristotelian 'causes' which were to be adopted in Christian science of the first 1,500 years: the final or ultimate cause (which could be equated with the Father), the formal cause which imposes the pattern or 'form' on created things (the Son), the efficient cause (the Holy Spirit) and the material cause or physical matter from which things are made. The early Christians accepted this way of thinking, that God, invisible and intangible, just beyond perception, is giving things a push in directions which say something about whatever is pushing. In other words the divine is to be known by the way it behaves and the way it behaves can be relied upon to have certain effects. When Thomas Aquinas pointed out that the existence of God cannot be a self-evident truth (or everyone would accept it on hearing it said that there is a God), he still thought it could be 'demonstrated' (that is, shown to be 'necessary') 'through the effects [of God] which are known to us'. Aquinas listed five 'ways' of proving the existence of God.[23] He depicts God as the divine Betterness-than-other-things, but also as the source of power. For Aquinas, God is the divine First Mover, the divine Cause, the divine Rule or Governance, as he argues from what we see and know to what he suggests 'must' lie behind, causing or shaping it.

All attempts to understand God in terms of the world and the world in terms of God are bound to be dogged by cultural assumptions and current fashions of expectation, but this basic idea has remained influential through dramatic changes of expectation and priority. 'It's all going to blow up, so why worry?' said a theology student overheard in an Oxford café in 2004 to a fellow student. They were discussing whether the ecological movement of the twenty-first century had theological implications. Perhaps, suggested one, if the rain forests were saved and the earth's ecology protected, there would be no need for the coming of a new heaven and a new earth promised in Revelation 21.1. If the natural world were 'managed' 'with a view to eternity', 'perhaps it won't need transforming', they speculated. Their idea was that if there was to be a transformation it would not involve a fresh creation. England would still look like England beyond the grave and even beyond the 'end of the world'.

'It's a completely fallen system,' one of them said, by which he meant that the poor tribes of the Amazon, exploited by the rich nations of the world, are arguably left with no alternative but to cut down the trees if they are to make a living. So they saw that the problem could be posed in terms of sin and 'fallenness'. But they also saw that it could be understood in terms of the mechanisms of nature, of natural consequences of actions in a framework of physical laws. And above all, they framed their questions and their answers in terms of the ecological assumptions of the early twenty-first century Western world of thought.

Yet their speculations were rooted in a distinction which these modern students shared – whether or not they recognized it – with some of the more radical theologians of the seventeenth and eighteenth centuries who proposed a 'natural theology'. The rational approach to which eighteenth-century thinkers gave the label of 'natural theology' lent itself to discussion of certain fundamental topics which had been defined as 'theological' by Boethius in the sixth century when he was trying to make it clear what aspects of God and his work can be tackled with the aid of reason alone. These were whether God exists at all; whether he is one or many; whether he can be both three and one and how; how he makes things other than himself.

The theme of the 'connectedness' of creation in its capacity to 'show the way' towards God and 'speak' of him appears throughout Christian history. Close to the year 1000 Ralph Glaber commented on the way God is 'plainly and beautifully preached' in the interactions of created things.[24] Yet everyone also thought there were limits to what could be found out that way. Bernard of Clairvaux discusses the inadequacy of the senses in matters of faith. 'Why do you ask the eye to do what it is not capable of doing?' He points to Jesus' words, 'Do not touch me' (John 21.17), and remarks on the fact that Jesus added, 'because I have not yet ascended to my Father'. That suggests to him that after the ascension some 'touching' might be possible. Indeed it is possible, he confirms, but it is a touching by 'affect' and not by hand.[25]

The theme of learning from nature about what lies beyond or behind nature was still a familiar commonplace in the sixteenth century, when Shakespeare referred to it, evidently considering it an idea any playgoer would make sense of. He speaks of 'Sermons in stones, books in the running brooks' (*As You Like It*). It was still familiar ground in the seventeenth century. In a seventeenth-century poem which became a hymn, George Herbert (1593–1633) tried to express the way in which spiritual perception can pass through matter, and matter enter into an exchange with spirit, in which some sort of transformation is brought about.

> A man that looks on glass,
> On it may stay his eye;
> Or, if he pleaseth, through it pass,
> And then the heaven espy

Pascal (1623–62) claimed that Descartes would have preferred to do without a God, but found he needed to postulate that he existed to initiate the world.[26] 'All understandings seek after God, and have a sense and feeling of God. If Reason did not apprehend God; Religion could not be learn'd. For there would be nothing in Nature to graft it on', commented the Cambridge Platonist Benjamin Whichcote (1609–83).[27] Another Cambridge Platonist, Ralph Cudworth (1617–88), in his *The True Intellectual System of the Universe* (1678), distinguishes between theists and atheists. Theists 'affirm that a Perfectly Conscious Understanding Being, or Mind, existing of it self from Eternity, was the Cause of all other things'.[28]

Joseph Addison versified the theory thus in a hymn which is still in use:

> The unwearied sun from day to day
> Does his Creator's power display,
> And publishes to every land
> The work of an almighty hand.

What though in solemn silence all
move round the dark terrestrial ball;
what though nor real voice nor sound
amid their radiant orbs be found;
in reason's ear they all rejoice,
and utter forth a glorious voice,
for ever singing as they shine,
'The hand that made us is divine.'[29]

It is against this very long-standing background of expectation that William Paley (1743–1805), writing the definitive 'natural theology' of the eighteenth century, discusses the 'evidences' provided by the natural world. His natural theology applies reason to observation of the world on the assumption that there is a relationship between creator and creation. If I stumble upon a stone, he says, I may postulate that it came there by chance, and the way it is, a shapeless lump, speaks of neither design nor designer; but if I were to find a watch lying on the ground I would be hard put to it to dismiss its existence as an accident or chance.

> When we come to inspect the watch we perceive – what we could not discover in the stone – that its several parts are framed and put together for a purpose, e.g. that they are so formed and adjusted as to produce motion, and that motion so regulated as to point out the hour of the day.[30]

It is not necessary for the rational observer to be able to penetrate far into the mechanics of the thing, suggests Paley, for him to be forced to conclude that it had a Maker. 'Ignorance [of the way it works] exalts our opinion of the unseen and unknown artist's skill ... but raises no doubt in our minds of the existence and agency of such an artist.'[31] He takes it as self-evident that a creation of great complexity, which it would take a supremely intelligent human being to put together, must show us a creator who is intelligent, resourceful and capable of working with things much better than we are. This God is, to put him at his smallest, Plato's craftsman at least.

The new breed of natural theologian frightened contemporary traditionalists. The eighteenth-century American reformer and Calvinist Jonathan Edwards (1703–58), alarmed at the implications, wrote that the Deists, 'are not like the Heretics, Arians, Socinians and others, who own the Scriptures to be the Word of God, and hold the

Christian religion to be the true religion, but only deny these and these fundamental doctrines of the Christian religion'. Ordinary heretics are 'wrong' only on specific points. 'The Deists deny the whole Christian religion. ... They deny any revealed religion ... and say that God has given mankind no other light to walk by but their own reason.'[32]

Kant tried to synthesize these traditional assumptions of natural theology with other modes of knowing. He ends his *Critique of Practical Reason* with the reflection that he is filled with awe and admiration whenever he considers the stars of heaven above him and the 'moral law' within him. These are satisfactorily 'present' to him, he says, and do not require metaphysical or speculative endeavour. They are things he really knows. The first lies within the reach of his senses, which perceive the world directly, and this first perception extends outwards into the whole vast connected system of times and places. The second begins inside his invisible self, but that is where his very consciousness resides. It is a direct intuitive knowledge.

The first major objection to natural theology as defined by Paley which had a substantial impact came with Charles Darwin's *On the Origin of Species*:

> The old argument of design in nature, as given by Paley, which formerly seemed to me so conclusive, fails, now that the law of natural selection has been discovered. ... Everything in nature is the result of fixed laws. ... But passing over the endless beautiful adaptations which we everywhere meet with, it may be asked how can the generally beneficent arrangement of the world be accounted for? [He now thinks it can be explained in terms of the laws of natural selection and the survival of the fittest.] It may be truly said that I am like a man who has become colour-blind. ... The state of mind which grand scenes formerly excited in me, and which was intimately connected with a belief in God, did not essentially differ from that which is often called the sense of sublimity; ... it can hardly be advanced as an argument for the existence of God. [But] I feel compelled to look to a First Cause having an intelligent mind in some degree analogous to that of man; and I deserve to be called a Theist.[33]

Nevertheless, Darwin did not entirely destroy the attractions of natural theology. Thinkers continue to juggle with it. In the twentieth century, Arthur Koestler suggests that the divine may be related to creation in some such way as this, in which God retains his 'position' at the 'top', is in control, and all change refers to him:

the term 'balance' or 'equilibrium' takes on a special meaning in the context of an organic hierarchy: it is not meant to refer to relations between parts on the same level of the hierarchy, but to the relation of the part to its controlling centre on the next higher level.[34]

We are moving away from the relatively simple structural options of the natural theologians here, to ask questions of the sort which have presented themselves in the modern world. It will be obvious that the attempt to state the questions in such new ways stretches the capacities of language as well as the conceptual frameworks the believer is invited to explore. Nevertheless, Koestler was really reminding his readers of yet another perennially recurring question, whether the nature of the universe and God's relation to it is dynamic or static. Robert Grosseteste in the early thirteenth-century 'scientific revolution' was already talking about the potential of the earth and earthly things to change and the power of the heavenly to bring about such change. Heaven and earth may be distinguished, he suggests, as the active and the passive creations, the creation in which things can be changed and the creation in which they cannot.[35] Heaven is mobile, but not necessarily in the same way as earth. Grosseteste cites the even earlier discussion of the Cappadocian Father and Christian Platonist Basil of Caesarea (c.330–79) on the way the heavenly spheres move, like a number of bowls one inside another.[36] This possibility takes us to our next section.

Unfinished business?

Growth and development

Did God make the world fixed and complete from the outset? Did God make the best imaginable universe? The possibility that he made his creation incomplete or imperfect was disturbing if it was taken a step further and allowed to include a degree of open-endedness or even the daring thought that God might not have been capable of making an 'already perfected' universe.

The 'fixed idea' that God was 'already' the imperturbable best he could be, had tended to encourage an equally fixed idea that the universe was made already finished, or with a built-in programme according to which it was bound to unfold. Anything else could scarcely be entertained in the Christian tradition until comparatively modern times. Even the thinkers who put forward the eighteenth-century ideas about natural theology, ahead of their time though they were, were mostly arguing from the assumption that they were looking at a completed design whose characteristics could be regarded as settled.

It seemed to Plato in the *Timaeus* that it was possible to separate two ingredients which appeared to have come together in the creation of the world. The first was matter, the physical stuff of which it was made. The second was the shaping of that matter into distinct 'created things' or 'creatures'. There was an 'orthodoxy' behind this, the belief that a God worth his name would not wish to get his hands dirty by having actual contact with matter. His having 'ideas' was another matter altogether, for ideas in the Divine Mind fitted comfortably with the belief that Godness was intellectual and rational and unbodily.

Matter was envisaged as the raw material upon which the 'forms' were impressed to make them into 'created things'. In the *Timaeus* Plato describes the creation of the world by a God who, like a great Craftsman, brings together pre-existing matter and form, so that only the world as we know it can be said to have had a beginning at his instigation, for the stuff which composes it was not made by the Maker of the world. Plato thought that God merely took over a disorderly state of affairs and made it tidier, turning everything that 'was' into the organism of this universe which was itself a living creature, in which all individual and particular living creatures subsequently have their being.

Christian thinkers were not content with that. It became an immoveable insistence of Christian orthodoxy that God was the origin of everything, matter and spirit. The assertion of the creation of the world 'from nothing' was important, not only because it elevated God from craftsman to creator, but because it denied any primordial existence to matter-evil as a power in the universe. Any other view would have significant consequences for our present enquiry. If matter were evil, it could not teach lessons about the Good God, and 'natural theology' would collapse.

So early Christians insisted that God as creator was incomparably more than a craftsman. The belief which emerged most definitively in the West was that God made everything in the created world from nothing (*ex nihilo*). He was no mere craftsman, but the very creator of the matter and form from which he fashioned created things. That seemed to be endorsed by Genesis when it says that at first the world was without form and void (Genesis 1.2).

Tertullian asks whether God made the world out of matter or out of nothing.[37] The North African Christian author Cyprian (d.258) and Lactantius both say that the world was made from nothing. The belief that God did not work with pre-existing matter was put on a firm footing by Augustine of Hippo. Ambrose, Bishop of Milan (c.339-97), was preaching on the creation story in Genesis when the young Augustine came to listen to his sermons and was overwhelmed with admiration at the way he was able to make intelligible and intellectually respectable a synthesis of the two traditions, the Christian and that of classical philosophy. Ambrose began his discussion of the first 'six days' by reviewing the debates of the day, in which this conflict between the classical philosophers who thought matter was primeval and the world eternal and the Christians who said God created it from nothing was a central question. When Augustine subsequently asked whether formless matter was made 'before' 'formed things' (in time),[38] he assumes that God made both.

The difference between this 'nothing' and 'something' was seen for a long time in terms of the question where the lumps of primordial stuff came from and the related question how the shapes which make it into created things were designed and imposed upon it. The material nature of the creation was still preoccupying thinkers beyond the Middle Ages. Thomas Hobbes (1588-1679) in his *Leviathan* (XLVI), is unequivocal that the created world is material. 'The ... Universe ... is Corporeall, that is to say, Body; and hath the dimensions of Magnitude, namely, Length, Bredth, and Depth.'

> From harmony, from heavenly harmony,
> This universal frame began:
> When nature underneath a heap
> Of jarring atoms lay
> And could not heave her head,
> The tuneful voice was hear from high:
> Arise ye more than dead.
> Then cold and hot and moist and dry
> In order to their stations leap.
> (John Dryden, 1687)

The usual assumption of Christian believers has been that 'completion' of the universe would be something like the casting of a plaster-of-
Paris garden gnome in a rubber mould. Unlike Plato's Craftsman, who
merely mixed the 'plaster' and poured it into a ready-made 'mould',
the Christian God designed the mould and invented the plaster. But
the outcome or result was, in neither case, going to be a surprise, for
questions of divine predestination and foresight make their presence
felt as soon as it is asked whether God had a plan for the world when
he made it, and whether he was able to carry it out satisfactorily.

The important early questions about the possibility of divine
involvement with the material world concerned time as well as space
and matter. The possibility of an incompleteness or latent perfectibil-
ity in the universe cannot even be proposed without taking some view
of the relationship of time and eternity. Some ancient philosophers
conjured with the possibility that the world is eternal, something
whose origins do not need to be explained because it has 'always' been
there, and that possibility continued to trouble Christian theologians
in later centuries. If the world or the universe is eternal all sorts of
possibilities open up, because it throws into question God's relationship to the world.

Genesis (1.1) says that God created the heavens and the earth 'in
the beginning'. What was God doing 'before' there was time? Is this
a meaningless question if there is no 'before' in eternity? It was not
appropriate for God to do anything *before* he did it, at which point
it was appropriate, one thirteenth-century commentator suggests,
juggling with this difficulty.[39] Or it could be argued that the beginning
of making things also made 'beginning' possible. It was the first tick of
the clock. It was, suddenly, 'fitting' for a linear temporal progression
to 'begin'.

On the face of it, time and eternity are incommensurable because
one is a perpetual condition and the other moves on. There need be
no progress in eternity, and perhaps there cannot be, if all is simulta-
neity. Whether or not the cosmos had a beginning, *time* must, of its
nature, have had a beginning. It is linear, runs only one way and must,
by definition, be in some sense 'progressive', for it moves ever onward.
Time has conventionally been taken to have had a beginning, 'before'
which God 'was'. Even on a traditional Christian view that God began
it, the created world is not necessarily all 'in' time. Earth may have

clocks but in a heaven made by the creator there need be no passage of time. Heaven may have had a beginning, but once made it could continue for eternity. So the modern believer faces a challenge not new in itself but presenting a range of novel difficulties in connection with ideas of development and completing in the progression of the universe.

The idea of an 'infinite universe' in the sense of a universe perpetually in change existed in an inchoate form before Aristotle. It is found in Democritus (460-370BC) and Epicurus (341-270BC), and Aristotle's criticisms of Democritus survive as do those of some of his pupils.[40] Nevertheless, it is suggested, this did not take over as a view which commanded general assent or interest until the end of the Middle Ages.[41] For the 'infinite universe school', the universe is in flow, moving dynamically. Epicurus wrote three open letters which may still be read in Diogenes Laertius' *Lives of the Ancient Philosophers*. The third of these letters, written to Menoeceus, was about human life (X.139). Death is nothing, it says, for when the body dissolves into the elements of which it is composed, it can feel nothing.[42] It has flowed on. The Stoics gave the world a beginning and an end but they envisaged it as being repeatedly reborn every time it ended.[43] In the traditional Christian view, the world would end indeed, but not merely to be reborn and begin another cycle, endlessly repeating itself. It would end, and a new heaven and a new earth would come into being, in which God's ultimate purposes for the universe would be fulfilled.

What is the modern believer to make of the possibility that God deliberately (or because it was the best he could do?) left the world 'unfinished' when he first 'made' it, leaving it to complete or 'perfect' itself? Robert Grosseteste in the thirteenth century thought Genesis described the bringing into being of the 'archetypal world'.[44] This world as first created, the world of the angelic hosts, was the world before mankind was made.[45] Genesis recognizes that things changed in the world after Adam and Eve ate the apple. This was regarded in Genesis as a change for the worse, but it was transformed by Christian theologians into a *felix culpa*, a happy accident. Grosseteste was not the only theologian to ask whether this was God's original plan, for there was an appearance of making the best of it about the rearrangement and rescue which came about with the Fall of some of the angels and then the creation of human beings, and their subsequent Fall,

and all the consequences which flowed from that as God set things
to rights and brought the creation round again, so that it could point
towards his originally intended conclusion once more.

The Bible warns that one must expect delay; one must expect to
have to be patient (Proverbs 20.21; Romans 8.22). But 'Christian hope'
is a notion presupposing a future to be looked forward to.[46] Eusebius
of Caesarea (c.260–c.340), one of the first historians of the Church,
set a Christian historiographical fashion for 'placing' this sequence
of historical events in eternity. Bede describes six 'ages' beginning
with Adam, and ending with the end of the world. This adds another
'dimension' to the question of the relation of time and eternity. Here
we are not merely thinking how the individual can progress through
time, but how the whole human race in history makes a journey
through time.[47] Bede, the calendar maker and measurer of 'time'
whose work became a uniquely important influence on the dating
practices of the Middle Ages, did not deal in such questions.[48] A series
of attempts to map this historical progression of the completing of the
world from Old Testament to New and on into contemporary history
was made by Rupert of Deutz (c.1075–1129/30) and his contemporary
Anselm of Havelberg, followed a generation later by Joachim of Fiore,
a latter-day prophet who set about announcing the end of the world
and attempted to put a date to it.

Nevertheless, some in the early modern world saw the possibility of
development and change in creation as an expression of divine power
as they understood it. The sixteenth-century 'Garden of Adonis' of
Edmund Spenser (1552–99) describes the rich creativity of a God eternally sending forth new designs. About his heavenly throne:

> Infinite shapes of creatures there are bred
> And uncouth forms which none yet ever knew;
> And every sort is in a sundry bed
> Set by itself and rankt in comely rew
> Some made for beasts and some for birds to wear;
> And all the fruitful spawn of fishes' hew
> In endless ranks along enranged were,
> That seem'd the ocean could not contain them there.
>
> Daily they grow and daily forth are sent
> Into the world it to replenish more;
> Yet is the stock not lessened nor spent

But still remains in everlasting store,
As it at first created was of yore.

Addison, too, saw it as a compliment to God to believe him capable of inexhaustible further improvements on an originally perfect theme. 'It being impossible that the great Author of nature should bound his own power, by giving existence to a system of creatures so perfect, that he cannot improve upon it by any other exertions of his almighty will.'[49]

Charles Darwin's theory of evolution explains the diversity of animal forms as something which has grown to meet the needs of the animals themselves. He did not accept that each animal was placed on the earth as we now have it, as if by a God playing with a toy farm. That presented a frightening challenge in the mid-nineteenth century. A God in whose mind lay the eternal pattern for making elephants would have had to adjust his thinking if elephants turned out to be not fixtures in the created world but a stage in a story in which mammoths came first.

> Under certain circumstances individual differences in the curvature of length of the proboscis etc., too slight to be appreciated by us might benefit a bee or other insect, so that ... the communities in which they belonged would flourish and throw off many swarms inheriting the same peculiarities.[50]

Process

A group of theologians half a century ago experimented in a novel way with the idea that God may not have a fixed plan whose working out he can ensure.[51] What came to be known as 'process theology' assumes that everything is in process except perhaps the idea that everything is in process.[52] It is tempting to point out a resemblance to the Ciceronian–Augustinian dilemma about the difficulty the Sceptics had in being other than sceptical about their own ideas, with the result that they could not say for sure that they were Sceptics at all.

Some members of this group took the idea of process into the doctrine of God itself. Charles Hartshorne, working among a cluster of theologians at Claremont and Chicago in the mid-twentieth century, suggested that God is somehow so much a union of the finite and the infinite that he is best thought of as a series of occasions rather than an eternal infinite being.[53] He suggested that there could be episodes in becoming when the 'process' pauses and 'is'. It was his colleague A.N. Whitehead's idea that such episodes are 'occasions of experience'.[54] This has the disadvantage that it seems to make God look like an electronic video recording, whose running has had to be interrupted by pressing the pause button in order to see what is happening at a given moment. Nevertheless, the idea of 'process' takes us once more into questions of sequence and of the meaning of 'time' in a cosmological context, with which a modern believer has to grapple.

Similarly, even the most sceptical of modern theoretical physicists is forced to recognize the fuzziness of the boundary between physics and metaphysics when it comes to questions about the beginning of the world. Modern science makes contributions which more or less consciously lie at the border between physics and metaphysics, for example that there was a Big Bang at the beginning and an expanding universe since. The Big Bang theorists are, after all, putting forward an explanation with change and development built into it. 'I suppose that Bishop Berkeley (1685–1753) [who questioned whether anything existed except minds and spirits and what they think or perceive] would have thought that in some sense the physical world emerges out of our mental world, whereas the more usual scientific viewpoint is that somehow mentality is a feature of some kind of physical structure'.[55]

Stephen Hawking adds:

> Roger Penrose and I worked together on the large-scale structure of space and time. ... We pretty much agree on the classical theory of General Relativity but disagreements began to emerge when we got on to quantum gravity. We now have very different approaches to the world, physical and mental. Basically, he's a Platonist believing that there's a unique world of ideas that describes a unique physical reality. I, on the other hand, am a positivist who believes that physical theories are just mathematical models we construct, and that it is meaningless to ask if they correspond to reality, just whether they predict observations.[56]

To the modern eye, then, there may be many further dimensions to this disturbance of the old confidence in cause and effect, like making like, and a generally settled air to created things. The old ideas of a certain sequential character to making and possibly to completing if completing is needed, have received a further jolt in modern science, where the laws of physics are observed to operate equally readily in either direction, forward or backward in time. Take the example of what happens when a glass of water is knocked off a table and breaks, splashing the water about. The sequence of events is easily understood as following the familiar laws of physics. But the observer would be surprised if the sequence reversed itself and the fragments and splashes reorganized themselves into a glass of water and put themselves back on a table. In physics the emergence of order, the coordinating move-ments, the sheer organization of the process, could work as readily backwards as forwards in time. Could they also turn the cause which in effect knocked the glass off the table into the effect which stands at the end of the process of reassembly running the other way? The possi-bility of a self-assembling glass of water, suggests Roger Penrose, ought to make us revise our assumptions that causation must always work in a particular direction. 'Highly-coordinated motion is acceptable and familiar if it is regarded as being an effect of a large-scale change and not the cause of it. However, the words "cause" and "effect" somewhat beg the questions of time-asymmetry.'[57] 'If we lived in a world where such occurrences were commonplace, surely we would ascribe the "causes" of such events not to fantastically improbable chance coin-cidences concerning correlated behaviour of the individual atoms, but to some "teleological effect" whereby the self-assembling objects sometimes strive to achieve some desired manifest configuration of an assembled and filled water glass.'[58]

Chaos

Modern science moves on to a more radical challenge still, but once more a challenge which is not essentially new, with the realization that the tidiness of the explicable may exclude significant aspects of reality and even quite profoundly misrepresent the way things are:

> Where chaos begins classical science stops. For as long as the world has had physicists inquiring into the laws of nature, it has suffered a special ignorance about disorders in the atmosphere, in the turbulent sea, in the fluctuations of wildlife populations, in the oscillations of the heart and brain.[59]

'The irregular side of nature, the discontinuous and erratic side'[60] interested Augustine, too. In the period immediately after his conver-sion to Christianity in 386, he retired with his mother and a group of friends to talk things through at Cassiciacum, on the north Italian lakes. One of the questions they tackled was whether 'there is any factor governing the movements of physical objects which lies outside human will and disposition'.[61] 'One night,' Augustine relates, when he lay awake as he 'often did, silently worrying', he heard the gurgle of water in the pipes and was struck by the way it stopped and started.[62] It was eventually ascertained by inspection that what was happening was the build-up of fallen autumn leaves in the guttering, which were then shifted by the pressure of the rainwater which flowed until another cluster of leaves formed, and was moved onwards in its turn. Augustine was glimpsing the problems to which modern 'chaos' theory proposes answers. So did the Cambridge Platonists, who regarded the parts of the universe as linked, 'limbs of one entire body', as Cudworth puts it in his *True Intellectual System*.[63]

To the modern scientist 'chaos ... is a science of the global nature of systems'. For the first truly modern chaos theorists, 'had a taste for randomness and complexity, for jagged edges and sudden leaps'. They were willing to 'speculate about determinism and free will, about evolution, about the nature of conscious intelligence. ... They believe they are looking for the whole', not the constituent parts of theory proper to distinct 'sciences'.[64] They were moving, consciously or not, close to crossing the boundary between natural and supernatural, physical and metaphysical. Modern 'chaos theory' embraces natural disasters and acts of living things, whether consciously willed or not. It is able to trace a route from the beating of a butterfly's wing to a car crash, thus uniting in a single chain of causation the willed actions of living things and natural disasters.[65] The earthquake of late December 2004 and the great tsunami waves which laid waste the litorals of South East Asia were a sharp reminder for many of the importance of certain questions which began to be asked again, insistently, and which overflow the boundaries of the study of the machinery of creation and open up ethical dilemmas. How can a good God allow all this damage and suffering? How can God be omnipotent if he allows these things to happen?

These issues still present themselves. It is just as much a question as it ever was whether the universe can be satisfactorily explained solely in terms of a physics in which everything can be measured, and measured by the same intellectual instruments. The study of the brain famously does not explain the mind. The advance of computers has not yet given them consciousness and it can be argued that it never could. 'Physicalism' and 'mentalism'[66] can still look like alternative ways of understanding the nature of things. 'It is essentially impossible that [conscious understanding] can have arisen as a feature of mere computational activity nor can computation even properly simulate it.'[67]

These are also questions central to the cosmology of other world religions. The basics may look different in Buddhism, Hinduism and Islam.

> It is God who splits the seed and the fruit-stone. He brings forth the living from the dead and the dead from the living. ... He kindles the light of dawn. He has ordained the night for rest and the sun and the moon for reckoning. Such is the ordinance of the Mighty One, the All-Knowing. It is he that has created for you the stars. ... It was He that created you from a single being and furnished you with a dwelling and a resting-place. ... It is He who sends down water from the sky with which We bring forth the buds of every plant.[68]

Unity is always best, Plato thought. Therefore, in his view, just as there must be one supreme being, there could not be multiple universes.[69] Christianity has tended to go along with him here, though modern hymns have played with the idea of many universes, each with its Christ:

> There is one beginning of things not many,[70]

> Such a vault of wonders she had never seen.
> The city hanging there so empty and silent looked new-made, waiting to be occupied; or asleep, waiting to be woken. The sun of that world was shining into this, making Lyra's hands golden.[71]

Lyra, the heroine of the novel, is provided with a bridge into a parallel world. Many worlds could be in parallel or inside one another, like Russian dolls. They and their parts need not all be the same size. Everything could be more relative than has yet been imagined.

The modern believer has to grapple with possibilities much more rich and various than was altogether foreseen in the centuries when God was seen as merely putting forth a paler version of his own perfection, allowing his own goodness to overflow. Yet all these later variations are inherent in earlier insights.

4

A high-risk strategy?

This is where we come to some of the most difficult questions any belief system has to grapple with. Life is a struggle. People fail at things they try to do. They hurt one another. Why is it all so difficult and often painful when a competent Maker of a really first-rate machine could surely have prevented all that? The manufacturer of a new car promises smooth fast running and there is a warranty that any mechanical breakdowns will be repaired if it does not live up to the promise. Why isn't life like that?

This chapter and the next will be concerned with the emergence of a system of explanation in Christianity which, once it began to crystallize, took on a life of its own. It encouraged the designing of a whole stream of requirements. The resulting theology of sin became a great burden to believers. Remove it and you take away a great many anxieties at a stroke. But is it possible to eliminate the notions of guilt and punishment, the machinery of repentance and absolution, all the conventional apparatus for 'dealing with' sin and be left with authentic Christian belief? And what replaces that machinery for the Christian believer who needs a way to deal with his own behaviour and the thoughts of which he is sometimes ashamed? How to think about and deal with 'wrongdoing', with its damage to oneself and others, the social aspects of the harm done by people whose behaviour damages others, remains a practical, daily, ethical problem for the modern believer.

The consequences of allowing choice

Living tends to be experienced, even by the most placid and level headed, as a continuing balancing act. Moods and the weather change. The first question for the modern believer is what to make of change and how to handle it. Charles Darwin suggested that it might be one of the 'laws' which govern the survival and evolution of species that living things make adjustments according to their environment. In that way plants and animals would grow to be comfortable with things as they are, even if that was not what they preferred. A giant redwood tree will remain a bonsai redwood but still a redwood if it is planted in a saucer. Is this a perfectly satisfactory open-ended way for the universe to go on, or, in adapting, are creatures making the best of a bad job?

The biggest 'change' and the most challenging to belief is change for the worse in a universe which has been created by a good and powerful God. Christian belief has mostly favoured the view that things are not all they might be and the universe is not at present in perfect working order. Yet even a mere missing screw or minor malformation in the universe presents a fundamental problem for belief in an all-powerful, omnicompetent God.

One possibility which began to emerge at the end of the last chapter is that there has been a high-risk strategy on the part of the creator in that he did not finish things off. Then the present imperfections of things are mere incompleteness and could be part of God's way of doing things, full of potential for perfection and scope for the making of contributions by creatures who want to join in. Creation would then be a growing thing, and the fact that it is not yet all it is capable of being (or as good as it could be) should cause no alarm. This explanation still allows God to be omnipotent, but it could be adapted to allow for the idea that he might not be, but was merely doing an imperfect best. 'Perhaps his experiment went spectacularly wrong, sir, Perhaps He's just baffled. Seeing the mess, not knowing how to put it right.'[1]

On the second hypothesis, the imperfections have to be regarded as 'evils', and then they begin to look like a worrying challenge to the traditional Christian view that the God who made everything is omnipotent. This hypothesis has it that the universe left the creator's hands perfect but something has since happened to damage it. That would of course mean that he allowed it to be damaged, or could not prevent the damage or had to build in a 'damage-and-repair' stage. It is on the second hypothesis that this was not the way things were *supposed* to unfold (even if God foresaw that they would) that Christian theology has created its enormous edifices of doctrine concerning sin, the consequences of sin, and what God did to rescue his creation from those consequences, so we shall begin there. The reader may like to notice the ways in which key passages of the Bible were woven in and out of the explanations as they developed, and give some thought to the ways in which Scripture was used to support arguments and 'prove' conclusions.

How to 'fall'

'It is obvious to anyone who reads the New Testament, that the doctrine of redemption, and consequently of the Gospel, is founded upon the supposition of Adam's Fall. To understand, therefore, what we are restored to by Jesus Christ, we must consider what the Scripture shows we lost by Adam',[2] said John Locke (1632–1704).

To the story half told in the Bible was applied a complex of ideas about the operation of the wills of rational creatures, and the expectation that in a world obedient to the laws of logic consequences would remorselessly follow. The 'disobedience' of the angels comes first in the story, although the 'evidence' for it in Scripture is very slight. In the writings of the fifth-century Greek author now known as Ps-Dionysius the Areopagite, who had strong views on the hierarchical character of creation, a 'natural history' of angels is teased from the scraps of information available in the Bible.

Genesis does not describe the creation of the angels. It became usual in the West to follow Augustine[3] and locate the events of the creation of the angels at the beginning of Genesis where God separates light and darkness.

The Bible mentions angels several times, angels of several kinds. Angels as a general class of created beings are discussed in the mention of the Fall of the angels in II Peter 2.4. There are many references to ordinary messenger angels, from the two angels of Genesis 19.1 who came to warn Lot of the destruction of Sodom and Gomorrah, to the angels who ascend and descend to and from heaven on a ladder in Genesis 28.12 and John 1.51. The angel Gabriel (Luke 1.19 and 26) is usually considered an archangel because of the special message he brought to Mary. There are specific mentions of archangels. I Thessalonians 4.16 prophesies that an archangel will blow the trumpet which will herald the Last Judgement, and Jude 9 refers to Michael the Archangel fighting the Devil. There are cherubim, principally in reference to the winged figures depicted in the mercy-seat of the ark of the covenant (Exodus 25.18–22, 37.7–9). There are the seraphim with six wings who dwell in the presence of God about his throne in Isaiah 6.2.

Angelic 'principalities' and 'powers' are mentioned in Romans 8.38.

Ps-Dionysius set these Biblical angels out in an orderly and comprehensive array. His idea was that angels were merely the lowest rank, the ordinary messengers of the universe, whom God would use to communicate with individuals in the normal way; archangels were for special messages, such as Gabriel's annunciation to Mary that she was to be the mother of the Messiah (Luke 1.26). Other higher ranks reflected concerns with power: thrones, dominions, powers, principalities. The supreme orders were the cherubim and seraphim (Isaiah 6.2).

The seraphim were conventionally held to be the rank of angels closest to God in the directness of their cerebral and purely rational love of God. They needed no aids to understand what God was saying to them. 'According to Isaiah,' says Peter Abelard, 'the seraphim do not cease to cry day and night, "Holy, Holy, Holy, Lord God of Sabaoth".'[4] Abelard's mid-twelfth-century contemporary, William of St Thierry, suggests that the seraphim burn the more brightly with love because they are closest to the divine presence.[5]

The first thing to 'go wrong' in the traditional story that evil originated with the wilful wrongdoing of rational creatures was the Fall of some of these angels. The Bible does not mention their fall, although fallen angels appear: the malevolent serpent in Genesis 3.1, Satan in Job (Chapters 1 and 2), Lucifer in Isaiah 14.12. What this 'fall' consisted in was also a matter of speculation throughout the history of Christian belief. The explanation was eventually 'modelled' on the fuller account available in the Bible of what went wrong for Adam and Eve. There were no known instructions to the angels about not eating fruit. So the idea emerged that the disobedience of the angels had been more like an inappropriate attitude, particularly perhaps a pridefulness, an angelic wish to rise to a height not appropriate to their nature. As Anselm put it in his book *Why God Became Man*, it was a case of wanting something good in itself (to be like God), but to a degree beyond the proper reach of angelic nature.

No death resulted for the fallen angels, as it is said to have done for sinful man (Genesis 3.19). In the Bible they continue their eternal lives, but estranged from God, prevented from turning back to him by their own irrevocable decision. The assumption has been that having given them free will, God respected their choice.

They are glimpsed from time to time plotting against humanity, as we shall see Satan doing in the Book of Job, as a further act of defiance of God. In Milton's heaven and hell a war is afoot. The arguments of Book I of *Paradise Lost* show the agonized fallen spirits resolving to do as much harm to God's cause as they can:

> To do aught good never will be our task.
> Consult how we may henceforth most offend
> Our enemy, our own loss how repair.[6]

'Offence' here is like the Latin *scandalum*; it means a stumbling block. Their objective is not to 'give offence' in the more modern sense, but to trip God up, prevent his doing what he intends. But the irony of evil is that it distorts perception, and the more actively Satan's crew oppose themselves to God the worse their situation becomes, for all their worst efforts are met by 'infinite goodness, grace and mercy shown' (I.215-19). Yet Milton's Satan has not lost hope of heaven. He would like to get back 'up' to what he once had. 'I give not Heaven for lost' (II.14). He imitates the glory to which he aspired with such fearful consequences. There are thrones in hell and he still has powers: 'neither do the Spirits damned/lose all their virtue' (*virtus*) (II.482-3).

It was a puzzle to some why God apparently did not do anything to rescue the fallen angels when he was believed to have taken so much trouble to restore humanity. Anselm's theory was that God could not have completed his original plan by making new angels to replace the ones who had fallen because the new ones would have been able to see what became of the rebels, and they would certainly not make the same mistake themselves. So there would have been two classes of angel, those who had loved God faithfully of their own free will and those who had seen where their best interests lay. The 'value' of the faithfulness of the second class would have been much less.

Angelic disobedience led, according to the narrative which Christian theologians constructed to explain things, straight into human disobedience, for Satan the fallen angel led Eve and then Adam, the first humans, to disobey God's instruction that they should not eat the fruit of the tree of the knowledge of good and evil. This story does not have to be taken literally to provide the basis for the unfolding of the trail of disastrous consequences which has always occupied so much Christian energy and concern. This second 'fall' is often portrayed as radically altering the relationship between God and man. A distance was created, and human beings became recidivists, repeatedly falling into further acts of alienating disobedience.

For the modern enquirer it is not easy to see how to move between this 'moral tale' in Genesis and the probable realities of the world of early man. The hunter-gatherers, the tribes Darwin and others describe as evolving from early primates not strictly human at all, cannot have been set down in a garden ready made, with a set of instructions. There were, it seems, processes in their coming to full human consciousness which are now beyond the reach of any speculation but that of the palaeontologist and archaeologist. There remain unanswered questions about the long-term biological future of the human race. Is humanity now on a plateau or capable of further change, with the next generation of children more or less intelligent? Beliefs about the implications of what the Bible says happened to Adam and Eve do not run at all smoothly in harness with this wholly different order of historical reality. In the case of the discrepancy between talk of the Fall of Adam and Eve and discussion of the 'real' history of the human race there is a frank incommensurability. One way of coming to terms with this problem is to treat the traditional explanation as describing a psychological or even a philosophical reality, to internalize it and try to relate it to experience for people now. This may be helpful to the modern believer, wondering whether the consequences for Adam and Eve are inevitably consequences for him or her.

Estrangement

The Old Testament records a series of episodes in which individuals have conversations with God, either directly or in the form of meetings with 'angels' acting as 'messengers'. With the exception of the commissioning of some of the prophets, these chiefly involve 'visits' from the heavenly realm to man, rather than human journeys of mind or body – in dream or reality – beyond this world. They were interpreted as depicting a process of estrangement and alienation from the point when Adam and Eve ate the apple.

These reported talks with God say something about the way 'relations with God' were understood in ancient Judaism, and the ways in which they have been interpreted indicate how these ideas were overlaid by the preoccupations of the Christian tradition. In Genesis, Adam and Eve speak to God and he speaks to them. As soon as he has made them, he tells them to be fruitful and multiply, to populate the earth and rule over all other creatures in the world (Genesis 1.28–30). They are placed in the garden with instructions not to eat the fruit of the forbidden tree (Genesis 2.17).

This talk seems to involve direct, even internal, communication from God to man. The lucidity of the understanding and communication they enjoy with God is exemplified in the little episode where Adam names the animals (Genesis 2.19–20), the words coming readily to his tongue. In the seventeenth century, John Milton, heir to the strong Christian tradition about the importance of the Word, picks up on this point in *Paradise Lost*, where Adam discovers he can speak, that language is 'in' him:

> But who I was, or where, or from what cause
> Knew not; to speak I tried and forthwith spake,
> My tongue obeyed and readily could name
> Whatever I saw.[7]

After they have disobeyed him, Adam and Eve hear God walking in the garden in the cool of the evening. They hide from him. But he calls out to them and questions them about what they have done. Then he curses them and excludes them from the garden. The Old Testament story is so framed as to leave the reader in no doubt that God is very powerful and has requirements. Yet there is no hint in the text of what God may have felt about the change of plan Adam and Eve had apparently necessitated, or whether it was not a change of plan at all, because he had put them in an experimental garden just to see what happened, or whether it was not a change of plan because he had known exactly what they would do.

In Genesis, it is God who makes the first humans tunics to cover the nakedness about which they have suddenly become self-conscious, and as he does so God is commenting to himself about what he is doing and no longer talking directly to the first man and woman (Genesis 3.8–21). The interpreters note a breakdown of communication.

Genesis records God as still speaking directly to human beings in the lifetime of Cain, but only to challenge the sinner. 'And the Lord said to Cain, where is your brother Abel?' (Genesis 4.9). Easy open conversational intercourse directly between God and man now fades from the Old Testament. Milton seems to have felt this left a gap. He gives Adam a conversation with the archangel Raphael (*Paradise Lost*,

VIII) in which Adam is able to satisfy his curiosity on a number of points – what heaven is like and how angels, being without bodies, are able to express love. Nevertheless, this is an 'ethereal messenger' (VIII.646). He cannot stay, but must return to heaven (VIII.652), and the perfect clarity of divine converse with man is lost. This notion is of some importance in connection with one of the mysteries we began with, why so much remains a mystery.

Direct talk between man and God after the Fall became something exceptional. When it happens in the Bible it is personal. God talks to certain individuals and they answer him back, in what can be a robust exchange of views. The behaviour of Sodom and Gomorrah prompts God to have conversations with Abraham. Abraham does not visit God's dwelling place for this conversation. God reveals himself to Abraham at Abraham's level and in a way which makes possible a more or less straightforward conversation. God comes to earth to see what is going on: 'I will go down and see whether what I hear is true' (Genesis 18.21). Abraham stands before God (Genesis 18.22) and pleads with him to spare the cities of the plain and, for the sake of the righteous who still remain there, not to destroy them. It is a lengthy conversation, in which Abraham pleads with God to spare the cities for the sake of an ever smaller and smaller number of righteous men. At the end God goes back to his 'place' and talk with God is at an end (Genesis 18.33).

Sometimes God communicates directly with individuals in the Old Testament through signs as well as direct speech, as though to underline the fact that his speaking to them is something extraordinary and numinous and the human recipient of the communication needs the assistance of these signs. This represents a still further symbolic step away from the intimacy of the first conversation in the Garden of Eden. The 'three' who appeared to Abraham at Mamre (Genesis 18.1–5) he greeted with the singular, 'Lord'. Augustine comments on this episode, asking what is to be made of the fact that the ensuing conversation moves from the singular to the plural, and canvassing the possibility that these three were angels or the alternative possibility that they were the three persons of the Trinity.[8] (Bede is quite clear in his own mind that this is a symbol of the Trinity.[9]) Ambrose of Milan, Augustine's contemporary, tries to express his own persuasion of the power of the symbolism to add to the plain story of the Old Testament coming of God to earth to talk to a human being. In the story Abraham is anxious to be hospitable and calls on his wife to prepare food for their guests with three measures of meal. Ambrose makes play with the notion of trying to measure the immensity of God, 'for even if God cannot be measured, he is the measure of all things'. He touches on the way one is able to hold and contemplate these paradoxes and draw understanding from them, in the inner secret place of the mind.[10]

In the story of Abraham and his willingness to sacrifice Isaac his son there is direct exchange between man and God, coupled with the use of signs to emphasize the immensity of the power of the divine partner in the conversation (Genesis 22). God speaks directly to Abraham, calling to him. Abraham answers. He is given direct instructions to set off with his son and prepare to sacrifice him, as an act of supreme obedience to God. When he has demonstrated his unquestioning obedience, it is an angel (*angelus*) who tells him that he has passed the test. Abraham raises his eyes and they fall on his next 'instructions'. A sacrificial animal is caught in a thicket and ready to hand to become a substitute for his son. This was taken by early and medieval Christian interpreters to be a significant indicator of the need for a remedy for the disobedience of the first human beings and a pointer to the kind of remedy it would have to be.

The story of Jacob and the ladder (Genesis 28.12-3) involves a vision or dream which Jacob experiences as he sleeps. Jacob sees a ladder standing on the earth and touching heaven and angels going up and down it. He sees God leaning on the top of the ladder and he hears him say, 'I am the Lord God'. Again, the conjoining of the sign and the speaking makes more powerful the impact of God's coming to talk to human beings. And once more God is distanced from man, remote at the top of the ladder.

With a similar use of a sign which is as much of a puzzle as a help, God 'appears' to Moses in the midst of a bush which burns and is not consumed (Exodus 3.2). It is from here and in this way that God asserts the mysterious mode of his existence ('I am that I am'). So it is with 'illuminating'. God is dazzling. But he is too bright to see or to see by. Exodus 3.6 describes Moses 'hiding his face', because he did not dare to gaze on God. The eternal light is 'inaccessible' and what is within it 'no man sees or can see' (I Timothy 6.16). This paradox of a brilliant illumination which hinders rather than assists the sight is seen by Christian commentators as an indication that even at his most reachable the God who begins to emerge after Adam and Eve have damaged the original relationship by their sin is distancing himself. Other indications seemed to them to point in the same direction. Moses, fearing to have the people too near, went up alone into the mountain to pray to God (Exodus 19.10-25). There he spoke to God and God answered him (Exodus 19.19). On the third day, the Lord came down before all the people 'upon Mount Sinai'. But he still kept his distance. There was an instruction not to touch the holy mountain (Exodus 19.12).

In a similar contradictory way, God is very loud and at the same time not at all easy to hear. God thunders from the mountain and there is lightning, and thick clouds cover the mountain (Exodus 19.16). In the episode when he spoke to Elijah the prophet and there was thunder and lightning and Elijah expected these to herald the mighty voice of God, a still small voice talked to him quietly and sent him about his prophetic business (I Kings 19.12). The story has great dramatic intensity from its very paradoxicality. God's manifestation in 'fire' on this occasion also had later parallels, which commentators adroitly picked up. Cyprian draws a comparison with the occasion described in the Acts of the Apostles (2.2-4) when there was a sudden sound from heaven and a strong wind, which filled the place where the disciples were sitting and it seemed as though they saw tongues of fire.[11]

So the story emerged that the actions of rational creatures, angelic and human, clouded the discourse between those creatures and God so that God 'withdrew', or appeared to withdraw, and communication was impaired. The picture of a breakdown of communication was very important indeed to the mindset of the early Christian world.

There was also some experimental exploration of aspects which are likely to present themselves more readily to modern readers. In the book of Job great questions about the human condition are raised and answered by the events described: the reasons why God allows the good to suffer, and lets his servants be tested to the limit of their endurance and perhaps beyond. Gregory the Great points to the fact that Job seems to have been a mere pawn in the exchange between God and Satan which was a battle taking place over his head, with him, its subject, in the middle.[12]

To the modern reader's eye there is a good deal of what we should now see as 'psychological' subtlety in the Bible's account of the attempt to undermine Job's trust in God not only by depriving him of health, wealth and family, but also by assailing his trust in his friends. What happened to Job was paradoxical. Human beings have a duty to obey God's laws, within the enfolding purposes of divine providence.[13] Here is Job, virtuous, blameless, humble, given to hospitality, generous to those in need. Why did he have to suffer so?

One explanation offered was that it was an act of divine benevolence to allow him to be tested so that his merits might be the greater. For some of Job's reported comments on what was happening to him have a sharpness (*aspera resonant*) which does not, on the face of it, betoken complete submission to the will of God. Perhaps, after all, there was something Job had to learn?[14] God gives Satan a limited power to act on earth. He may go so far but no further in testing Job (Job 1.12).[15] Gregory the Great says that God permits Job to be tested, but the testing is kept under God's control.[16] Satan goes out from before God's face (Job 1.12 and 2.7). But how can this be, asks Gregory, for God is everywhere and no one can leave his presence. There must, however, have been some alteration of the mode of that presence, for Satan could not do his wicked deeds before God's face.[17] Later, when that first testing has not caused Job to curse God, Satan returns and asks for more powers and God allows him to afflict Job physically, but not to take his life (Job 2.6). In this story the relationship of the child to his divine parent proves resilient enough to survive the ultimate severing which took place when Satan sinned, for Satan is permitted an active role in events. The breaking and testing of human beings, in this case of Job, is his task.

The story is retold in a recent novel, *Mr. Golightly's Holiday*, from another viewpoint, involving God in a degree of participation he had not (in this version of the story) foreseen. In this modern allegory, God has all the appearance of an ordinary middle-aged man (except about the eyes, in which infinities may be glimpsed). The days of being almighty and angry have passed. He spends a holiday in an English village with the intention of rewriting his 'bestseller', the Bible, so as to freshen it and make it more accessible to future readers. He is endlessly distracted from this task by the small surprising realities of particular human lives.

During his time in the village, Mr Golightly is emailed by Satan with quotations from Job. Satan eventually appears for a conversation in which Mr Golightly, a modest, unassuming and not always actively omniscient God, begins to understand what has been happening to him: 'You might say I was being playful – part of your holiday recreation. It is what today I believe is called "consciousness raising". One of the older of my functions.' Mr Golightly – who had not previously recognized the quotations – 'said nothing but stood sunk in thought. It was true – hedged about, safe from turmoil, he had not been tested by life, and he had come to see that he had been the poorer thereby.'[18]

Cosmic consequences

> A robin redbreast in a cage
> Puts all heaven in a rage.
> (William Blake, *Auguries of Innocence*)

According to the story, the first humans had a free choice to do what God told them to do, or not. Could some human act of disobedience really have damaged a well-constructed universe? Genesis speaks of the arrival of a certain prickliness in thistles after the Fall of Adam and Eve (Genesis 3.18). It also says that Adam and Eve were altered in what in the modern world we should describe as their very genes. Eve and her female offspring were going to suffer labour pains in giving birth. Adam was going to spend his days working hard and tilling the soil. Both were eventually going to die, returning to the ground from whose dust they had been taken when God created them. So the metaphor of the sprouting of the thistles bespeaks a far more extensive alteration of all things for the worse (Genesis 3.14–19).

And why should the extreme punishment of death come to Adam's progeny, or prickles to thistles, since the eating of the apple was not their fault? We are coming now to the arguments which have made some Christian lives so burdensome and worrying over the centuries. Protecting the position of the creator, so that he did not look weak or incompetent, was seen as extremely important. Blame had to rest elsewhere. If Christianity could not entertain the thought of a rival God, a powerful source of original evil in the universe, somehow it must all be the fault of misbehaving angels and human beings, for they were the only possible agents of the destruction.

But another hypothesis is required. This is that God's proper

Godlike response to this misbehaviour was angry and retributive. In the older part of the Old Testament the leading themes are of God's 'choosing' of his people and their duty in response to adhere to a code of laws in obedience to God's wishes, at first a simple code mainly expressing the character of the cult. But divine anger soon makes its appearance. The Old Testament, taken as a whole, describes a furious and demanding God, who punishes those who do not obey him or uses his power to ensure the downfall of his people's enemies. Joshua 11.20, for example, says that God himself hardened Israel's enemies against Israel so that they might be destroyed.[19]

This characterization of God as 'angry' is foreign to the philosophers' idea that he never gets upset, but it is a vital part of the Old Testament story. The philosophers' 'diminution by separation' is transformed into an opposition of wills, as God's human creatures are seen to defy him and ignore his wishes. That is what God is taken to be angry about, and the Bible assumes that it is all 'our fault', as it must have been if from its creation the rational human creature's role was obedience to his will and to his laws, clearly set out in due course on tablets of stone (Exodus 20.1–17). The Old Testament contains texts which emphasize the personal responsibility of individuals for their own avoidance of wrong actions understood in this way. Ezekiel 18 and Jeremiah 31.29–30 discuss whether a son ought to be punished for his father's sins or rewarded for his father's virtues and conclude that the answer is no.

Yet there are hints that this was not to be the obedience of machines. God's law was not necessarily conceived as restrictive in the Old Testament. God's ordinances are 'Sweeter also than honey, and drippings of the honeycomb' (Psalm 19.11). The essential reasonableness of the requirements was emphasized by Jesus when he spoke of the light burden and yoke (Matthew 11.28). The idea of the 'inwardness' of sinfulness, the way it reflects a person's nature and habits (Matthew 5.21–5 and 15.18), began to emerge in the New Testament, moving the emphasis away from the drama of disobedience and 'just' divine anger to the notion that human beings should quietly behave themselves because that is the kind people they are, or wish to become. James 2.10 says that he who offends in one thing is guilty of all offences. One sin makes a person as much of a sinner as another. This line of argument tends to turn the consequences of sin back upon the sinner, making his inner and personal economy the theatre of sin rather than the universe.

In the formative period of early Christian theology, this mild New Testament shift of emphasis and expectation was soon elbowed out of the way by a series of alternative explanations.

On one view, sin has automatic consequences. That would mean that sin is like a breach of the English law of trespass. It is an action for which there is a 'strict liability', that is a liability which does not depend on motivation or any other circumstantial feature. It is like knocking over dominoes. Once one falls they all follow. This has been the traditional main line of Christian theological argument. It goes with the belief in the creation of a fixed perfect universe, damaged by the actions of rational creatures, and it leads on to the theories of punishment and rescue we are now beginning to consider. Buddhism too accepts 'an unavoidable moral responsibility' and the idea that 'every act is inevitably accompanied by its corresponding conse-quences'. 'Neither by tears nor by prayers, neither by hymns and songs of praise, nor by the mournful melody of a Miserere, can a man avoid the just consequences of every wicked deed he has ever committed – much less by the vicarious sufferings or the propitiatory sacrifice of another, even of a perfectly innocent person.'[20]

On another view, ethics is situational and many layered; a given action is sometimes bad and sometimes good; there is motivation or intention to be taken into account as well as action. When Jesus said (Matthew 5.28) that a man who merely lusts after a woman has already sinned, he meant that sin lies in consenting to a wrong act as much as in actually doing it. The Bible also recognizes that it is possible to do the right thing for the wrong reason. I Corinthians 11.27 says that anyone eating the bread and drinking the wine of Holy Communion 'unworthily' will be answerable. As Peter Abelard enquired in the mid-twelfth century, and situational ethics might ask today, does it matter with what motivation the act was done?[21] Then there is the question of context or point of view. Are there actions so wicked that their motivation or context becomes irrelevant (genocide, child abuse)? My bad things might be your good things. If we both run in a race and you win I am likely to regard that as a bad thing (for me) but you would probably consider it a good thing (for you). On the proverbial principle that every cloud has a silver lining, an apparently bad thing might turn out to have (some) good consequences. Suppose I had been your running coach and I had hopes that you might run in the next Olympic Games; the discovery that you could now beat me would become a good thing.

A third 'model' bases its explanations on the belief that bad things are ultimately good for us. Balancing the severity with which disobedience was 'taken seriously' has been the equally strong sense that it must somehow not be allowed to thwart God's plans.

> For the creation was subjected to futility, not of its own will but by the will of the one who subjected it, in hope that the creation itself will be set free from its bondage to decay and will obtain the freedom of the glory of the children of God. We know that the whole creation has been groaning in labour pains until now (Romans 8.20–25, RSV).

The belief that humans 'fell' when Adam and Eve ate the apple meant that the apologists had to apologize further and say that the divine plan either gave way to some sort of 'happy thwarting' (the *felix culpa* again), or had to be thought of as having always contained within it the certainty that it would be thwarted, that God would subvert the consequences of things going wrong and set all to rights. So to one side of the logical sequence of entailments of a theology of predestination stands a thread of argument of immense importance in the Middle Ages. This is the idea that the Fall of Adam and Eve was (or God turned it into) a fortunate event. Through it, all creation paradoxically benefits in the end, man gets a better deal than angels in the end, a 'crown such as angels know not'.[22] Dorothy Sayers describes it thus:

> Man says, 'you say I mustn't know – but I intend to know.' God replies, 'Very well. If you insist, I shall not prevent you; nor shall I annihilate My creation or stop My work on that account. But I have to inform you that the price of that particular kind of knowledge is toil, suffering, renunciation and death.' 'And since I made you with free-will (and what we make we love), I will stand by you. I will go every step of the way with you. Further, I will turn your evil to good, so that, in the end, and by holding on to Me, you will attain all, and more than all, I originally intended for you, and a crown such as angels know not.'[23]

These uncertainties as to whether anything has gone wrong, and, if so, what it is, and what if anything needs to be done, contributed to a great deal of energetic discussion of the divine strategy and its high risks.

Omnipotent goodness and the problem of evil

> It just seemed flatly inconsistent to say that the universe was created by an omnipotent and perfectly good being.[24]

Another way to approach the problem was favoured in early Christianity under the influence of the classical philosophers. It asked what is meant by 'bad' and why it is 'bad'? Belief in the 'existence' of anything evil appears to deny either the goodness or the omnipotence of God. If bad things happen and God is good he cannot be omnipotent. If bad things happen and God is omnipotent he cannot be wholly good. Either he must be making them happen or he must be allowing them to happen. One obvious answer to the question where evil comes from is that it has always existed, just as the good has always existed. That saves compromising belief in God's goodness. But it involved a radical departure from the insistence that there is only one God and from the concomitant belief that he is omnipotent.

This required the believer to admit the existence of two opposing Principles in the universe, the Good and the Evil. A colourful Gnostic mythology full of stories and character surrounded these from before the birth of Christ. A Manichean Psalm-Book survives, probably from the fourth century,[25] in which dualism can be seen in its contemporary context of an elaborate mythology of battles involving supernatural powers:

> Let us worship the Spirit of the Paraclete ...

> When the Holy Spirit came he revealed to us the way of Truth and taught us that there are two Natures, that of Light and that of Darkness, separate one from the other from the beginning. The Kingdom of Light, on the one hand, consisted in five Greatnesses, and they are the Father and his twelve Aeons and the Aeons of the Aeons, the Living Air, the Land of Light; the great Spirit breathing in them, nourishing them with his Light. But the Kingdom of Darkness consists of five store-houses, which are Smoke and Fire and Wind and Water and Darkness. ...

> Now as they were making war with one another they dared to make an attempt upon the Land of Light, thinking that they would be able to conquer it.[26]

The two powers thus envisaged are eternally at war, for their natures are diametrically opposed. For the dualist, it is not a foregone conclusion that good will win, so there is work for believers to do in striving to add to the chances of the ultimate victory of good.

The Christian was sure that God will win, but not necessarily without a battle. The Devil or Satan is the supreme evil but he is a mere fallen angel and not considered to be an equal and opposite First Principle to God himself. God is ultimately in charge of him and his activities. A main theme of the Book of Revelation is cosmic warfare, in which God and his servants overthrow the power of evil after a great battle.[27]

Dualism persisted, however, and it kept cropping up in Christian communities and challenging orthodoxy. A common dualist school of thought, debated in Augustine's time and still current in the Middle Ages, held that the Bible is divided into an Old Testament which is the book about the Evil Power and a New Testament which is the book about the Good. Those who held this view considered that the Old Testament describes the creation of the material world. The New Testament describes the rescue of the universe from the bad effects of its materiality and its transformation into something spiritual. The Old Testament was the Book of the Father-Creator of the material world and the other the Book of the Son whose reign was spiritual. It was in reaction against such teaching that the creeds began by emphasizing the unity of God and the fact that he made absolutely everything, the Nicene Creed with 'I believe in one God the Father Almighty, Maker of heaven and earth, and of all things visible and invisible', and the Apostle's Creed with 'I believe in one God, the Father Almighty, Maker of heaven and earth'.

This 'dualist challenge' reappeared century by century, with variations, among the Manichees of Augustine's time and the medieval Albigensians, Cathars and Bogomils. Dualism even underlies belief in witchcraft, for the witch who worships the Devil is joining in the war of good and evil on the side of Satan.

Spirit good, matter bad

One of the most consistent assumptions of the dualists was this notion that the Good was to be identified with spirit and the Bad with matter, and consequently with the body, the material habitation of the soul. Christian apologists were thus presented with the task of purging the bad reputation of matter. Irenaeus (c.130–c.200) saw heaven as a glorified but still somehow material world. Tertullian says that the soul has its own solidity by means of which it can feel and suffer.[28] The fourth-century Firmicius Maternus, in his *Mathesis* and other works, assumes that the heavens (physical) are also the heavens (celestial, supernatural). Augustine admitted he found it difficult to envisage the spiritual as anything but extremely refined and fine-textured matter. The Cappadocians of the fourth century went to the other extreme in reaction, and suggested that 'material beings are produced by a meeting of purely spiritual and intelligible qualities and that there is no material substratum apart from these qualities'.[29]

The attempt to improve the reputation of matter in Christian thinking was not wholly successful. From dualism sprang Christian asceticism, which was doubtful about the body because it is made of matter. Medieval writers talk disparagingly of the body as a dung-heap. The spiritual and intellectual were highly valued in classical thought, and the serious minded were encouraged to subdue the flesh and behave as far as possible as if they had no bodies at all. It was very widely believed that the body was at war with the soul and a dangerous potential distraction from the kinds of thing a soul ought to be thinking about. The theory was that the body is drawn to pleasures inimical to the higher life of mind and spirit. It likes getting drunk and overeating and having casual sex. And the mind and soul are drawn along with it into vicarious enjoyments of pleasures of the senses, of a kind and to a degree, which interfere with the contemplation of the purely spiritual and intellectual, but in the end inseparable from Christian tradition too. The New Testament too is shot through with the assumption that the body is like an animal which tugs the Christian away from his heavenward ascent. 'I buffet my body and bring it into bondage.' These are the terms in which I Corinthians 9.27 speaks of the need to keep the body under control. The subjugation of the flesh implies a recognition of the uppity character of the body's demands and the way they run counter to the reasonable wishes of the soul.

On this understanding, it is the body's fault that we get distracted. We are not 'free' to go apart to consider the divine and the eternal future because of the battle our souls must engage in with our bodies before they can go on holiday from the body in this way.[30] This is the explanation regularly offered in the early and medieval Christian world for the tendency for the mind to wander, the ease with which human beings are distracted. The mind which goes away from God drifts into inappropriate thoughts, warns Isidore, Bishop of Seville (c.560–636), and its owner will find that the thoughts with which it has been preoccupied keep recurring when it turns to prayer, and prevent it from 'lifting' itself freely in its desire for heaven. Isidore's argument is that the human mind's natural milieu is heaven and it can only get there (in prayer) when it is impeded by no earthly cares.[31]

This chimes well enough with ordinary human experience of being tugged in opposite directions and especially by appetite of one sort or another. A small boy makes model aeroplanes, or plays computer games; hours pass in a concentration and absorption which seem to be highly satisfying to human beings. With more years comes a more distracted scene, the conflicted willing which has dieters and cigarette smokers reporting that they did not do as they meant, that they ate the chocolate cake or smoked the cigarette while intending not to. Regret comes after the cake is eaten and the cigarette smoked with the realization that the 'giving up' is all to do again. The patterns are obvious from observation but the reasons are not. It is a plausible explanation, or at any rate one regularly adopted over the centuries, that each person is really two and the two, body and soul, have contradictory expectations, and that of the two the body is the better at getting its own way. Modern physiological explanation involving addiction, and psychological explanations involving obsessive-compulsive disorders, partly replace these earlier observations, but they do not go below the level of the mechanics of an explanation of the universal human experience any more than does the ancient and medieval tale of the war between body and soul.

A lingering early modern heritage of dualist mistrust of matter is to be seen in Ralph Cudworth, who thought a tendency to see all existence as material was what defined the unbeliever of his own day. He suggested that theists 'derive all things from Senseless Matter, as the First Original, and deny that there is any Conscious Understanding Being Self-existent or unmade'.[32] The idea seems to be that atheists are conveniently to be divided from believers by their unwillingness to accept that anything exists if they cannot kick it or lick it.

Yet more has been heard in recent generations of the suggestion that bodily nature is our proper context and should be entered into enthusiastically and enjoyed. This returns to some of the assumptions Cicero was making when he said that souls inhabiting matter are put there to look after it. Within the parameters of the thought of the classical period, this presents a kind of 'incarnational' and 'ecological' view. A recent comment by Rowan Williams as Archbishop of Canterbury robustly asserts the place of the body in the eternal scheme of things. 'Living religiously is a way of conducting a bodily life. It has to do with gesture, place, sound, habit; not first and foremost with what is supposed to be going on inside.' He goes further and takes the very process of believing to involve the body. The 'fundamental mistake is to consider belief ... as more or less exclusively a mental event'.[33]

This problematic character of the body is recognized in Eastern religions too, sometimes in terms the Hermetic tradition would have warmed to. Nisikânta Chattopâdhâya explains that from the Buddhist perspective, the individual is mixed, compounded of opposing and irreconcilable elements, in which the bodily parts have pleasures which muddy the aspirations of the higher, spiritual parts:

> A man who gives himself up to pleasure, who does not strive after high wisdom, is like a vessel full of dirty water in which are many beautiful things; so soon as one shakes the water one cannot see the things it contains; thus pleasure and desire cause confusion and disturbances in the heart, and are like sediment in water; they hinder us from recognizing the beauty of sublime reason. As soon as we remove the impurities the original form reappears.

He links what he is saying with the way, as he understands it, Christianity 'lays similar stress upon the inviolability of the moral law, and upon the necessity of first purifying the inner man, or the soul'.[34]

Is evil the absence of good?

The traditional Christian explanation of evil sought to emancipate itself from all this, though it was never wholly successful, and hang-ups about the body remained strong. The Christian rationalization began from the 'immovable pillars' of the beliefs about the divine nature we saw emerging from late antique philosophy. Augustine of Hippo in the late fourth and fifth centuries proposed a solution. God could not be omnipotent and wholly good if evil existed. So in this titanic confrontation of incompatible assertions about fundamental features of God and the universe, it was evil which must 'move'. He suggested that evil is a mere absence of the good, a failure of things to be as they ought to be.[35] This became the orthodoxy of the West. 'Evil is the corruption of good,' claims Peter of Poitiers, and 'Evil had a good cause, for all that exists is good.'[36] The argument can be summarized thus:

> God is good.
> God is omnipotent.
> So God made everything which is exists and everything which exists is good.
> Therefore evil cannot exist.
> Therefore evil must be an absence of good, in effect nothing at all.

The Augustinian solution was not entirely satisfactory, either. The 'evil is nothing' version of events still does not really explain how this damaging nothingness comes about or why 'not-God' should be bad. The God whose creatures are deemed to be less than him and moving away from him has also been held to be so entirely good that he can give rise to nothing which is not also good. Creation cannot have built-in tendencies to evil. So how can there be evil? To say evil is a mere absence of good does not stop it being experienced as immensely powerful and destructive. It has been seen as a black hole into which all that is good and beautiful is sucked, becoming distorted on the way, so that humans and angels in its grip can no longer think straight.

Morality and mechanical faults

Christian theology early confused moral 'wrongdoing' and mechanical breakdown in its attempt to get to grips with the problem of evil. A belief in the omnipotence of God made it hard to see that any breakdown in the smooth running of the universe could be the result of poor manufacture. The cosmos of the classical philosophers and the natural theologians has to be adapted if it is to accommodate the idea of error in the machine. The possibility is not necessarily built-in to the system. Rather the reverse, for the real force of this type of argument is that a smoothly running universe bespeaks the good design of a powerful and competent God. Augustine was intent on fixing the 'blame' for things being not quite right by locating the origin of evil in the misdirected wills of rational creatures, men and women and angels,[37] but he admitted that it is not easy to explain natural disasters such as earthquakes in that way.

For this group of thinkers, evil is not so much 'nothing' as 'of no or little account', except insofar as it is a disruption of the orderliness of the universe. Natural theology does not need an 'explanation of bad behaviour' to make sense. It can restrict itself to the classical philosophical questions concerning the proofs for the existence and nature of God and the mechanics of his creation. As William Paley put it,

> Neither ... would it invalidate our conclusion, that the watch sometimes went wrong or that it seldom went exactly right. The purpose of the machinery, the design, and the designer might be evident, and in the case supposed, would be evident, in whatever way we accounted for the irregularity of the movement, or whether we could account for it or not. It is not necessary that a machine be perfect in order to show with what design it was made: still less necessary, where the only question is whether it were made with any design at all.[38]

Nevertheless, even among the rationalists of the eighteenth century, there was a strong temptation to move into the realm of moral questions and to import into the simplicities of the machinery hints of the Christian theology of sin. Joseph Butler moves rapidly in his *Analogy* from the neutral territory of a system of natural religion to the idea of a 'moral government of God' by rewards and punishments. 'As the manifold appearances of design and of final causes in the constitution of the world, prove it to be the work of an intelligent mind; so the particular final causes of pleasure and pain distributed amongst his creatures, prove that they are under his government.'[39] Some, Butler says, think 'the only character of the Author of Nature to be that of simple absolute benevolence'. That does not seem to him to be enough. In his view, 'the perfection of moral government consists in' rewarding and punishing 'with regard to all intelligent creatures, in an exact proportion to their personal merits or demerits'.[40]

A.A. Cooper, Third Earl of Shaftesbury (1671–1713), wrote in *An Inquiry Concerning Virtue* that it seems to him 'impossible to suppose' a 'mere sensible Creature originally so constituted and unnatural, as that from the moment he comes to be try'd by sensible Objects, he shou'd have no one good Passion towards His Kind, not foundation either of Pity, Love, Kindness or social Affection'.[41]

'Going wrong', then, has been taken to embrace a number of things which easily become conflated or even confused, such as:

> the philosophers' and hermetics' idea of 'departing from the best' or 'lowering oneself' in a hierarchy of being;

> 'unintended by God in his original plan' or some other form of running out of control or disorderliness, perhaps prompted by the too-free use of the wills of rational creatures;

'harmful to creatures or to the creation'.

'The problem of evil is a problem of human suffering,'[42] wrote John Coventry in the late twentieth century, trying to bring his readers back to what is really important. Is that what matters here or were the Oxford theology students right when they said that the right way to look at it all in the modern world is from an ecological perspective? Both options are some way away from the set of connected concerns which drove the discussions outlined above, and which laid the foundations for the Christian belief in sin and the need for to do something about the consequences of sin, for the world and for each 'fallen' human being, to which we come next.

5

Repair

If what really happened in the dawn of the world was that apes grew into people, and Adam and Eve exist only in a story, how can it all be 'our' fault? What explanations have been on offer about what has been done to put right the wrongs of the world? If God made the world so imperfectly that it could 'go wrong' should there not have been a manufacturer's guarantee? In what way has God made things 'better'? If it is all our fault, ought there to be a contribution from us to putting things right?

Does something need to be put right?

> There's a famous seaside place called Blackpool
> That's noted for fresh air and fun
> And Mr. and Mrs. Ramsbottom
> Went there with young Albert, their son.

But Albert poked a lion at Blackpool zoo and the lion swallowed him whole. His parents went to complain to the management.

> The manager wanted no trouble;
> He took out his purse right away,
> Sayin' 'Ow much to settle the matter?'
> Pa said 'Wot do you usually pay?'
> But Mother 'ad turned a bit awkward
> When she saw where 'er Albert 'ad gone.
> She said 'No, someone's got to be summonsed!'[1]

The zoo managers accepted liability for the loss of Albert, asked what price would satisfy Albert's parents, and offered to compensate them. His mother did not think that was good enough. She was anxious to see someone punished.

Her natural indignation makes a number of suppositions. Albert had disappeared inside a lion which ought to have been kept by the zoo with due regard for the health and safety dangers it presented. There had been negligence which compounded her loss and made her disinclined to think that a sum of money paid in compensation would make up for it, even a large sum. She wanted someone 'punished'. Similar ways of thinking have coloured the answers to the question what had to be done when things 'went wrong' in the universe. If it was really the 'fault' of rational creatures who 'disobeyed' God and if the consequences were truly cosmic, it seemed natural to a human sense of justice to expect God to want compensation and also to want to punish those who had created this undesirable situation. And they were sure he could.

Yet this punishment requirement ('someone's got to be summonsed!') needs examining; the analogy quickly breaks down. In a family a child's misbehaviour is seen as part of a learning process, inevitable because of immaturity. As a rule the first act of childish defi-ance is not taken to alter for ever the relationship of parent and child, to require the selling of the family home and the ejection of the child to live by its wits on the streets, hungry and at risk. Why would God behave with less understanding than a human parent? And even if it was appropriate for him to react in such a draconian manner, an all-powerful and omniscient God was in a better position than a human father, for he could have designed his creatures so that this cosmic drama could have been avoided.

> Aristotle ... would have said that if God had really been concerned with human behaviour he would have made us behave according to his own way.[2]

So the 'scenario' of sin and disobedience creates a dilemma for the modern believer as it has always done. The idea that God could have been in any way helpless in the face of the breakdown of his crea-tion into a rebellious muddle went against the entrenched assump-tions about divine omnipotence and goodness. It seemed an affront to God's dignity even to suggest it. Yet any suggestion that he might simply let things take their course in an open-minded willingness to see how they turned out has also been hedged about with the many restrictions which Christian theologians have been convinced must govern the finding of an acceptable solution. For it would seem to throw God's foresight and powers of planning open to question.

For many centuries, the option which seemed the most satisfactory was that God had made things the way they should be, and had been defied by his rational creatures, angelic and human. The question which then had to be addressed was what he had done, or was going to do, about it. The consensus of early Christian explanation was that God could not just throw away the world and start again, or that even if he could have done (being omnipotent) he would not (being a God of compassion, or a God who can bring good out of evil, or a God too mighty to allow his will to be frustrated). The idea that God's very 'majesty' does not allow him to forget in the sense of *ignoring* what had happened assumes that it would be a breach of right order.

So God will not tolerate this state of affairs, it was suggested; something had to be done. Various interdependent reasons have been given: because it is not in his nature to do so, because he intends his original plan for creation to be realized and God's intentions are always carried into effect, because he is merciful and wants his creatures to be restored to the state and mode of life he had intended for them or to the relationship with him which he originally planned for them.

One way out of this dilemma was to argue that God knew perfectly well what would happen and made the best of it. What went wrong has been presented as the happy mistake (*felix culpa*) already mentioned, a bad event which God foresaw (although he was not its author), built into his plan and now turns to good, so that the end result is better than it would have been if nothing had ever gone wrong. The New Testament makes room for this idea that this could have been deliberate and 'for the best':

> For the creation was subjected to futility, not of its own will but by the will of the one who subjected it, in hope that the creation itself will be set free from its bondage to decay and will obtain the freedom of the glory of the children of God. We know that the whole creation has been groaning in labour pains until now (Romans 8.20-5, RSV).

This would be in tune with the theory that God did not make the universe fixed and complete, but made it in such a way that it could be perfected, and was somehow dynamic and not static. Jerome thought that the first human beings were created full grown,[3] but he considered that that did not necessarily mean that they were fully 'realized', their potential all actual from the beginning, merely that they did not have to grow up physically. The way the story is told in Genesis makes sense only if Adam and Eve were capable not only of choice but of development. The thirteenth-century Robert Grosseteste, discussing why Adam and Eve were forbidden to eat the fruit of the tree of knowledge, cannot accept that there was anything wrong with the tree, for everything God made was good. But the command provided them with an opportunity to understand the meaning of obedience and a way of winning God's praise and thus to grow or develop.[4] The options thus opened up led, predictably, to more squabbles. There was a good deal of pamphlet warfare in the early modern period about what would have happened in the Garden of Eden if Adam and Eve had not sinned. Would they have been 'translated' to heaven in some way without having to pass through death, for Genesis suggested that it was only their sinfulness which made them mortal? When would that have happened? Would more human beings have been created in some way before then, and how? For sexual reproduction was seen as an unfortunate necessity resulting from their sin. Perhaps, some suggested, children would have sprouted from the ground like seedlings.

The hypothesis that God gave rational creatures 'room to deny themselves' assumes a capacity for change and improvement not only in individuals but in the universe itself. This process of completion remains a logical possibility, whether there is held to be a directing and foresightful omnipotence or a God looking on rather helplessly and merely making a contribution. It usefully makes room to accommodate the quite different account of the emergence of the human race which would now be taken as the norm. Built into this line of explanation is the recognition that human beings may not have been a fixed quantity from their creation.

The options

The major emphasis throughout the centuries has been on the need to put right something which had gone wrong but there have been changing explanations why this was so important.[5]

The war between good and evil

Early Christians tended to see the putting-right which was needed in terms of 'the war between good and evil', a great battle in which God, in the person of the incarnate Christ, defeated evil and rescued humanity from bondage to it; in which Christ was the Victor but

He died in winning. This was a picture undoubtedly influenced by the dualist or Gnostic idea, which was never thoroughly extirpated from Christianity, that good and evil are eternally at war. Prudentius (348–c.410) wrote a 'soul battle' (*Psychomachia*) involving a battle of the virtues and vices, which had numerous sequels.[6]

Redemption

The next fashionable emphasis to emerge was on the 'Albert and the Lion' approach. 'Redemption' literally means 'buying back'. Medieval and Reformation theologians tended to see the problem in terms of a debt owed to God, whose honour, and indeed his very nature, demanded that it be paid, for it is not in the nature of God to allow sin to go unpunished or simply to disregard it. This is Anselm of Canterbury's explanation in his 'Why God became man', the *Cur deus homo*. It is echoed in Milton's *Paradise Lost*:

> Die he or justice must; unless for him
> Some other able, and as willing, pay
> The rigid satisfaction, death for death.[7]

The first principle which had to be established here was that the 'buying back' required God to become man. Christian theology has insisted that this was 'necessary', the only way. Sinful human beings were not capable of doing what was needed. Anselm of Canterbury's explanation was that God alone could do it, but his doing so 'required' human action too, for he could not logically simply pay a debt to himself, when it was human beings who owed it. 'And setting Christ aside, as though he had never been, [this book] proves by necessary reasons that no man could have been saved without him ... and that it was necessary that this should have been done by a man, but by none but a God-man' (Anselm, *Cur deus homo*, Preface).

> In flesh at first the guilt committed was;
> Therefore in flesh it must be satisfied:
> Nor spirit nor angel, though they man surpass,
> Could make amends to God for man's misguide,
> But only man himself, who self did slide.[8]

Perhaps the most important and complex idea which developed to underpin the theology of redemption has been the theory of 'sacrifice'. This needed adjusting from its well-established Old Testament role to fit the new Christian account of things.

In ancient Greek and Roman paganism the gods accepted sacrifices intended either positively to please them or to placate their anger. Such gods gave rewards. It was a straightforward *quid pro quo* transaction. The Jewish tradition of obedience to the Law, with its considerable emphasis on sacrifice, fed this habit of thought and pattern of expectation about what was required, and although the Old Testament God Yahweh was no petty godling to be bribed, sacrifices were expected to please and placate and satisfy him, and the reward was his good opinion and pleasure. Leviticus sets out in considerable detail the right way to make offerings to please God, offerings which will be acceptable to him, especially when there is sin to be purged.

The idea of sacrifice, of an act of voluntary suffering or self-denial which obtains its reward, is central to the Judaic tradition. The sacrifice of his son Isaac, which seemed to be required of Abraham until God provided him with an alternative animal conveniently caught in the thicket, was to have been costly indeed. Sacrifice is paradoxically both self-less, because costly, and an action far from disinterested, because it is a purchase.

The core idea of sacrifice is that of 'offering'. In Judaism this is coupled with the idea that obedience to the Law and doing the will of God are an important factor in the making of the sacrifice. There is sin-offering in reparation and expiation, such as the atonement made by the sacrificed bull in Leviticus 16.6. This is the area where sacrifice is closest to penance. The Old Testament tends to see sacrifices as fixed quantitative gifts appropriate for particular purposes (so many lambs or goats) to placate an angry God. There are also various possible 'offerers'. An offering may be from a community on its own behalf. It may be made by an individual for his own sins. The 'heave-offering' of the Old Testament involves the lifting up of one's own hand with the offering in it.

There is a strong underlying doctrine of 'intention' in the descriptions of sacrificial requirements in Leviticus. An animal is sacrificed in a particular way for a particular purpose for the benefit of the intended individual or category of individuals. The death of the animal in an Old Testament sacrifice has no effect in itself. The sacrificial action follows the killing, for example, the sprinkling of the blood in the holy places and thus before God.[9] The sacrifice, to be effective, must involve more than merely going through a series of ceremonial steps.[10] There are various possible modes of offering, depending on the intention. There is the thank-offering, which may be personal or on behalf of the community. In the Old Testament sacrificial meal, God is given parts of the animal as a thanksgiving and the offerer's family or community shares it. There is the offering by way of 'rent', a payment for goods received. This presents itself in the Old Testament as a payment of tithes and first fruits and the offering of first-borns.

Biblical tradition suggests that putting right the relationship of man and God has to be a bloody business (e.g. 'there is no forgiveness without the shedding of blood' (Hebrews 9.22)), or at least it seemed so in the earliest Christian tradition. For these are notions deeply embedded in the story as 'revealed' in the Bible, and forming core elements in Christian liturgy from ancient times. In the prayer said over the bread and the wine in the Eucharist, the words of Jesus at the Last Supper are repeated: 'This is my blood of the new covenant which is shed for you and for many for the forgiveness of sins' (cf. Matthew 26.28 and I Corinthians 11.25).

> Almighty God, our heavenly Father, who of thy tender mercy didst give thine only Son Jesus Christ to suffer death upon the Cross for our redemption, and who made there (by his one oblation of himself once offered) a full, perfect, and sufficient Sacrifice, oblation and satisfaction for the sins of the whole World, and did institute and in his Holy Gospel command us to continue a perpetual memory of that his precious death until his coming again

echoes the Prayer of Consecration in the 1662 Book of Common Prayer of the Church of England, underlining several points which had become matters of controversy, notably whether Jesus' death on the Cross had done all that needed to be done, eternally speaking, and what exactly was achieved in the innumerable 'celebrations' of the Last Supper in which the Last Supper before the crucifixion was re-enacted.

It is in this context of history and assumption that talk of Christ's 'sacrifice' has tended to be set:

> Glorious now behold him arise,
> King, and God, and sacrifice.
> (Carol: 'We three kings of Orient are')

Various liturgical examples make it clear that the idea was not merely that Christ made a sacrifice in a way which was familiar within an ancient Jewish tradition. First, he did not make it for himself but for humankind.

> And with his blood mankind hath bought.
> (Carol: 'The first Noel the angel did say')

The theory that it is possible to make a sacrifice on behalf of someone else is a development of the basic theory that sacrifice 'works'. Buddhism rules out the idea of vicarious satisfaction. Christianity could not do so if it was to entertain the belief that one enormous and fully 'satisfactory' vicarious satisfaction had been made in the death of Christ. In the New Testament it is only in Hebrews that there is much talk of Christ's death as a sacrifice.[11] But if it was a sacrifice, it must have been vicarious, because it was obvious that it was made for others.

In the Judaic tradition, what sacrifice 'buys' does not necessarily have to be a personal advantage. It may be the good of the community or the benefit of someone else that the sacrifer has in mind, or simply to please God. The scapegoat of Leviticus 16.9–10 and 16.21–2 was sent out into the desert 'carrying' the people's sins. Aaron the priest confessed all the people's sins over the goat with his hands on its head and then the beast was sent out into the wilderness to go free. Yet Christ's dying 'for' us and what that might mean was the subject of endless analysis in succeeding centuries.

In Christianity this unfolded into the conception that all life is a sacrifice and should be lived as such, with the Christian offering to God everything he does and doing all things in God's name.[12] Whereas the Judaic and Christian theory of sacrifice rests on an idea of covenant, some agreement between God and man with 'terms' which can be 'fulfilled', the Hindu idea is closer to the notion of restoring 'right order'.[13] A pattern emerged in the Upanishads as it did in Christianity, involving a similar interiorization and emphasis upon the 'intention' of what remained an external and visible act involving deity and material.[14]

In the Thirty-Nine Articles of the sixteenth-century Church of England, Article 2 states that Christ suffered 'to reconcile his Father to us, to be a sacrifice, not only for original guilt, but also for all actual sins of men'. This is close in wording to Article 3 of the Lutheran Augsburg Confession, and it reflects debate of the preceding half

century or more in which the 'sacrificial' character of the Eucharist
had been hotly denied by reformers. The anxiety prompting this was
a sense that the institutional Church in the West was trying to claim
powers for its priests to 'add' to Christ's sacrifice every time they cele-
brated the 'memorial' of the Last Supper when Jesus had broken bread
before his crucifixion and said to his disciples, 'This is my body which
is given for you.' The reformers argued that Christ's sacrifice had been
complete and all-sufficient and could not be added to by an act involving human agency, such as the saying of masses. By now the prelimi-
nary question had almost been lost sight of – whether any sacrifice was
necessary or appropriate or could be efficacious.

Mr Golightly, the homely God, muses in his conversation with
Satan:

> 'I have been wondering very much about suffering and love. You see – '

Satan indulges in a little dig at God's 'Platonic' impassibility:

> 'I understand,' the companion at his side interrupted, 'as the fountain-
> head yourself, you had no individual experience of it and yet.'

> 'And yet there is my son,' Mr. Golightly broke in, not wanting the other
> to broach the name.

> For the first time, his old rival turned to face him fully and his eyes looked
> like ruined stars. 'I was going to say,' he suggested mildly, 'that, from my
> rare observations of the phenomenon, to love another means in some
> sense to put oneself in their person; and for that to be possible there must
> first be the extinction of the self. I offer the idea in pure humility' – Mr.
> Golightly gave a slight nod – 'this, perhaps is what your son ... . '[15]

Mr Golightly, it will be remembered, is a modest and unassuming
God, short on omniscience, to whom a great deal comes as a surprise
and revelation. He has suffered the loss of his Son. It is now being
'suggested' to him by a mildly challenging and quite amicable Satan,
in a reworking of the conversation recorded in the Book of Job, that
Jesus gave up 'himself' in an act of supreme love for others. His Father
suffers because of his own love, is made vulnerable, and only now, on
his holiday, begins to be changed.

This modern allegory has the unorthodox implication that in the
incarnation the Father became as 'human' as the Son in his capacity
to suffer, but it contains familiar modern insights into the 'psychology'
of sacrifice which make it more than the mechanical 'offering' of one
thing to 'buy' another.

Reconciliation

Biblical sacrifice can be associated with celebration, thanksgiving, joy, as well as pain and loss. The language is of a sweet odour (Genesis 8.21).[16]

> We'll crowd thy gates with thankful songs,
> High as the heavens our voices raise;
> And earth, with her ten thousand tongues,
> Shall fill thy courts with sounding praise.[17]

A third explanation, likely to be more congenial to modern Western tastes, recoils from the idea of fighting a war in heaven, and from mechanistic requirements of redress and recompense, and concentrates on the idea of peacemaking. It sees God as kindly and generous, entering into a transaction with the believer in which there is forgiveness on one side and response and grateful acceptance on the other, 'God making peace between himself and humankind'.[18]

This allows for the possibility that God would have become incarnate anyway, even if Adam had not sinned.[19] A theology of 'at-one-ment' has emphasized a different purpose, in which God made an approach to humanity which had more to do with mending and improving things, perhaps by setting a practical example of how to be what a human being is supposed to be. This idea is summed up in some words of the twelfth-century Peter Lombard, 'Because his death commended God's love to us, so that we were stirred to love God in return and by that we are justified which means freed from our sins.'[20]

There are pointers in the Bible which accord with the notion of a complex and profound and even cooperative relationship between creature, creation and creator. The 'fear of the Lord' emerges as something better translated as respect. Psalm 2.11 calls on the believer to 'serve the Lord with fear'. In Luke 5.26 the watchers are all filled with fear and awe. Servants are encouraged in Ephesians 6.5 to obey their masters with fear as they would Christ. In Philippians 2.12 is to be found the call to work out one's salvation with fear, and that does not mean fright but awe.

Such an understanding of the nature and purpose of the 'work of Christ' is echoed in many hymns and carols which speak of a sort of solidarity (at-one-ment):

And he feeleth for our sadness,
And he shareth in our gladness
(Carol: 'Once in royal David's city')

Peace on earth, goodwill to men,
From heaven's all-gracious King!
(Carol, 'It came upon the midnight clear')

Peace on earth and mercy mild,
God and sinners reconciled
(Carol: 'Hark the herald angels sing')

This line of explanation fitted well with the idea that Jesus set an example, though it did not preempt the question whether human beings
could follow that example if they tried or needed some divine help
(grace). The debate Augustine started with the followers of Pelagius
made this a burning question for many centuries, erupting from time
to time into real controversy. Pelagius was a late fourth-century 'society
preacher' – and one of the few Britons to make a mark in the early
Church – who had been persuading the Roman upper classes that
they could get to heaven by working hard at living a good life and
obeying God's commandments. Augustine disapproved. He thought
this tended to make believers arrogant, believing that they could safely
rely on their own efforts to please God. He argued for the opposite
view, which was that nothing anyone could do could please God at all,
for all are sinners. God is not only entitled to reject them but is acting
in accordance with the requirements of his goodness and justice if he
does.

This 'helplessness' theory has remained attractive to many. Most
importantly of all, it requires a strong doctrine of sin and its consequences. As we shall see in the next section, it underlies the teaching
that the believer 'needs the help' of the Church and the sacraments
in order to make up for sinning, as much as the belief that he or she
simply needs direct action of God's grace to do any good act.

The Pelagians and their successors continued to believe that being
good was just a matter of behaving well. Anyone could do it. It just
took a little effort. But they conceded that this 'self-improvement'
needed a role model, and it had, in their view, been God's reason for
becoming man to show people how:

For he is our childhood's pattern
(Carol: 'Once in royal David's city')

Teach us to resemble thee
In thy sweet humility
(Carol: 'See amid the winter's snow')

The modern believer can now begin to see the shifts of emphasis and take stock of them. Each was seen in its time as an explanation of the nature of the need and the way it had to be met to set things right in the universe. But they differ, and their range of fundamental assumptions seems to set the modern believer free to consider what the need to be met really was and is, for all these 'ways of putting things right' assume that things 'went wrong' in the particular ways discussed in the first part of this chapter.

Damaged goods?

Why be bad if the reasons to be good are so persuasive? The most convenient answer is 'I cannot help it'. That was, essentially, the conclusion the Western Christian tradition came to. It moved during the first centuries from the reproving talk of Old Testament times about the way 'bad behaviour makes God angry' (so stop it), to a doctrine that bad behaviour is inevitable (so what is God going to do about it?).

It was impossible to maintain that the work of Christ, whatever it had been, had made all human beings better people or visibly mended them as individuals at all, even if it had made it possible for God honourably to disregard their imperfections and consider them 'justified in his sight'. It is a matter of common observation that people have gone on making mistakes and struggling and getting their lives in a mess. They have gone on complaining that the spirit is willing but the flesh is weak (Matthew 26.41). It could not even be said with any certainty that things could not go wrong again as badly as they were said to have done when the first 'sin' was committed.

The theory that all human beings are inevitably going to misbehave had two parts, involving liability (guilt) for 'original' and actual sin respectively. The doctrine of 'original sin' is hinted at in Romans 5.12–21 ('Inasmuch as all sinned') and I Corinthians 15.22 ('as in Adam all men die so in Christ all men will be made alive'), but it emerged as a fully fledged doctrine in the West only gradually from Augustine's time and it was never accepted in the same way in the Greek-speaking Eastern half of the old Roman Empire.

A certain 'solidarity' of human beings with Adam is assumed in the passages from Romans and I Corinthians just quoted. The Fall of Adam and Eve is then held to have led to permanent damage to human beings, of a kind the modern world would call 'genetic'. It was hereditable. This damaged 'gene' means all human beings cannot help being sinful. Original sin was deemed to be culpable in itself. Even a baby which lived only a few minutes and did not have time to commit any actual sins would be punished for its 'original' sin for eternity, said Augustine, prompting the debate we touched on earlier. The contemporary acceptance that that was simple justice on the part of God underlines how seriously the implications of sin were being taken.

One of the effects of original sin, Augustine argued in his disputes with the Pelagians, is that human free will is damaged so that humans cannot freely choose the good any more. The only choice which remains truly 'free' is the choice of the wrong option. So again and again the individual will 'helplessly' commit actual sins for which he or she is also to be blamed.

The painful consciousness of sin

Christian believers have thus been encouraged to be painfully sensitive about their 'sinfulness'. 'The Sense of Mens Minds, the Guilt of their Consciences, and their own heart Misgiving Them',[21] have been vividly pervasive in Christian theology.

Despite the lack of an exact equivalent of the Western doctrine of original sin, a desperate sense of the seriousness of sin is to be found in the Orthodox tradition too, sending the early hermits known as 'stylites' to live in solitary and visible discomfort on the tops of columns, and the 'desert fathers' out into the wilderness to wrestle with their sinfulness alone with God. St Theodore of Sykeon (seventh century) understood, his biographer says, that the friend of the world is the enemy of God (James 4.4) and that no one can serve God and Mammon (Luke 16.13). As a boy and young man he practised extreme self-denial and eventually retreated from the world, taking up residence in a pit, and later in a cave in the mountain, where he continued to refuse food. Such athletic spiritual exercises and extremes of mortification were a wonder to the population and he began to make a reputation. Dragged forcibly out of his cave by his family he was found to be covered in sores and pus; his hair was matted and full of worms; his bones stuck out and he smelt so strongly that no one could bear to stand near him. 'In short, people saw him as another Job,' comments his biographer.[22]

In the Roman Catholic tradition of the West, the heightening of anxious feeling on the subject in the faithful became a deliberate pastoral policy. Guido de Monte Rocherii wrote the *Manipulus curatorum*, just before the Reformation, to urge on priests and people the importance of coupling an intense love of God with a passionate detestation of sin.[23]

And despite their historical origins in a protest movement against the burdening of the faithful with fear, the Protestant traditions have tended to place a heavy emphasis upon the seriousness of sin and the danger of not turning to God and the fear of hell.

> Suddenly this conclusion was fastned on my spirit. ... That I had been a great and grievous Sinner, and that it was now too late for me to look after Heaven; for Christ would not forgive me.[24]

On one definition, then, guilt, liability to be punished for being sinful or committing sins, is simply the universal human condition since the Fall of Adam, for all humanity is now under the 'strict liability' entailed by original sin; everyone is guilty, even a new-born infant, and the guilt is pervasive, contaminating the whole person. James 2.10 says that he who offends in one thing is guilty of all offences. On another way of looking at things, it is the inward sense of guiltiness which is the important thing. It makes people uncomfortable and restless and fearful, as a dog which knows it has misbehaved expresses a wish to placate its master which has every appearance of a consciousness of guilt. Guilt, then, can be both 'being answerable' for having broken some law or rule (*being* guilty) and a sensation within of being 'out of order' (*feeling* guilty). This way of describing things relies on the following hypotheses:

> that in a moral universe there is right behaviour and wrong behaviour;
>
> that God invigilates;
>
> that God takes a reproving interest in the behaviour of his individual human creatures;
>
> that God imposes sanctions on individuals who offend him.

This theory of 'human helplessness', coupled with a strong doctrine of divine justice, made it necessary to devise a theory of divine 'grace' (*gratia*), in which grace is God's free exercise of generosity. Grace has nothing to do with human deserving. There was room for the idea that God is generous because Christ died.

> He sent his Son with power to save
> From guilt and darkness and the grave:
> Wonders of grace to God belong,
> Repeat his mercies in your song.[25]

> When sin departs before his grace,
> Then life and health come in its place.
> (Carol: 'On Christmas night all Christians sing')

Or perhaps God is just generous. But above all, a doctrine of grace made it possible to keep to a strict theory of human incapacity while allowing it to be understood how God might intervene to assist people to do what they cannot do for themselves. It is by 'grace' that the unnerved arm of human choice is enabled to opt to do the right thing.

This doctrine did not reconcile the polarities or diminish the absoluteness of the choices as they had come to be understood. As late as the mid-twentieth century, the Evangelical C.S. Lewis (1898–1963) still saw 'salvation' as a decisive removal of the individual from hell. In *The Great Divorce* Lewis rewrites Blake's *The Marriage of Heaven and Hell*. Lewis's idea is that there can be no admixture of the two, that 'if we insist on keeping Hell (or even earth) we shall not see Heaven'. 'I believe, to be sure,' he adds, 'that any man who reaches Heaven will find that what he abandoned (even in plucking out his right eye) has not been lost: that the kernel of what he was really seeking even in his most depraved wishes will be there, beyond expectation, waiting for him in "the High Countries".'[26]

Nevertheless, from the eighteenth century there has been a diminution of the importance of this theory of original sin and its consequences in the West except in those communities which have continued to define themselves in terms of a theology of sin and its consequences. Another important line of thought which can be traced from New Testament then had room to develop. This looks at the inwardness of sin and its effect not upon God (in making him angry) but upon the sinner (who suffers detriment in himself). 'The law written in their hearts, their conscience bearing witness therewith, and their thoughts one with another accusing or else excusing them; in the day when God shall judge the secrets of men' (Romans 2.14–6, RV).

The Epistle of James stands out among the letters preserved in the New Testament for its freedom from many of the complications generated by Paul's anxieties about the inevitability of sin and its awful consequences. James sets out again and again the simple idea that the faith of a believer will naturally issue in a certain kind of behaviour. There is a similar cutting through to the essentials in the letters of John. 'Love means following the commands of God. This is the command which was given you from the beginning, to be your rule of life' (II John 6, NEB).

Just deserts?

What do I have to do to be saved?

'What do I have to do to be saved?' When the gaoler in the Acts of the Apostles (Acts 16.30) asked Paul and Silas this question, they told him he only had to believe in Jesus. For John Locke this notion of a saving faith lingered at the heart of his attempts to cut away the unnecessary complications of the Christian belief of his own day: 'What we are now required to believe to obtain eternal life, is plainly set down in the Gospel. St John tells us, "He that believeth on the Son, hath eternal life; and he that believeth not the Son, shall not see life."'[27]

Yet the Gospels contain passages suggesting that belief will lead to a pattern of *conduct*, much as James and John taught, but with the additional expectation that it will in some way 'count' in favour of the believer. Luke 17.29 speaks of leaving home and family for the sake of the Kingdom of God. The prospective dwellers in heaven will be faithful keepers of the Law, for not one element of the Law's requirements will be abolished until the end comes, says Matthew's Gospel (Matthew 4.17). They will live their lives virtuously, not allowing disputes to remain unresolved, not committing adultery even in their hearts, not harbouring or giving any quarter to any habit or part of themselves which is leading them astray (Matthew 5.21–48). This expectation is, however, nuanced. Those who live rightly by doing the right thing will not be rigid or demanding of others. Forgiveness of others is expected of those who are to enter the Kingdom (Matthew 18.23). And the learned teacher of the law will have to learn that he has everything to learn before he enters the Kingdom (Matthew 13.52). The notaries and Pharisees shut the door of the Kingdom of Heaven in people's faces but do not seek to enter themselves (Matthew 23.13).

Jesus' account of the Last Judgement (Matthew 25.33) describes a separation of the sheep from the goats which contains surprises. The sheep have 'done' the right things. They have visited the sick and those in prison and supported the poor and widows. The goats have not done these things. This encouraged some to believe that God approves of people because of the way they behave. But the same passages emphasize that the sheep acted without knowing that they were doing something credit worthy. 'When did we see you hungry and fed you, or thirsty and gave you drink, a stranger and took you home, or naked and clothed you?', the righteous ask in puzzlement (Matthew 25.38-9).

So it seems to be important that though the 'work' which is approved of in this story consists of the adoption of certain patterns of behaviour, what really matters is that it reflects fundamental attitudes or stances towards God and other people. It is an expression of an inward reality in the believer, speaking of what he or she 'is'. If that is the way it should be read, it would not be the doing but the spirit in which it was done which 'counts' with God. On one construction, God rewards the sheep and punishes the goats. On the other, he merely recognizes each for what it is in a process mainly 'revelatory', for sheep and goats alike are surprised to find out which they are.

Much of the medieval literature exhorting the faithful to prayer and effort had been based on the idea that people could please God by their actions or at least 'work with' or respond to his grace so as to grow into persons who please him in a much more mechanical and even quantitative way. 'Good works' could be reckoned up to the believer's credit. This all encouraged a habit of seeing the whole problem of sin in terms of accounting – so much reward for so much right-doing. Martin Luther, wishing people to feel free of the burden of obligations to do the right thing, with or without divine assistance, argued that God 'counts' people acceptable because of their faith, not because of anything they do (justification by faith).

Another answer, favoured by Augustine and by Calvin, has been that God does not keep such a count anyway, but rewards whom he chooses, regardless of their deserts (predestination). Does providen-

tial care, divine foresight and predestination extend to individuals?
Boethius had long ago, sitting waiting for execution as a political
prisoner in the sixth century, asked about this in a conversation with
'Philosophy' in his book *On the Consolation of Philosophy*. Boethius
confesses that he has come to believe that no benevolent divine provi-
dential care extends to the affairs of individual men and women.[28]
This leads them on in their talk to the famous picture of Fortune's
wheel, and a discussion of the way Fortune can behave, bringing a
man or woman down at her whim and then tossing him up again,[29]
a very different fate from being directed to a particular end by a firm
reliable God who knows what he intends and will bring it about, but
leaving people just as helpless.

Does God have preferences? Yes, the Bible seems to say. God's
people are special, a 'holy people' (Exodus 19.6).[30] 'Many are called but
few are chosen,' warns Matthew (22.14).[31] The number of those God
chooses is said to be smaller than the number of those he does not
choose (Matthew 22.14). 'Narrow is the gate,' admonishes (Matthew
7.13–14; Luke 13.24). The company of heaven is to be a 'chosen' people
(I Peter 2.9). Romans 8.28–30 goes from the mention of foreknowledge and predestination to speak of the calling, justification and glori-
fication of individuals. Ephesians 1.3–14 mentions God's 'choosing'
when it speaks of his foreknowledge and predestination. II Timothy
1.9 adds the idea that this is at God's gracious wish.

There is, then, plentiful support for the idea that entry to heaven
will be selective. The doctrine of predestination has remained optional
in the scheme of Christian doctrine. Christianity in the East tended to
accept Origen's idea of God's universal will to save. In the West, the
story was very different. Under the pervasive influence of Augustine,
it was very widely held that the choosing was God's, and that he had
made his choice concerning each individual at his or her creation, but
this never became an official position. In early Western Christianity,
the adherents of a doctrine of predestination laid all the onus on God
to choose and accepted that his choice might be mysterious. Grace
had its favourites, who might appear to their neighbours to be very
uncertain candidates for sanctity.

To Augustine it was of the first importance that no one could be
sure whom God would freely pardon, and if it had been a straightforward matter of being confident that one could tell from people's

visible behaviour, there would have been no mystery about it. On that presumption, that God awards the 'gift' of heaven for his own reasons, rather than rewarding the soul which has effortfully earned it, careful keeping of a tally becomes irrelevant.

With this school of thought went another idea, that all sinners 'deserved' only hell. No human effort could be great enough for anyone to be able to 'work his passage' to heaven. Indeed, some argued that no sinner could make any effort towards the good at all without the aid of grace. Augustine and Anselm were both pessimistic about the numbers of humanity which could hope to be saved. If individuals are predestined, an elaborate penitential process seems redundant, for the predestined must enter heaven whatever they do, and those God does not 'choose' will not enter heaven however hard they 'try', and this, as Augustine insisted, will be perfectly just.

This is another of the points on which the Church never officially made up its mind, for there is an obvious conflict between the main considerations. Luther's doctrine of justification by faith fitted readily with a doctrine of predestination, for it allowed a direct link between faith and salvation in which there were no particular expectations of growth or development in the individual. Calvin, Luther's younger contemporary, added to Augustine's theory his own conviction that those who are 'saved' know it. Pastorally, this could be disastrous, for it left those without that happy inner conviction in a state of despair. 'Are you saved?' asks the modern evangelist you meet in the street. He is the heir of Calvin's conviction that God has chosen some individuals and that these 'elect' are conscious of the favour in which they stand with God.

If there is to be a selection, can it be predicted what kind of people will be admitted? There are many hints in the Bible that God's preference is for the broken and vulnerable and unassuming. The Sermon on the Mount indicated that the Last Judgement would be a surprise, to observers and participants alike. There will be the weak and the foolish, for God chooses such in order to shame the strong and the wise (I Corinthians 1.27). Augustine, in his *Confessions* (XIII.xix.25), takes this theme and uses it to make a link with I Corinthians 1.27. God's chosen people will be a surprising selection when they can be identified and stand revealed.

The modern believer can stand back from these disturbing

discussions, since they proved as inconclusive as they were passionately argued. The important thing about them was the degree to which they reflected the insistence upon an action-based valuing of human beings, lives weighed and found wanting, sin as something demanding punishment, and reward as something earned or awarded within that framework. If God could give it regardless of individual deserts, that simply meant that he chose to disregard the framework, not that the framework was not there at all. The modern believer can think this through afresh.

The Church and the sacraments

Baptism and celebratory 'memorials' of the Last Supper Jesus ate with his disciples were practised by the early Christians. A formal belief in a more extensive system of sacraments 'administered' within the Church was slow to develop as something considered to be 'necessary to salvation'. Confirmation, ordination to the ministry of the Church, marriage, the anointing of those who were sick when they seemed likely to die were all gradually added to the list, and there emerged in the course of the later Middle Ages a particular emphasis on the penitential system and its requirements. 'Sacrament' originally just meant 'mystery'. Augustine had seen the sacraments as outward and visible signs of an inward and spiritual reality and capable of pointing the enquirer-after-God in the right direction. They were increasingly seen in the late Middle Ages as powerful, able to affect people's spiritual destiny, even bring about a person's 'salvation'.

Martin Luther said that such 'human' requirements were mere impositions, constructions of the 'power-brokers' of the institutional Church who wanted 'control' over the faithful; yet he and reformers of the sixteenth century and after who have thought as he did were not discarding the idea that there was any need to 'deal with' or 'pay for' sin. The removal of Church control from the equation has not proved easy to maintain. Protestant Churches have sometimes turned out to have a lust for power too. Puritanical Protestant sects have been known to be repressive and threatening to members who step out of line and do not conform to the 'requirements' of the group or sub-group (for their membership has frequently divided on disputed points of detail). Some modern American television evangelism, which holds itself out as controlling the gateway to heaven in return for cash, seems to have a similar concern with power and control in its approach to salvation.

This is perhaps an unavoidable legacy of the adoption of the doctrine of original sin and a preoccupation with God's insistence on punishing people for it. When Martin Luther was still a monk, he says, he began to have extremely negative feelings about the text of Romans 1.17, with its assertion that the righteous are those who *live* by faith. This went on so long as he believed that God would punish all those whose actions did not come up to his required standard of behaviour. However irreproachably he was living as a monk at the time, he says, he had no confidence that he was pleasing God, and saw himself only as a sinner with a troubled conscience. He could think of nothing but his failure to do what was expected, until he became angry with God for putting believers in so intolerable a position.[32] His eventual solution was to formulate his doctrine of 'justification by faith' and remove himself and those who followed his lead from the intolerable battle to be good by declaring it unnecessary.

Many sixteenth-century reformers read Jesus' summary of the Ten Commandments of Exodus 20 with anxiety too. 'Thou shalt love the Lord thy God with all thy heart, and with all thy soul, and with all thy mind. ... Thou shalt love thy neighbour as thyself' (Matthew 22.38–9, RV). Did that mean that love earned salvation, and, if so, exactly what did someone have to do to fulfil this obligation?

None of these reforming challenges to the institutional stranglehold of the late medieval Church in the West removed sin from the equation. It merely removed it to a place where it could be declared to have been comprehensively dealt with already by the death of Christ. Luther belongs firmly in the camp of those who have held that God is an angry God who expects a lot and imposes sanctions if his requirements are not met. The situation was still being summed up in terms of the repercussions of original sin by John Locke in the seventeenth century.

> Nobody can deny, but that the doctrine of the gospel is, that death came on all men by Adam's sin; only they differ about the signification of the word death. For some will have it to be a state of guilt, wherein not only he but all his posterity was so involved, that everyone descended of him deserved endless torment in hell-fire. ... To this they would have it be also a state of necessary sinning, and provoking God in every action that men do: a yet harder sense of the word death than the other.[33]

Nevertheless, awkward questions were in his mind and we have already seen him challenge these fundamental suppositions. 'It is obvious to any one who reads the New Testament, that the doctrine of redemption, and consequently of the gospel, is founded upon the supposition of Adam's fall.'[34] This 'would have all Adam's posterity doomed to eternal infinite punishment, for the transgressions of Adam, whom millions had never heard of, and no one had authorized to transact for him, or be his representative'. 'How doth it consist with the justice and goodness of God, that the posterity of Adam should suffer for his sin; the innocent be punished for the guilty?'[35] 'Perhaps it will be demanded, why did God give so hard a law to mankind, that to the Apostles' time no one of Adam's issue had kept it? Answer. It was such a law as the purity of God's nature required. ... The law was ... holy, just and good [Romans 7.21] and such as it ought, and could not otherwise be.'[36]

The modern believer may perhaps reread James and John at this point and consider the alternative of simply behaving in accordance with the hopeful simplicity of the kind of believing Jesus spoke of, without this complex of anxieties.

Best behaviour

'Greet all the saints' (Hebrews 13.24) is a salutation apparently referring to all the Christians in the place where the letter is being sent.[37] The word 'saints' subsequently narrowed until it had a particular reference to those who were thought to deserve to be called 'saints' because of their outstanding holiness.[38]

In the course of the later Middle Ages saints became a distinct and identifiable group of the especially good. The Orthodox Churches have legions of them in the calendar. In the West they were identified by a formal process of canonization, with monasteries hiring biographers to write the life stories of their dead abbots in the hope that they could be put up successfully for canonization and a profit could be made from the tourist visits of pious pilgrims to their tombs. Eventually – after Bonaventure in the thirteenth century had gone into the matter – saints were deemed to be so abundant in goodness that there was a positive surplus over what they themselves 'needed' to enter heaven, and they were held to be able to contribute to a 'treasury of merits' on which others might be able to draw. These canonized saints were never thought to be the only future inhabitants of heaven. They are 'examples to us all' precisely so that others may aspire to be like them and follow them thither. The whole scheme of aspiration and expectation outlined in such talk presumes the survival of the individual.

It has been a comforting idea that one might turn out to belong to the category of people who, though obviously not saints, were nevertheless capable of being made fit for heaven with a little further adjustment.[39] To the Christian tradition, it has seemed obvious that human beings, in general, would not 'do' as they were. It was readily accepted as the penitential system evolved that comparatively few people when they died were 'ready for heaven'. The individual was thought to emerge perfected before death only in rare cases, the 'saints' whose excess of holiness leaves the world in no doubt that they died acceptable in the sight of God.

The twelfth-century West saw the full working out, of a notion of which there had been only glimpses before, of some provision divinely made for those not 'saints', who would, nevertheless, be spending eternity with God. Jacobus of Voragine gives a convenient thirteenth-century list of the three categories of those 'in need of purgation'. They are 'those who have died before they complete the penance imposed on them', those who have completed it but it was not sufficient in the eyes of God because the priest imposed too light a penance, those who take with them beyond the grave the 'wood, hay, stubble' of worldly attachments.[40] He thought that a period of expiation after death could win pardon for such as these.[41]

By the middle of the twelfth century, this sort of argument had encouraged the development of a doctrine of purgatory. It was a response to the expression of a pastoral need for reassurance that all might not be lost for the majority of ordinary people who died without obvious 'sanctity' and whose relatives were uncertain that they would be able to pass muster with God and be let into heaven. Technically speaking, purgatory in the later Middle Ages was defined as the 'place' in which for a 'time' souls already saved (guaranteed heaven in the end) served out their remaining required penances after death. Purgatory was the anteroom to heaven, a place of transformation, in which the individual was fitted for the company of God in heaven.

The emerging doctrine took it that provided an individual had repented before death, confessed and been absolved by a priest, there was hope. There would be outstanding penalties to discharge. These were of their very nature quantitative and temporal. Indeed the penitential codes emphasize that aspect, for it is the only way of providing for proportionate punishment for more or less serious sins. So there came into being a general expectation that for a good proportion of the Christian community a period of 'time' in purgatory would serve to fit them for heaven, that to die and find oneself there was good news, since it carried an absolute assurance that heaven would come later.

Purgatory, once invented, provided a device for tying off loose ends, but it will be apparent that it prompted a good many questions. It assumed a whole apparatus of expectations and devices for meeting them. It rested heavily on a set of beliefs about sin and punishment. It also 'materialized' the afterlife, putting 'time' and measured penalties into eternity, so as to 'save' the self of body-and-soul.

The modern believer can take a view of all this from the distance of some centuries of changing expectations. In the Roman Catholic Church and a number of other communities the penitential system is still pastorally important. It can be a comfort because it seems to contain and measure the problem of sin and its consequences and provide the believer with something he or she can do about it.

The question for the modern believer is whether all this apparatus is necessary. For serving one's sentence, doing one's penance, places a heavy reliance on the assumption that repentance is not enough. The formal penitential system made repentance central. It required confession to a priest, not simply to God. It entrusted the priest with two duties. He would grant absolution and he would impose a penance for the penitent to perform to show that his repentance was sincere. So simple forgiveness became overlaid with other requirements.

Forgiveness

If sorrowfulness for having offended a loving God and willing confession of one's guiltiness were stressed in the Latin West, in the Greek East the emphasis lay upon *metanoia*, a change of mind, with a concomitant expectation of amendment of life. The experience of *personal conversion* has often been the moment of recognition of a strong sense of one's own sin and sincere repentance for it, accompanied by a simultaneous sense of release, a new freedom and being accepted 'regardless'.

Forgiveness is (technically) an act of generous giving up of an entitlement. It is the action of the person who has been injured or to whom the debt is owed. It makes it possible to treat the injury done as if it had never been. It remits a debt. By asking for forgiveness (pardon) the sinner recognizes that God has expectations which the sinner has not met. Forgiveness has also been taken to mend or renew a damaged relationship between persons. The need for such mending is a frequent preoccupation of the Gospels. When Peter asked him how often someone should be forgiven if he offended, and suggested up to seven times, Jesus told his disciples to forgive those who injured them generously and as often as necessary, up to seventy times seven (Matthew 18.22).

Jesus told the story of the unjust steward whose own debts were forgiven but who refused to forgive a fellow servant (Matthew 18.23–35). He encouraged his disciples to mend quarrels at once. Even if someone is going on an urgent errand he should stop and reconcile himself with his neighbour before he goes, he urged. 'If, therefore, thou art offering thy gift at the altar, and there rememberest that thy brother hath aught against thee at the altar, leave there thy gift before the altar, and go thy way, first be reconciled to thy brother, then come and offer thy gift' (Matthew 5.23–4).

The modern believer will have experience of offending and being offended at the human level and will have learned some lessons both about the difficulty of forgiving and forgetting and the almost automatic consequences which unfold within such situations without forgiveness.

A range of rewards?

> Were I an Infidel, Misfortunes like this would convince me, that there must be an Hereafter: For who can believe, that so much Virtue could meet with so great Distress without a following Reward.[42]

The perceived unfairness of the present life has been persuasive for many in encouraging them to believe that heaven will provide compensation or rewards. The idea is older than Christianity. The logic of Cicero's position too was that he could not see any other reason why men should strive so hard during their lifetimes unless there was to be an enduring future of enjoyment of their achievement.[43] The theme is also there in the Bible. 'The angel spoke to me words of consolation' (Zacharias 1.13). 'Lazarus the beggar who once lay at the rich man's gate now lies in the bosom of Abraham while the rich man burns in hell' (Luke 16.20–31). The New Testament contains other passages comforting for the disadvantaged. The rich man would find it more difficult to get to heaven than the poor man. It would be as hard for him as it would be for a camel to pass through the eye of a needle (Matthew 19.24; Mark 10.25; Luke 18.25).

Cyprian thought there would be many possibly different rewards in heaven, and it was one of the strong themes of Augustine's *The City of God* that heaven would be the place where the order of such things would be put right. Even if this life seems burdensome the load is much more easily borne than it was in Old Testament times, when the gates of heaven remained closed and when few cared to set their sights on heaven,[44] says Thomas à Kempis (c.1380–1471). So heaven was to be consoling, because it would make up for things, rebalancing life's inequities. For many centuries the social effect of the belief that everything would be all right in the end, but in a future life, continued to be felt in a general lack of interest in anything more than the direct relief of the poor and afflicted, the visiting of those in prison, and so on. There was not seen to be any need to improve general conditions of earthly life and even up social inequalities until comparatively modern times. Only in the late fourteenth century did William Langland (c.1330–c.1400) explore the idea of a differentiation of rewards in heaven, in the context of the budding concerns for social justice of some late medieval anti-establishment thinkers preaching a kind Christian socialism heavily laced with class hatred, such as the Waldensians and Lollards.

The promise of 'reward' is held out by Christian authors not only as compensation, but also as an *enticement* to the virtuous life. Cyprian in the *De lapsis* argues that those who seek the heavens should not allow themselves to be weighed down or held back by earthly desires. God invites us to despise earthly goods by offering rewards in heaven (I Corinthians 15.10).[45] As Gregory the Great puts it, the heavenly crown on the brow, the crown of victory, is experienced as the divine 'remuneration' (*merces*).[46] Ailred of Rivaulx certainly thinks that to find oneself in heaven is a reward.[47] William of Auxerre in the thirteenth century speaks of the 'gifts' given to the resurrected.[48] He identifies these (knowledge, enjoyment and love) with the 'measure pressed down and running over' of Luke 6.38.[49]

Those thinkers of the classical world who believed in a life to come had also tended to believe it would involve reward and the meting out of punishment on a proportionate basis. The just punishments of the gods (*poenas*)[50] were adapted to fit the offences of those who lie deep in Virgil's Hades in the *Aeneid*. There is a strong underlying principle in the *Aeneid* that one gets one's deserts for what one has done wrong, and with some exactness. Anchises is counting *moresque manusque* when Aeneas comes upon him.[51] Some have hated their brothers (*invisi fratres*), or were killed for committing adultery, or were guilty of fraud (*fraus*), or kept for themselves money they should have shared with their kindred.[52] These are social misdeeds, but the gods have been offended. There is some wider classical authority for the idea of a tailor-made life to come, fitting exactly the deserts of the individual, or perhaps simply enabling him to be fully himself. Cicero's sense of just reward included the idea that each should receive his 'due', at least as a citizen in this world.

The expectation that there will be different rewards for different kinds of life is also there in the Bible, in the Sermon on the Mount. 'Blessed are those who suffer persecution for righteousness' sake, for theirs is the Kingdom of heaven' (Matthew 5.10). Yet this idea of 'achievement' and its 'reward' could not be transferred into Christian theology without a good deal of debate, despite Cyprian's Ciceronian echo in the *De bono patientiae*, with its hint of a reward for each according to his deeds.[53] The 'great' reward in heaven of the Sermon in the Mount (Matthew 5.12) is specifically promised by Ambrose of Milan to those who love their enemies,[54] together with the assurance that they will be sons of the Most High (*filii altissimi*) (though in fact the text in Matthew 5.12 makes this particular promise to those who are persecuted and condemned for righteousness' sake).

How does this affect the question why the individual should 'be good'? The first reason, that you will be punished if you do not behave well because God will be angry with you, fits in with the 'redemption' theory. 'Fling the useless servant out into the dark, the place of wailing and grinding of teeth' (Matthew 25.14–30). 'Thy destruction is of thyself' (Hosea 13.9). This was a favourite theme of the Cambridge Platonists too: 'All Misery arises out of our selves.'[55] 'Hell arises out of a Man's Self.'[56]

The second reason which has been advanced is that it is an end in itself. It is simply 'the right thing to do'. The rather Aristotelian idea that things 'ought' to be themselves so as to arrive at the end that is in them and fulfil their purpose has merged in Christian theology with the Judaeo-Christian notion that each individual human being has a relationship with God and can act 'against' him. Any such act has to be turned round in some way to bring things back to their right balance. This 're-balancing' idea fits comfortably with the hypothesis of 'atonement', the idea that God became man to restore order and to bring about reconciliation between himself and humankind.

The *Expositio totius mundi et gentium*[57] is a description of the world and its people by an author of some intellectual pretensions, and perhaps a Christian, probably writing in the fourth century. He begins with the land of the Magi (where better?, he says).[58] He moves on to the Camarini (IV) who live in the part of the Orient which Moses described as Eden. The people there have no need to labour to produce food. Each day bread rains down upon them and they have wild honey to drink. They enjoy sunshine so warm that they are obliged to go and bathe in the river while the sun is at its height. They need no government because they do not need to organize a common system of food production (V). And since they enjoy such a great happiness they suffer from no sicknesses. They die, but they know the day of their deaths (VII). As it approaches, each makes for himself a coffin of scented wood and lies down in it and serenely takes his leave (VII). This is a calm, conscious leave-taking, a finishing of unfinished business.

No such happy resignation and sense of completeness was possible within the early Christian scheme once the theology of sin had begun to develop its ramifications. The Christian tradition has made much of the idea that for each individual a fearful and irreversible end awaits if his or her sinful condition is not attended to in this life. The implications are not confined to Christianity. Some of the suicide bombers emerging in modern Islam seem to have been led to think in terms of the pleasing of an angry and punishing God by personal sacrifice. Question the traditional concepts of sin, punishment and redemption, and an entirely different landscape opens up in all directions.

PART III. LIFE'S ENDS AND PURPOSES

Death has been portrayed as the great fixer and the end of opportunity. Early Christianity came to accept that the ultimate outcome for each individual was fixed at the moment he or she died. This gave rise to a Christian literature of last-minute hope, in which the most unlikely individuals were suddenly transformed by repentance at the moment of death. Nevertheless the approach to death is sometimes described with critical realism: 'That stupid Symptom observable in divers Persons near their Journey's end ... that is, to become more narrow-minded, miserable and tenacious, unready to part with anything when they are ready to part with all, and afraid to want when they have no time to spend,' as Thomas Browne cruelly put it ('To a Friend, upon the occasion of the death of his intimate friend', *Religio Medici*, p 161).

The seventeenth-century English Metaphysical poet and Dean of St Paul's, John Donne, was much preoccupied with death's paradoxes, its role as both an end of life as we know it and a gateway to life as it will be.

> I runne to death, and death meets me as fast,
> And all my pleasures are like yesterday,
> I dare not move my dimme eyes any way,
> Despaire behind and death before doth cast
> Such terror ... (*Divine Poems*, p 434).

In the twentieth century, still playing paradox with this most serious theme, T.S. Eliot (1888–1965) is more downbeat, pointing to the 'warning' which sounds within the ordinariness of life:

> Webster was much possessed by death
> And saw the skull beneath the skin.
> (*Whispers of Immortality*)

So what comes next?

6

A nice place to be?

The traditional landscapes of heaven

I know not, O, I know not
What joys await us there.[1]

What is it possible to write about heaven, since no living reader can judge the reliability of anything that is said? If there is a heaven, its reality stretches away out of sight. We may have our ideas, but how do we know they are God's ideas, 'not such as are conceived and imagined in ourselves', as John Donne put it?[2] The relatively modern notion of a rather vapid heaven, peopled by figures in white nightgowns plucking harps, is partly a legacy of English Sunday Schools and of a moral children's literature of the nineteenth and twentieth and twenty-first centuries. It is not surprising that this sounds as though it would be boring and why it seems unattractive. A more adult and challenging approach must be possible.

Again and again even the most radical and forward-thinking have declared themselves to be nonplussed and have fallen back upon the familiar conventions. 'When I lay sucking at my mother's breasts, I had no notion how I should afterwards eat, drink, or live. Even so, we on earth have no idea what the life to come will be,' admits Martin Luther. Luther, for all his aggressive certainties on many points, had none here. What he had were assumptions, held within a climate of thought which had been shaped over many centuries. So he draws a conventional picture:

> It will be no arid waste, but a beautiful new earth, where all the just will dwell together. There will be no carnivorous beasts, or venomous creatures, for all such, like ourselves, will be to us as friendly as they were to Adam in Paradise. There will be little dogs, with golden hair, shining like precious stones. The foliage of the trees, and the verdure of the grass, will have the brilliancy of emeralds; and we ourselves, delivered from our mundane subjection to gross appetites and necessities, shall have the same

form as here, but infinitely more perfect. Our eyes will be radiant as the purest silver, and we shall be exempt from all sickness and tribulation. We shall behold the glorious creator face to face; and, then, what ineffable satisfaction will it be to find our relations and friends among the just.[3]

Writers were still having difficulty in getting away from the familiarities of the tradition in the twentieth century. Dorothy Sayers put the classical ideas beside the Christian images and could not see how to reconcile them:

> Dante never read Plato properly; he might have found the Platonic Heaven a bit more adult. But wouldn't he have thought it too impersonal? Too much like being absorbed into the infinite? I don't know much Plato, but would he have had much use for the 'glorious and holy flesh', or said, 'Behold our city, how wide its gyres, how great the company of its shining robes?'[4]

In *The Great Divorce* C.S. Lewis takes the reader into the 'country' of heaven by way of a metaphysical bus ride, the mid-twentieth-century equivalent of the medieval vision or dream-sequence. In the allegory he unfolds, his fellow passengers and he mount the bus in the mean streets of a rainy town in twilight. The bus takes off; it flies. He finds himself 'in a larger space, perhaps even a larger sort of space' than he had ever known before, 'as if the sky were further off and the extent of the green plain wider than they could be on this little ball of earth'.[5] This new world is more real, too, in the sense of being more solid. He tries to pick a daisy and finds it hard as diamond. Yet the description does not get imaginatively beyond the same patterns of reconstruction and improvement of familiar things. Heaven is still no more than earth writ larger and brighter. Augustine had admitted frankly that he did not really have any clear idea what eternal life would be like because he did not know how it was to be related to any present sense-experience.[6]

A good way to begin, then, is to assemble the conventional pictures so that the reader can form a view of their satisfactoriness and their limitations as a focus of hope and belief.

Heaven as a kingdom turned upside-down

The leading Old Testament idea was that God reigns in heaven, sitting on a throne and surrounded by angelic 'courtiers', as he does in Isaiah 6. There is a good deal of talk of military power in the Old Testament too. 'Hosts of heaven' are really 'armies' in the Latin of the Vulgate (II Esdras 9.6). This is a repeating theme of the Old Testament (IV Kings 17.6, 21.3, 21.5, 23.4–5). Deuteronomy warns against mistaking the sun and moon and stars for the heavenly armies and worshipping them instead of God (Deuteronomy 4.19 and 17.3). This language came to be used of spiritual warfare. Cyprian addresses himself to the Christian who is God's soldier and longs to be in the heavenly 'camp'.[7] In his own discussion of these ideas, Jerome remarks in his commentary on Isaiah on the sight of 'all the army of heaven' standing to God's left and to his right (III Kings 22.19).[8] Gregory the Great asks 'and how is the army of heaven described if not as the multitude of the angels'?[9] Bede has the constellations as 'the armies of heaven'.[10]

The 'kingdom' to come is a particularly strong theme in Matthew's Gospel (4.8). Satan shows Jesus all the kingdoms of this world and their glory, and he resists the temptation to rule such kingdoms. But John the Baptist preached the coming of the Kingdom of Heaven (Matthew 3.2) in something of the spirit of Old Testament prophecy. 'Repent for the Kingdom of Heaven is at hand!' he calls (Matthew 3.2; cf. 4.17, 10.7). Jesus' own favourite image of the world to come was also that of a kingdom. 'Many will come from all directions to feast in the Kingdom of Heaven with Abraham, Isaac and Jacob' (Matthew 8.11). Jesus is recorded as promising the disciples that they will sit on 12 thrones judging the 12 tribes of Israel with the Son of Man in his majesty (Matthew 19.28).

Yet this was going to be an unexpected sort of kingdom. The disadvantaged will no longer be disadvantaged there. The servant will rule. 'The least in the Kingdom of heaven will be greater than John the Baptist' (Matthew 11.10–11). The humble and meek of the Sermon on the Mount (Matthew 5.5) are apparently going to reign in heaven, for 'theirs is the Kingdom of Heaven' (Matthew 5.3). When the disciples came to Jesus and asked him who was to be the greatest in the Kingdom of Heaven, he set a small child in front of them and told them that unless they became like children they would not enter the Kingdom of Heaven, for there the greatest will be those most childlike. And there must be particular care not to damage the faith of children (Matthew 18.1 and 4). The citizens of heaven will be quiet and unassuming and not show off about the visible signs of their faith and their charitable deeds (Matthew 6.1–18).

Jesus put forward as the natural citizens of the Kingdom not the mighty and powerful, but the poor in spirit and the persecuted, and this is at least in part because they have no material ties to earth. The 'treasure' of those who are to enter the Kingdom of Heaven is already stored there, and not on earth, for where someone's treasure is, there he will feel most at home (Matthew 7.21), and the rich keep what is important to them here in this world. The Kingdom of Heaven is of such value that it would be worth losing all one had to have it (Matthew 13.44 and 45), and the rich and powerful do not find that easy to accept. The New Testament thus insists that God prefers the underdogs, and when I Peter 2.9 speaks of a 'royal priesthood' it seems to be in the expectation that it will be open to the faithful without social discrimination.

Heaven as a garden

Gardening was a pleasure classical authors commonly looked forward to when they contemplated retiring in old age to live 'by oneself' and 'with oneself', duty done and passion spent, in a rural retreat.[11] The theme of quiet reflection in beautiful country surroundings appears repeatedly in late Roman literature. Cato, and Varro in his book *On Agriculture*, are both very practical on the pleasures of the country life for the man who enjoys a country estate (but has a gardener to do the work). The two pleasures of leisure, as Pliny identifies them, are reading and relaxation.[12] A bookish landowner needs only enough land to refresh himself by strolling along perhaps one pathway. On a modest estate he can know every vine and every bush.[13] Leisure in the garden may be, for the classical author, the realization of a lifetime's desire for time to think and enjoy, or a time and place of preparation for death. 'The Fields of the Blessed' or the Elysian Fields were thought of as a garden too. Virgil's *Aeneid* contains a description of certain 'happy places' to be found even within the gloom of Hades. These seem once more to be simply a beautiful landscape, a wide space with good air and light, where there is sport and music and the blessed may continue to enjoy themselves in ordinary human pastimes.[14] So there was a plentiful classical 'garden' literature on which to build in any Christian interpretation of heaven, which took it to be an eternal 'version' of Eden's garden of delights, and somehow prefigured by that pleasant garden in which Genesis says that God placed the first human beings at their creation.

The Book of Revelation has a reference to the Tree of Life which is said to be in the midst of 'paradise' (Revelation 2.7). Paradise[15] has often been taken to be (or perhaps confused with) the Garden of Eden, where God planted the Tree of Life and put Adam and Eve into dangerous proximity with it (Genesis 2.8). Paradise is mentioned in the Song of Songs, in relation to the sister who is a 'walled garden' and a 'sealed fountain' (Song 4.13).[16]

Bernard of Clairvaux celebrates the 'spring' imagery of the Song of Songs, the passing of winter and the appearance of flowers on the earth. The flesh 'sown' like seed in death bursts into flower again in its resurrection and the scent of these flowers fills the earth.[17] This kind of imagery is attractive in every age, although the beauty of nature had varying appeal as the conventions of garden design changed century by century, admiration for knot-gardens mutating into an apprecia-tion of a grand landscape with a long view.

Heaven as a city

The Book of Revelation speaks of the 'great city', the 'New Jerusalem', descending from heaven and from God, like a new bride arrayed for her husband (Revelation 21.2). Eusebius, Constantine's biographer and one of the Church's first historians, takes up the theme as he describes the city 'above' the heavens, the heavenly Jerusalem, the heavenly mountain of Sion, as the city of the living God, in which myriad choirs of angels celebrate, in theologies beyond our describing or comprehending, their Creator and the Lord of the Universe (cf. I Corinthians 2.9).

The idea of a 'city' of God received its fullest development in Augustine's book on the subject. There the emphasis is on the city as a 'community of citizens' rather than on the 'architecture of a place'.[18] Augustine is not describing a city which is entirely other worldly. He wants his readers living in this world to experience fully the sharing of their citizenship with those already in heaven and those not yet born. Augustine did not know whether he or his friends were fellow citizens of that city. God alone knows who they all are, he claimed, for he has chosen them unbeknownst to the chosen themselves. If he is right, you do not know whether those you love best are with you or against you in the perspective of eternity.

In the Middle Ages citizens of heaven are commonly seen as stones in the city wall,

> Living stones, by God appointed
> Each to his allotted place.[19]

This modern hymn, with its first stanza representing Christ as 'Corner Stone' and 'sure foundation', describes the building of the heavenly city out of its very inhabitants. They are the walls; they form the city.

The image of the Heavenly Jerusalem also belongs here. King David decided to make Jerusalem God's dwelling place with the House of the Lord within it and 'the glory of the Lord filled the house of the Lord' (I Kings 8.10–11).[20] Psalms 9.11, 74.2 and 135.21 also have God dwelling in Zion or Jerusalem. Ezekiel has a vision of the glory of the Lord entering the Temple (Ezekiel 43.1–5). There is the promise of a new temple in Jerusalem even more glorious than the old (Haggai 2.9).[21] Nehemiah and Ezra speak of restoring Jerusalem to its former glory.

There are many indications of double thinking in the patristic and medieval centuries, many hints of a poetic willingness to mutate the earthly into the heavenly Jerusalem, so as to make this going back to Jerusalem symbolic as well as real. When the crusaders set out in the late eleventh and twelfth and thirteenth centuries for the earthly Jerusalem in the crusades which combined pilgrimage with holy war, a number of those who went took themselves to be going to the heavenly as well as the earthly Jerusalem.

The garden and the city were sometimes conjoined in a single landscape. The fourteenth-century poet William Langland begins *Piers Plowman* with a description of a great plain full of people – this world – from which can be seen at a distance both heaven and hell. Hell is a dungeon. Heaven is a splendid tower on a hill in the sunshine. John Bunyan (1628–88), too, has his Pilgrim 'progressing' through landscape to a citadel in the seventeenth-century *The Pilgrim's Progress*.[22] Nevertheless, these are really distinct images, for the garden is above all a beautiful 'place' and the city may be more of a 'society'.

The problem which faces the modern believer will perhaps be obvious by now. The archetypal images have lasted. They provide ready-made pictures of heaven capable of being adjusted to fit the cultural norms of Christians in changing societies. But essentially they are limited conventions. Can the believer go beyond them into another realm of possibilities?

Something new?

The Bible talks about 'renewal' a good deal. 'You renew the face of the ground' (Psalms 104.30, RSV). God creates a pure heart and renews an upright spirit (Psalms 51.12). 'He who is not reborn cannot see the Kingdom of God' (John 3.3). 'We are buried into Christ's death in baptism and rise with him from the dead' (Romans 6.4). 'The trumpet shall sound and the dead shall be raised incorruptible, and we shall be changed. For this corruptible must put on incorruption and this mortal must put on immortality' (I Corinthians 15.52-3, RV).

It is not always clear whether the Bible promises 'renewal', in the sense of a restoration of lost freshness and faithfulness to the creator's intentions – perhaps a rebirth – or something 'quite new', altogether beyond what was before. It does not say consistently whether the 'renewal' is to be like the retreading of a worn tyre, or whether it is to be a 'newness' without precedent.

'Ending and beginning again' is to be found in I Corinthians 15.52-4. The theologian and poet John Donne borrows the theme in *Deaths Duell*. 'In an instant we shall have a dissolution, and in the same instant a reintegration, a recompacting of body and soul, and that shall be truly a death and truly a resurrection.'[23] He borrows from the same place the idea that death is to be swallowed up in victory as a triumphant ending.

A 'complete newness' is also promised in the Bible. 'And I saw a new heaven and a new earth' (Revelation 21.1). 'I saw the new holy city of Jerusalem descending from the sky from God, prepared like a bride adorned for her husband' (Revelation 21.2). 'He who sat on the throne said behold I make all things new' (Revelation 21.5). Augustine seems to say that the new will wholly supersede the old in the heavenly city, so that 'No vestige of the old will remain'.[24] Gregory the Great in his commentary on I Kings discusses what it would mean for all the old things to disappear so that we shall have so many new things to say (*tot nova*) that saying the 'old things' would be quite crowded out.[25] These debates about the possible newness of heaven remain, then, within the parameters of the familiar imagery and assumptions without really breaking free into a truly new set of ideas about the unprecedented possibilities of heaven. Nevertheless, they lay a foundation for such a departure.

'Where' would God be in the wholly new? For there is a strong tradition of Christian belief which is confident that 'going to heaven' must involve 'returning to God'.

Getting (back) to God

Let us make man in our image, after our likeness
(Genesis 1.26, RV).

In pre-Christian times Cicero was already canvassing the question whether man is made in the image of God or makes God in his own image.[26] Christian belief has leaned all one way on this point. 'What glory it is to become like God!' exclaims Cyprian.[27] Augustine speaks, in a very rare use of an ambitious Latin word, of 'being made God' (*deificari*).[28] How 'ambitious' is this idea? Can Cyprian or Augustine have meant that those who enter heaven will not merely be in God's presence but actually become gods themselves?

Christian belief sees the individual human being restored to the image and likeness of God (Genesis 1.26), but with definite limitations. Descriptions of the faithful as 'children' of God are commonplace in Scripture, but they are not seen as 'gods' themselves. Galatians 3.26 describes the faithful as 'children of God'. Romans 8.15 also assumes the children of God are the Christian faithful, not children in any bodily sense, but rather 'adopted' as God's children according to his promise (Romans 9.8). According to Philippians 2.15, the children of God are to stand out in the midst of a 'wicked people' for their simplicity of life and their lack of quarrelsomeness. Matthew 5.9 expressly identifies the sons of God as peacemakers. By contrast, in III John 3.10 the 'children of Satan' are unrighteous and do not love God. Yet a human 'child of God' thus 'adopted' becomes the child of being indescribably 'other'. A human being cannot 'grow up to be God'.

Plants and animals generally flourish and develop in the manner of their kind when they are given the conditions they need and do not meet impediments to their growth, such as slugs and mildew. This is a matter of mechanisms not of moral imperatives. Plants do what they 'ought' to do as far as they can, as may be observed in any struggling buddleia whose seed has lodged in the crevice of a wall. That is roughly the way Aristotle saw things tending to their 'end' and fulfilling their 'purpose'.

Return to God?

Could it be inherently different for Christian believers? Again and again over many generations, Christian souls are portrayed in via, merely on their way, in the hope of a resurrection not yet vouchsafed, a state not even glimpsed. This 'journey' reflects a running theme of the late Platonic–early Christian tradition. This is the idea that where we are now, the world as we know it, is not home, that we long to 'go home', and that means getting back to the God from whom we departed when we were created and thus made other than God. The Christian tradition added that we had taken ourselves still further away by our wilful disobedience or 'sin', putting us in a painful condition in which the creature is always restless because it is in the wrong place.

That this wrong place we are in now is a 'region of unlikeness' (regio dissimilitudinis) became an important idea.[29] It seems to take its Latin origin from the reference in Augustine's Confessions (VII.x.16) to Augustine's discovery, by self-examination, that he has strayed far from God, into a 'region' where he has lost the likeness (similitude) of Genesis 1.28, the image and likeness to God in which God made his human creatures. This metaphorical or spiritual 'distance' becomes a semi-literal 'distance' for some commentators. Bernard of Clairvaux places the 'realm of unlikeness' on a 'map' on which he identifies 'this present life'. On the map are also other regions: purgatory, hell and heaven (the regio expiationis, the regio gehennalis, the regio supercaelestis).[30]

This is not mere exile from a place but alienation from the intended 'human condition', on the assumption that that is the only possible satisfactory condition for human beings. Ailred of Rievaulx suggests that this is a useful clue affording an explanation of God's divine purpose in allowing his people to linger miserably in exile in this world.[31] People need the opportunity and the time to find their way back, and indeed to realize that they want to. Thomas of Chobham uses the idea of the regio dissimilitudinis in connection with the Prodigal Son of Luke 15.13. 'Often the strangers and outsiders who return from a far distance like the prodigal son, praise God more than those of his household who remain in his house.'[32]

William Langland's Piers Plowman ends with a beginning. Conscience decides to begin on a pilgrimage and walk through the world.[33] 'Is the [Divina] Commedia [of Dante] the most nostalgic poem ever written?' asks Dorothy Sayers. 'From beginning to end everybody is homesick. ... It's a poem by an exile, about exiles, for exiles.'[34] John Bunyan describes in The Pilgrim's Progress the journey of the human soul through life in this world. He called the book and its hero after the centuries-old tradition of Christian pilgrimage, in which the faithful journeyed in the body to a physical place which was holy by association with some saint or event of Christian significance and by analogy journeyed in the soul to a spiritual place.

This is the motif which lingered in Christian consciousness despite the unpromising unfolding of the distinction between mankind and a God eternally displeased with him, and quite other than his creature. Moses glimpses the Promised Land across the Jordan but he will never enter it. It is not merely a matter of getting back to the right 'region' from a place of exile. The driving force of the pilgrim's journey, the journey from the region of unlikeness, is the relief of the pain the creature feels while it is separated from God.

There is, then, a strongly marked thread in the Christian tradition which sees this life as a departure from the place where we ought to be and heaven merely a return. The return is often seen as the restoration of a 'primordial' relationship with God. Our perception of things encourages us to see time as flowing in a single direction. We cannot go back to yesterday except in memory. To 'return' to God has always been conceived of as involving a fresh journey, a going back which is also a going forward.

> Till man's first heavenly state again takes place
> (Carol: 'Christians awake, salute the happy morn')

It is salutary to remember here that for the modern scientist 'return' is not necessarily like that. 'All the successful equations of [modern] physics are symmetrical in time. They can be used equally well in one direction in time as in the other.'[35] This perception of the possible reciprocity of such 'movements' is a useful reminder that the conventions of the Christian tradition may have more stretchiness in them than was needed in earlier centuries. 'Returning to God' might feel like arriving somewhere quite new.

Hiding in God?

The longing for what has been perceived as a something lost to ordinary direct common human access, some singleness of heart, some purity, a chaste eroticism, an internal 'right order' which is in accordance with the order God intended for (and designed into) the universe, has appeared in Christian writing century after century. The soul, which has been practising by withdrawing into what the Vulgate calls the *cubiculum*, the inner chamber, of its own self, learns in the Song of Songs of another chamber into which the Bridegroom (Christ) leads the Bride (the soul).[36] Ambrose of Milan says that this leading into the chamber of the self describes the overshadowing of the self by the Holy Spirit.[37] Then there is the 'sanctuary', the holy place into which the soul goes in search of the presence of God (Psalms 72.17).[38]

Another strand of Christian belief favoured the idea that 'knowing God' is a swallowing up in darkness, that in the secret place where the believer is before the face of God, he is hidden (Psalms 30.21–2), a passage Augustine was particularly drawn to.[39] Cassiodorus (485/90–c.580) borrows it too, and interprets it as referring to the resurrection, when the righteous will have their reward and will see God.[40] These Biblical themes, powerfully interpreted, take us deep into the mystery of a 'deification' which seems to have been widely understood in the Fathers and in medieval authors as involving some sort of getting lost in God.

This conception of what 'is to come' as a state of union or changed relationship with God rather than a literal or figurative 'place' has its imagery of journeying too. The soul goes forward step by step into this new relationship, just as though it were travelling to a place. William of St Thierry, in his 'Book on the Nature of Body and Soul' (*Liber de natura corporis et animae*), sets out a programme of progression for the soul pace by pace.[41] In his 'Journey of the Mind to God' (*Itinerarium mentis ad deum*) a century later, Bonaventure begins by recommending to those who would take this journey that they dispose themselves in the right way inwardly by beginning with prayer.[42] Augustine in the *Confessions* and Anselm in his *Prayers and Meditations* taught much the same practice of preparation for being changed.[43]

So the modern believer may envisage heaven as the ultimate in 'getting lost'.

An eternal exchange of views?

Although in the story of the Prodigal Son (Luke 15.11–32), the father runs towards his son when he eventually comes home (having squandered his inheritance), and the old family closeness is restored with feasting and welcome, discussion of Christian belief in a 'return' has concentrated on the son's journey, not on the father's response. The human reader visualizes the child falling with relief upon its parent's breast, where there is comfort and reassurance and safety.

But among the 'relational' notions of the 'what is to come' is a strong thread of expectation derived once more from the classical philosophical tradition, and summed up in the New Testament in 'I shall know as I am known' (I Corinthians 13.12). Cicero explains that he follows Pythagoras in his belief that human minds (*animi*) are emanations of the divine mind (*universa mens divina*) (*De senectute*, xxi.77).[44] Cicero's idea of the 'immortal mind' is intellectual. This notion of a somewhat cerebral afterlife has its counterpart in Augustine's picture of an eternity of 'enjoyment of the mind of God'. Augustine's aspiration, conditioned by the philosophical assumptions of the late antique world, was to live in open, full, perfect knowledge. This bright clear light of understanding is his main idea of what it means to be in the 'sight' of God.[45] Augustine remarks that it was on his birthday that he and his friends came to the conclusion, after three days of discussion, that there would be no future happy life without perfect knowledge of God, that indeed the happy life really consisted in that 'knowing'.[46] He meant by this something like a truly successful conversation with a friend, which is exactly how he talks to God in the, admittedly rather one-sided, 'telephone' conversation of the *Confessions*. It is anxious and ecstatic, but still a conversation. A subtle but important movement from *animus* to *anima*, mind to soul, is involved. That was still being made in the early thirteenth century. William of Auvergne asserts that the highest faculty of the human soul is that which apprehends and knows.[47] For the contemplative tradition in Christianity, the divine presence affords interest enough for eternity, for, they asked, how can God not be sufficient, indeed, how can he not be all in all? This 'presence' of God makes life in heaven a perpetual 'feast', say some, an everlasting 'celebration'.[48] This relational and conversational friendship with God is another heavenly possibility for the modern believer to consider.

A cosmic dance?

Would a joining-in God who interacted with human beings in an open-ended way, not acting as a comforting backstop or a partner in dialogue, but a God himself in progress, be a lesser God and would it matter if he was?

> I danced in the morning
> When the world was begun,
> And I danced in the moon
> And the stars and the sun,
> And I came down from heaven
> And I danced on the earth
> At Bethlehem
> I had my birth.

In Sidney Carter's hymn, the divine joins in the enterprise of the universe. God the participant in this dance is also God the leader, but in a manner which seems to leave the created world free to follow him or not.

> Dance, then, wherever you may be;
> I am the Lord of the Dance, said he,
> And I'll lead you all, wherever you may be,
> And I'll lead you all in the dance, said he.[49]

Some modern Christian theology has made bleak claims that if the old certainties about the 'completed' and 'reliable' character of God are given up, or even questioned, that is tantamount to saying that God is 'dead'. 'The death of God is the death of a transcendental signifier stabilizing identity and truth. It is the death of identity, telos, and therefore meaning in anything but a local and pragmatic sense.'[50]

But there is another possible outcome, where loss is balanced by gain, when the old 'static' metaphysical assumptions give way to potential for movement and change and an infinitely variable possible relationship of God and creature,[51] 'God is not to be treated as an exception to all metaphysical principles to save their collapse.'[52] That idea can also be read as allowing the old fixities to be questioned without fear of a consequential collapse of everything. The question is where the brake can be applied once the story begins to run away in this direction. What stops the vulnerability of God becoming the destructibility of God and the world ending in collapse and failure?

We are faced with something of the same difficulty if we want to suggest that there are other ways to heaven and other sorts of heaven to be looked forward to within the Christian tradition than those outlined with such fervour by so many over the centuries, or if we want to challenge the pervasive understanding that the whole business of each human life is the perfecting of an individual human creation who will continue to be a 'who' and an 'I' in a heavenly future of 'personal', if 'shared', enjoyment – or merely other ways of looking at all this.

> A painter of the Umbrian school
> Designed upon a gesso ground
> The nimbus of the Baptized God.
> The wilderness is cracked and browned
>
> But through the water pale and thin
> Still shine the unoffending feet
> And there above the painter set
> The Father and the Paraclete.[53]

This poem of T.S. Eliot depends upon a tradition, old in art as well as in thought, to make its glimpse of the 'unoffending feet' of the incarnate Christ at once startling and familiar.

Paradigm shifting requires not merely an intellectual breaking out but a 'validation' of that breaking out, an acceptance of a wholly different way of envisaging things. Radical challenge has had its periods of being fashionable. Leaders of intellectual fashion in the eighteenth century were prepared to throw out a great deal. Yet the grit of the old assumptions can still be detected in the writer's shoe; it affects the way the feet are put down, gingerly and with proper care to avoid stubbing the toe on the old non-negotiables. The question for the would-be believer is what to take from the old ideas and what to leave behind, how far he or she can dare to venture in conceiving of a heaven more and better or at any rate different from anything mapped out before.

7

Is there a future for 'me'?

'"Love the Lord your God with all your heart, with all your soul and with all your mind." That is the greatest commandment. It comes first,' was Jesus' summary (Matthew 22.39). Who are 'you'? Are 'you' always going to exist? A great deal of Christian ink has been used in urging self-abnegation, and the notion of the loss of 'self' has a respectable ancestry in the most orthodox teaching. The challenge to modern expectations about the self comes next for the believer.

What is a person?

The Book of Revelation shows the newly arrived in heaven actively 'ruled' by the Lamb, but with a rule which is really a series of acts of pastoral tenderness. They are led to the waters of life and their tears are wiped away (Revelation 7.17). The 'rest' depicted in Revelation is a freedom from hunger and thirst and the heat of the sun (Revelation 7.16). Those who pray for the dead request for them quiet and a peaceful eternal dwelling place.[1] To the busy person whose life is full of stresses, the prospect of a rest is attractive. So is an easing of fears and anxieties. There was a well-developed desire to be 'free' from self-reproach and dissatisfaction. Romans 8.21 describes the creature 'freed' from slavery to this 'corruption' 'into' the freedom of the glory of the children of God (Romans 8.21). But this seems a conception of freedom very largely characterized by relief. It relies on the expectation that the newly arrived will still be concerned with their present problems and discontents, and feeling that they need a holiday. It looks backwards not forwards.

After a rest the blessed no doubt feel better. In the sixth century Cassiodorus, retired senior civil servant, describes 'paradise' in his commentary on the Psalms as 'a very pleasant place' where there is a certainty of everlasting joy. He uses several of the Latin words for happiness or pleasure available to him, often in the superlative. The promise is of *great* happiness, *extreme* pleasure.[2] On the traditional assumption that they still remain much the same persons as they always were, the blessed then turn to an eternity of doing what? Is there anything more for the blessed to look forward to? Is there anything to do in heaven? What is there to be happy about?

That question probably makes sense only if 'I' am going to be much the same and so are 'you'. 'I love to range through that Half of Eternity which is still to come, rather than look on that which is already run out; because I know I have a real Share and interest in [the future],' asserted *The Tatler* in 1710.[3] What is the force of that 'I'? Might some quite different relation to the universe be entered into at death in which 'I' do not feature?

The conceptions of 'self' and 'person' familiar in the modern West are comparatively recent and quite 'local' to that culture and frame of reference. The early Christian debate took place in a world of thought which almost wholly lacked the conceptual apparatus with which we can now discuss such concepts as 'personal identity', 'personhood and 'personality', let alone the associations and categories brought to it all by modern Western sociology and psychology. There was no general idea of 'doing your own thing' or of 'personal development' in the modern sense. A man or woman tended to be valued for conformity with an ideal rather than for any interesting personal variations. A virtuous human being was above all 'typical'.[4] The Greeks approved of certain characteristics, such as moderation, and striking a proper balance between intellectual activity and physical fitness, which they thought befitted a good citizen. There was a list of approved virtues, the Roman 'good citizen' virtues of prudence, temperance, justice and fortitude listed by Cicero and adopted by Christianity, and the faith, hope and charity contributed by Christianity (I Corinthians 13.13).

In the classical world, the leading idea was that good people had things in common. This was not thought of in quite the modern Western way (sharing an interest in skateboarding or chess), but rather as a common way of looking at things from the point of view of the general good. When Cicero described friendship as 'a common mind in divine and human things', coupled with affection, he had in mind a bond which extends beyond individuals to benefit the whole community.[5] A similar emphasis is there in Acts 4.32, which speaks of the Christian believers as a 'company' of those who were of one heart and mind and who had everything in common, including property; it was repeated in the early ecumenical councils of the Church, which began by stating that the assembled bishops are of one mind with those who have met in previous councils, as they are with one another.

The idea of the 'person' began to develop some centuries after the beginning of Christianity, with the emergence of the doctrine that the Father, Son and Holy Spirit are three 'Persons' in the Trinity. Such a 'Person' was not at all the same as the human 'person' of today's thinking. It had no 'personality' in the modern sense. *Personalitas* remained a rare and limited word until at least the twelfth century. There was scarcely even an adequate Latin vocabulary in that same century in which 'individuality' could be discussed. *Individuum, individualis, singularis*, belong chiefly to the world of logic, where questions about what made a separate entity were quite technical.[6] Even in the later Middle Ages, limited importance was attached to the particularity and distinctiveness of the self.

The early modern period got to grips with some aspects of the question, as it was realized that this affected eligibility for heaven. Joseph Butler writes, 'personal identity has been explained so by some, as to render the inquiry concerning a future life of no consequence at all to us the persons who are making it'.[7] He cites John Locke's idea that a person is to be defined as 'a thinking intelligent being' and personal identity as 'the sameness of a rational being'. 'Mr. Locke's observations upon this subject appear hasty,'[8] he notes critically. Butler was interested in the very modern question of continuity of personal identity in the present with the identity of the person in question in the past, and with the role of personal memories in maintaining a recognizable identity.

This slow evolution and uncertain unfolding of the idea of a person must give us pause when we come to ask how fundamental the modern idea of a human 'person' is. Many of the associations and categories brought to the idea of a 'person' by modern Western sociology and psychology are remote from these defining debates of early Christianity. Talk of 'personal development' and the concept that each individual is not only to hope for heaven but also to aspire to be a bigger and better version of himself or herself on arrival there has seemed natural only to the small proportion of the Christian believers of history living in the modern West or influenced by its assumptions.

The modern believer may choose to be modern about this and hang on to his or her sense of self, or feel free to return to the less constraining options of earlier ages.

Death and the separation of soul and body

One respect in which people are undeniably individuals in this life is in their possession of one body each. Christian believers have been fairly consistent in envisaging this body as being inhabited by one 'soul'. There are many difficulties when it comes to agreeing what this soul is, its relationship to the body and whether the body is an integral part of the individual or merely a temporary vehicle.

There have been two main theories in Christianity about the way the individual 'soul' gets into a particular body, integrating its atoms and somehow inhabiting and animating them.[9] But partly because so much remained uncertain about exactly what two things were being brought together, neither has ever been formally adopted as the orthodox view. The first ('creationism') was the idea that God creates a new human soul at the moment a child is conceived (or perhaps allocates a soul from a stock he had already prepared). This seems to have been the poet Wordsworth's idea:

> Our birth is but a sleep and a forgetting:
> The Soul that rises with us, our life's Star,
> Hath had elsewhere its setting,
> And cometh from afar:
> Not in entire forgetfulness,
> And not in utter nakedness,
> But trailing clouds of glory do we come
> From God, who is our home.[10]

The creationist hypothesis has to 'locate' the taint of original sin in the body, for the good God could not be thought to be creating infected souls.

The second idea (traducianism) asserts that the soul comes into being with the begetting of the body and is somehow handed on by the child's human parents. This had the advantage that it easily explained how the new-born child could be already tainted with original sin – the infectious first sin of Adam – even before it had lived long enough to do anything wrong, for its soul is directly 'inherited' from Adam and Eve.

The Christian tradition has tended to believe that the soul once in the body did not merely wear it like a coat. That the body with its senses and the soul with its divinely implanted 'ideas' interacted was not much disputed in the early and medieval centuries. Otherwise the body could not have led the soul astray. On the positive side, the soul adds to its innate ideas and comes to understand them better through the bodily senses, thought Augustine. He devised an explanation involving the mind drawing upon sense perceptions to allow it to make comparisons and additions, and build up its 'database' held in the memory. This gave rise to much complicated argument in the Middle Ages, on topics we should probably examine today in connection with the difference between the mind and the brain. Ailred of Rievaulx discusses the Augustinian theory that the memory is like a great container in which a large number of 'places' provide storage slots for various items. 'The memory is a certain great hall [aula], containing, as it were, innumerable treasure-chests. ... Everything is stored there sorted into categories.' John, who is Ailred's companion in this literary dialogue, asks how the soul can store bodily images if it is itself incorporeal. Ailred takes him on a tour of his inner realm. He asks him how large his own reflection in a mirror seems to him. He answers that it is the same size as the original. Ailred invites him to consider his inward image of the city of London, in all its vast extent, held in his little head.[11]

Everyone is going to die and one of the things that means is that the body will stop working. True philosophers practise dying by trying to separate themselves from their bodies in this life, claimed Plato.[12] This is where it is necessary to ask whether the body is essential to the individual being of human persons, for the great test of the persistence of the 'embodied individual' takes place at the death of the body. Modern science might use different terminology and other concepts but it is a recognized scientific conundrum that analysis of the physical working of the brain does not entirely explain what 'mind' is, nor can science yet quite explain how millions of single cells become an 'organism' in which their individual material separateness is swallowed up in a single collective identity. The relationship 'within' a human being of those things which can be measured and located and what cannot is still unexplained.

The classical dead were thought to hang about as shades in a shadowy world because they lacked the concentrated focus a body gives.

Cicero had taken his stand at the 'optimistic' end of the classical spectrum of ideas about life and its aftermath. He thought there might well be a life to come. But the public funeral oration tradition in the ancient world was gloomy. Life is mostly suffering and death a happy escape, it thought. Consider how much worse it is for others and you, who still live, will be comforted. The person who has died is as much cut off from life as a person who has not yet been born. At the end of the fourth century, Ambrose of Milan wrote a number of funeral orations for his brother Satyrus and for Valentinian and Theodosius.[13] Even as late as the end of the fourth century, the tone of this Christian leader is one of sorrow: life is short and those things the world prizes are ultimately valueless. Jerome, Ambrose's contemporary, is confident that the Christian dead have gone to a better life in a better place, but he does not find this a theme to be treated lightly or merrily. He wrote to Paula on the death of Blesilla, a letter which has some of the features of a classical funeral oration hanging about it still.[14] Another such letter, to Theodora on the death of Lucinus, begins with the grieving messenger who has brought the news. There are more letters of condolence, chiefly to Jerome's female correspondents.[15]

The question whether the 'soul-self' is ultimately independent of the body and can 'go on' without it lingered. Gregory the Great's interlocutor in the *Dialogues* (Book IV) describes how he once saw someone die. He did not observe the spirit leaving his friend's body.[16] While he was speaking, his spirit suddenly left him, and the eyewitness saw the man who a moment before had been talking to him suddenly extinguished (*extinctum*), but he did not actually see his soul go. It is very hard, he comments, to believe that something 'happens' if no one can see it. Gregory does his best to convince him that this is no reason to doubt that the soul can become separated from the body at death. He asks him why he is surprised. The soul cannot be seen while it is in the body, so why should it be visible when it leaves it? Yet we accept that there is an animating force in the living body, and we know it is present by the movements of the body it occasions.[17] This is, Gregory suggests, analogous with the way God moves invisibly in the visible world, creating and ruling, filling and surrounding, transcending and sustaining, himself boundless and invisible.[18]

The literature of deathbed scenes over many centuries continued this sense of puzzlement at the absoluteness and at the same time the ambivalence of what can be seen to take place when the body ceases to move and speak and appear 'inhabited'. Late eighteenth-century and early nineteenth-century deathbed scenes[19] exploited the awe natural to the moment, emphasizing the way it created receptiveness to final messages and the exaction of promises of amendment of life from those who were to live on, so that the moment of departure 'for another life' became a gateway to that life in a different sense for those who witness it but were not themselves to experience it yet.

Unconcerned with Christian orthodoxy but with a scientist's curiosity, Aldous Huxley described the dying of his wife:

> I told her that I was with her and would always be with her in that light which was the central reality of our beings. I told her that she was surrounded by human love and that this love was the manifestation of a greater love, by which she was enveloped and sustained. ... Now she must go forward into love, must permit herself to be carried into love, deeper and deeper into it, so that at last she would be capable of loving as God loves – of loving everything, infinitely, without judging, without condemning, without either craving or abhorring. And then there was peace. ... And where there was peace and love, there too there would be joy and the river of the coloured lights was carrying her towards the white light of pure being, which is the source of all things and the reconciliation of all opposites in unity.[20]

The 'out-of-body experience' has frequently been reported in terms which resemble those Huxley describes, and often without any context of religious expectation. It seems to follow a pattern. Someone dangerously ill, whose heart has stopped perhaps or who is undergoing a life-threatening operation, sees his or her body stretched out below while the consciousness in the person of the 'self' floats above. The conscious self is drawn into a tunnel with white light at the end, and sometimes emerges from that tunnel into the light, to find the welcoming faces of dead friends and loved ones waiting with greetings. Then the process is reversed, the 'soul', or consciousness, returns to the body and it turns out that the operation has been survived or the heart re-started, and death is not to be yet. These modern descriptions are a useful reminder that the old dilemma about the possibility of individual survival without the body, or the need for it, are as fresh now as they were in the first Christian centuries. The modern believer still has to decide what to think.

Death and disembodiment

The body ceases to function. The person who used to be met in the street is met there no more. So what form could 'survival' take? The first possibility which has been canvassed is that it is the soul alone which continues. Some of the philosophers of late antiquity thought that souls were like sparks of the divine fallen into bodies, and their emphasis was upon the continuing essential unity of those sparks with the unity of the divine from which they were shed. That seemed to them much more important than the continuation of individual selves. 'In the human soul, the deepest layer of existence reaches back to the foundation of the universe,' says Plotinus.[21] That might allow individual souls to vanish back into a great sea of souls, to 'become God again' in that way. Cicero suggested something similar, that the gods might have planted souls in human bodies so that there might be beings who would care for the earth and look after it, and that they brought with them recollections of heaven in a continuity of their individual being.[22]

This idea that human souls are fragments of the divine embedded for a time in matter is still to be found in much later literature. In the seventeenth century John Donne depicts the human being as matter and spirit, using the conceit (also a serious scientific proposition for many centuries) that the material world is made up of the four elements of earth, fire, water and air:

> I am a little world made cunningly
> Of Elements, and an Angelike spright.[23]

The eighteenth-century poet and artist William Blake in *The Marriage of Heaven and Hell* took the idea to a logical bold extreme and asked himself whether the human is the divine, so that to honour and love the divine in other people is to worship God: 'Men forgot that all deities reside in the human breast.'

The Christian tradition has insisted that the body is ultimately to be resurrected. 'The phoenix is a bird in Arabia which, when it knows it is time to die, lays itself down among fragrant odours and then it is born again. Therefore this bird teaches us by its own example to believe in the resurrection.'[24] In this passage, Ambrose uses the phoenix to make a case for the reality of the resurrection of the body, but there was scarcely any need, for it was far too central to Christian belief from the outset. Christ had led the way by his own bodily resurrection and ascension. Thomas, the disciple who doubted, was invited to prod the resurrected Jesus in his side to convince himself of the continuing solidity of his body (John 20.27). I Corinthians 15.13-19 maps the trail of consequences. If Christ is not 'raised', the Gospel is in vain and so is our faith and we are lying witnesses and you are still in your old state of sin and the Christians who have died are all lost, Paul tells his readers. In this way faith in the resurrection of Christ transformed for Christian authors all subsequent understandings of what would follow death. For if Christ was raised from the dead, so might they be. It could almost be said that this 'was' the faith. Tertullian puts it at no less. 'The faith of Christians is the resurrection of the dead. In believing that we are what we are.'[25] Augustine comments on the importance to the faith of belief in the literal resurrection of Christ's body.[26]

Augustine called Plato in aid as an authority for the idea that souls cannot be without bodies even in eternity,[27] but in reality this early theorizing about the implications of the death and resurrection of Christ taught that humanity was 'engaged' with the cosmos in a manner which was without classical precedent, and which had a new high seriousness. Tertullian argues that it is inconceivable that God 'should abandon to eternal destruction the work of his own hands, the queen of his own creation, the heir of his generosity'.[28] The resurrection could now explain the whole purpose of the world. For had not God himself entered human life and died like any other man, and then risen from the dead like no other man before him, so that others might then do the same? So the assumption from the earliest Christian period was that the soul and the body were to journey together into heaven.

This 'certainty' still left a big uncertainty, however, and that was whether the resurrected body would be a body in any sense with which we are now familiar. 'It is sown a natural body; it is raised a spiritual body' (RV). In this passage I Corinthians 15.44 holds out the expectation that the natural body will be raised, even if in some 'spiritual' form. What can it possibly mean to talk of a resurrection of the body? Gregory the Great discusses the debate about the nature of the resurrected body. Those who think it will not be a body which can be touched, but an invisible 'subtlety' of a body are, he thinks, in error.[29] Gregory was much preoccupied in his *Dialogues*, Book IV, with suffering in hell and the question whether the damned will need physical bodies if they are to experience the pain necessary to make their punishment as agonizing as justice requires. These may be the concerns of a mind with a relatively limited notion of a real 'difference of kind' between natural and supernatural, this world and the next. It is to be found in visible form in the medieval depictions of the Last Judgement, in which the resurrected are seen springing out of their graves in the original bodies they left there.

Belief in the resurrection of the body has therefore been every bit as challenging an idea as the theory that human beings are compounded of bodies and souls. For example, the possibility of the passage of a physical body across the boundary separating a natural (physical) world from a supernatural (spiritual) world raised from an early stage many questions about the nature of the boundary on the other side of which lies the transcendent. If there are going to be human bodies in eternity, talk of time and place begins to be relevant to a 'world' beyond time and space. There were many questions which mocking dualists asked in an effort to ridicule the whole idea of the continuance of a physical body which would somehow be the same as the body which had lived on earth, asking how people would manage in eternity with immensely long hair and fingernails when a lifetime's growth was restored to them.[30]

Peter Abelard, writing in the twelfth century, poses this question of the future of the body from another direction, and in a revolutionary way. Why is it necessary to talk of being 'in' heaven at all? He proposes that the supreme eternal happiness of the vision of God should be able to be enjoyed 'anywhere', for example, in an inward and spiritual manner, so that it is not going to be necessary to come to a particular 'place' (heaven) to enjoy it to the full. God is everywhere so surely he can be enjoyed everywhere?[31] Abelard's contemporary, William of St Thierry, also discusses the 'place' (locus) where some will be called the 'children of the living God' (Romans 9.26). Where is this place, he asks? It is not Rome. It is not Judaea. It is a 'higher place' where it will be fitting to speak to God, and possible to do so. This he 'locates' within the mind of man, his reason and above all in the heart which was for medieval thinkers the seat of thought as well as of feeling.[32] This is not far from the Miltonic position, that 'the mind is its own place, and in itself, can make a Heaven of Hell, a Hell of Heaven'. It has a hint of George Berkeley's disinclination to believe in any reality but that of thought. It begins to take us from the mechanics of the event of death when soul and body appear to separate into the more intricate questions which lie within.

Many have already died. Can they be said to 'have a life' before their bodies are restored to them at the Last Judgement (Matthew 25.33)? This too has been the subject of a great deal of debate. Gregory the Great discusses whether the souls of the blessed can even be received in heaven before the Last Judgement. If they cannot, where are they 'now' while they wait? It became a commonplace to point to the text in Revelation which speaks of the 'martyrs under the altar' (Revelation 6.9), and suggest that this is Scripture's description of the state of even the holiest of the dead, while they wait somewhat forlornly to be reunited with their bodies. If this is not right and the disembodied dead are already in heaven, the question is what they will receive at the Last Judgement if they have already been enjoying the bliss of heaven. The answer, says Gregory, is that they will add to that the joy of their resurrected bodies, and so they will experience a double joy.[33] He considers the text of Revelation 6.11, where the bestowal of the white 'stoles' is a token and promise that when they have rested a little time the martyrs will be joined by their fellow martyrs. The single garment will then become a double garment.[34]

Such energetic defending of the conception of a human being as an individual entity eternally composed of body and soul was partly an attempt to rebut the contentions of those who thought the spirit in each body simply disappeared into the divine or into some sort of spiritual generality, a soul-soup of the sort evoked by Aldous Huxley in his words of comfort to his wife on her deathbed. The Christians held on to the body as an eternal feature of the human individual.

Again the modern believer has to make his or her own mind up.

Living the death of self

Phlebas the Phoenician, a fortnight dead,
Forgot the cry of gulls, and the deep sea swell
And the profit and loss.
           A current under sea
Picked his bones in whispers. As he rose and fell
He passed the stages of his age and youth
Entering the whirlpool.[35]

We are left, then, with difficult choices among beliefs held by a range of Christian believers over the centuries, from a literal reuniting of the soul with its original body, or the provision of some new 'sort' of body, more at home in a non-material heaven, to the disappearance of the individual soul into a sea of spiritual stuff or into God himself. There is a strand of God rather demanding comfort in the tradition. God told Abraham to leave all that was familiar to him, country and kindred, and go where the Lord would direct him. The instruction was accompanied by an enticing promise. Abraham was to have more than he had given up, though the reward was to take a rather worldly form. A great nation was to come of him and he was to be famous (Genesis 12.1–2).

The 'desert fathers'[36] and their counterparts in late antique Italy, were hermits who cut themselves off from company and food and sex. They were the conspicuous non-consumers of their age. Albinus, who never travelled anywhere without a heavy load of books so that he could open them and teach the people wherever he went, always chose the most broken-down beast of burden in the monastery to transport them, and thus encumbered and disadvantaged himself in the very discharge of the mission for which his soul 'burned'.[37] The giving up of what is most enjoyed is rarely seen as a disinterested abandonment of self-will, rather as a paradoxical giving up of what you want so as to have what you want even more.[38]

This is recognized to be hard work. Enthusiasm for it could be hard to maintain. Gregory the Great wrote in his *Dialogues* on a theme he often recurred to, the strain of being tugged both ways, by his administrative duties and his desire for God. The depression he experiences comes, he says, from the dreadful familiarity of the problem as it grows daily worse and worse, and ceases to be a stimulus to further effort.[39] Richard Rolle, the fourteenth-century English mystic, writes of this *accidie*, the unforeseen interruption to what had seemed a promising beginning in the spiritual life,[40] which could strike the contemplative as he grew bored as readily as the man of business experiencing stress symptoms or 'burn-out'.

The most demanding of devotional Christian literature has consistently pointed to something which goes even beyond the deliberate giving up of self-interest, to the very end of 'self'. What can the end of self possibly mean? Somewhere in the unmapped territory of what we are may lie the possibility that we may, individually, cease to be, or at least cease to be the selves we are. The call to 'die to self' has sometimes been a shorthand for a mere 'dying' to selfishness. German writers such as Lessing, Herder and Goethe developed from the late eighteenth century the idea that a human being might become his or her own work of art, perhaps perversely strengthening selfhood in the completion or perfecting of the individual. Friedrich Schleiermacher made this line of thought both powerful and influential in his *Speeches on Religion to its Cultural Despisers* (1799). His idea was that the individual should seek the widest possible range of experience but also try to unify its diversity in what he 'became', so that he was at one with reality. He holds out hope of fulfilment by means of this process of synthesis. There is the alternative possibility that to remain an individual 'self' is essentially a limitation.

Will individual consciousness survive?

Lactantius proposes one reason why the Christian tradition has been so insistent that the *vita animi*, the life of the mind, is everlasting (*sempiterna*), that the individual enjoys the fruits of immortality or suffers perpetual punishments and endless torments, in a continuing separate existence at the heart of which is an 'I'.[41] The assumption has been the driving force of a huge literature of exhortation to individuals to take seriously the importance to each personally of the eternal destiny which awaits him or her.

Bede points out that the Bible contains a number of passages in which the individual's personal point of view seems to be important. 'Only Isaiah saw the praises of the hosts of the seraphim' (Isaiah 6.1–5).[42] Moses, fearing to have the people too near, went up alone into the mountain to pray to God (Exodus 19.10-25), and the mountain was obscured by cloud, shutting him off alone with God. Daniel *alone* remained among the angels when his companions fled (Daniel 10.1ff.). *Only* Ezekiel wondered at the cherubim and the buildings of the heavenly city (Ezekiel 1.1). Paul *alone* was snatched up to see the third heaven and the delights of paradise (II Corinthians 12.2). Bede's idea is that when the individual soul 'shuts the door' so as to be alone in prayer, it is the single turtle dove of the Song of Songs.

Anselm of Canterbury, in the late eleventh century, recognizes that my heaven may be different from your heaven, though not in the sense that it would actually be a different 'place' or different in itself.

His idea is that individual experience of heaven may vary, with each individual continuing to enjoy what he has enjoyed most in this life. Anselm says enticingly in the *Proslogion* that in heaven one will be able to enjoy (but much more fully) anything which has been a legitimate pleasure in this life. 'There will be good things for body and soul! ... If beauty delights you', remember 'The righteous will shine like the sun' (Matthew 13.43). If speed or strength or unhampered bodily freedom is your special joy, think of, 'They will be like the angels of God' (Matthew 13.22, 30). If it is a long and healthy life you look for, there is a healthy eternity before you.[43] Anselm thus depicts in the final chapters of his *Proslogion* a heaven in which each individual will continue to enjoy those things which were in themselves good and which he or she particularly enjoyed in this present life. His idea seems to be to make heaven attractive by making it familiar, a promise of recognizable enjoyments.

Anselm seems to see these pleasures as something individual and personal. Someone who has especially taken pleasure in beauty or speed or strength or bodily freedom, or a long and healthy life, will find that same pleasure in eternity, for example, a healthy eternity and eternal health (*sana aeternitas et aeterna sanitas*). This is the *gaudium plenum*, the fullness of joy, the Lord promises, and it will fill the heart and the mind and the soul, the whole man (*pleno quippe corde, plena mente, plena anima, pleno toto homine gaudio illo*).[44] Anselm may be saying no more here than that the individual will recognize old familiar pleasures in a common joy, that there is no need to fear the unfamiliarity of heaven or the loss of any legitimate satisfaction of the present life. Or he may be suggesting that the key lies in individuality of experience, that my heaven will not be your heaven.

There are individual souls in Dante's heaven whose selfhood persists in the new atmosphere of divine glory and in the presence of God:

> *Vita beata che to stai nascosta*
> *Dentro alla tua letizia*
> 'Blessed living soul that dwells unseen within your happiness.'[45]

The contemplative soul is a 'holy lamp' (*sacra lucerna*). Its brightness and gladness (*letizia*) are coupled again and again in Dante's *Paradiso*, with the brightness itself uniting brilliancy of colour and light with ardour (Canto XXIII). One such soul, later identified as Peter Damian, dwelling in its cloud of happiness, explains to Dante that 'divine light is shed upon me' (*luce divina sopra me s'appunta*), and the light pierces the cloud of happiness so that it seems to merge with the soul within:

penetrando per questa in ch'io m'inventro,
la cui virtù, col mio veder congiunta

In this way, the soul is raised above its creaturely limitations (*mi leva sopra me tanto*) and in that way it sees *la somma essenza*. The contemplatives' region is rather severe in the extreme of its beauty and brilliance. This is not a truth which can be described on earth. What is seen as light here is mere smoke or cloud there (*in terra fumma*). Dante's wickeder 'selves' seem to display a higher level of differentiation from one another, variety being a bad sign or a sign of the bad.

Seneca had seen the happy man as making his own happiness within his own mind. It springs up perpetually from its inner source, and the man who possesses it is drawing his happiness from what is most profoundly his own.[46] Milton, with his notion that the mind is its own place and makes a heaven of hell a hell of heaven, advances a similar argument about the paradoxical 'objectivity of the subjective', the ultimate 'reality' of the individual's perception of its own good.

The call to 'know thyself' (*Scito teipsum*) in antique philosophy is not really concerned with the kind of thing which would now be described as 'personal development'. *Gnothi seauton*, 'Know yourself,' says Juvenal, preferring the Greek version to the Latin.[47] But he follows the quotation with a robust Roman restatement. 'Take stock of yourself and describe yourself to yourself as you really are.'[48] This is a form of self-knowledge useful to those in public life. It is also a way of getting on terms with the world without self-deception, and so it can make the boundaries of the self less confining as they become less defining. The emphasis is not upon the distinctiveness or uniqueness of an individual. It does not invite the enquirer to 'find' himself or herself. This is not the modern Californian idea of self-fulfilment. It has more to do with being realistic and honest with oneself.[49]

The survival of individual consciousness has been questioned hard only in more recent centuries. Spinoza suggested the theory that the individual mind (*mens singularis*) ceases with the death of the body.[50] Perhaps the mind is not in space, he ventures? Leibniz rejected this idea. In an early work, the *Confession of Nature against the Atheists* (1669), Leibniz was already exploring the immortality of 'minds'. Ten years later, in April 1676, Leibniz was saying that no soul has ever 'begun' or will ever 'cease', but his notions of what might be involved in saying this did not run along the same lines as those favoured by Aristotle and his medieval successors.[51] Kant wrestled with the relationship of the self to its self-awareness. He asked whether the self could be a simple and persisting substance, or, at the opposite extreme, some sort of unification of diverse representations of the world.[52] Leibniz had formed the view that every impression which occurs in a body has some effect which proceeds or continues to infinity. He was also arguing that certainty depends upon a perception or embracing of the whole of that of which one seeks to be certain.[53]

Hegel (1770-1831), taking forward Kant's exploration of this territory of mental experience, traverses it, pausing to inspect it from each new vantage point, where consciousness itself proves to have changed into something it was not before, or, perhaps more accurately, to have realized or experienced itself in terms of something which was at first other than itself. First, he thinks, comes consciousness of self. Then there is consciousness of an object which the conscious mind knows to be different from itself. Then there is a uniting of the consciousness with its object, making the self also the object it is contemplating in some way, which makes it 'certain of itself' in that object.

The end of this process in Kant's view is a universalization of the individual consciousness, for this self-consciousness becomes a consciousness of all the world. Hegel sees the whole process of evolution of religious understanding in similar terms of a progression of the mind, which increasingly embraces what it contemplates, allowing it to move from the subject matter of natural religion to that of revelation.[54]

The Kant–Hegel 'self', which learns from experience in this way, uniting itself with and becoming what it understands, is capable, says Kant, of emerging from the process with principles of conduct which are 'impartial'. 'For Kant, while moral virtue presupposes a feeling of affection for humanity, this feeling only takes on its distinctively moral character when it issues in impartial principles of conduct.'[55]

This more modern understanding of the merging of individual and universal has been picked up in more recent discussion of the notion of selfhood. Ludwig Wittgenstein (1889-1951) asked what 'inner' can mean, how what is going on 'inside' 'me' can be related to the 'outer' world through sense perception (or in any other way). Nevertheless, like medieval linguistic theorists he was sensitive to the movement of language in and out of reality. 'In saying that the idea of our visual field being located in our brain arose from a grammatical understandings, I did not mean to say that we could not give sense to such a specification of locality.'[56] Wittgenstein was sceptical of the possibility that there could be any such thing as an inner entity, something private and accessible only to the individual concerned.[57]

John MacMurray challenged in his Gifford Lectures of 1953 the traditional idea that the self is a pure subject for whom, or to which, the world is an object.[58] He, seeking to take further Kant's ideas about Pure and Practical Reason, was also interested in the relationship of the theoretical and the practical in relation to the future of the self: 'A way of life must be a relatively satisfactory adjustment to Reality, exhibiting a systematic structure, and, to a considerable degree, a consistency of direction.'[59]

The implications of this line of philosophical enquiry may take the debate outside the domain of Christian orthodoxy. Nisikânta Chattopâdhâya's lecture on Buddhism and Christianity suggested that in the universe as understood in Buddhism, souls migrate about the universe from one 'life' to another as the balance is adjusted. 'There is no God who judges actions and dispenses reward and punishment, but reward and punishment are simply the inevitable consequences of Karma, which works of itself.'[60] No God is in charge of this process. Christianity has postulated a purpose for the universe in which, sin removed and evil banished, it will be what it was meant to be, the best possible, while Buddhism, our author suggests, envisages an end in which, with everything corrected and brought back into balance, the universe and all things in it will cease to be.

For the individual self in Buddhism the end to be desired is the end of self. From the Buddhist text, the *Milinda Pracna*, the author of our lecture on Christianity and Buddhism describes it thus: 'Nirvana is; it is a perception of the mind; the pure, joyful Nirvana, free from ignorance and evil desire. ... Nirvana ... removes the infinite pain of the world, and presents itself as the chief felicity of the world, but its attributes or qualities cannot be explained.'[61]

Yet among the quotations from the Buddhist Scriptures with which Nisikânta Chattopâdhâya illustrates his account of all this, is one which makes some of the assumptions which also drive the Christian explanation of the nature of the self. He explains that the individual is mixed, compounded of opposing and irreconcilable elements, in which the bodily parts have pleasures which muddy the aspirations of the higher, spiritual parts:

> A man who gives himself up to pleasure, who does not strive after high wisdom, is like a vessel full of dirty water in which are many beautiful things; so soon as one shakes the water one cannot see the things it contains; thus pleasure and desire cause confusion and disturbances in the heart, and are like sediment in water; they hinder us from recognising the beauty of sublime reason. As soon as we remove the impurities the original form reappears.

He links what he is saying with the way, as he understands it, Christianity 'lays similar stress upon the inviolability of the moral law, and upon the necessity of first purifying the inner man, or the soul'.[62] Christian teaching has often assumed that there is also some requirement to repair the damaged 'self'. For why should God 'put us through' what looks very like an obstacle race on the way to heaven unless repair is necessary? And if repair is necessary, the 'self' to be repaired begins to appear valuable, a thing to be preserved.

There appears to be room for the hypothesis that some quite different relation to the universe might be entered into by the Christian soul at death. 'If the process constituting our world were a single smooth flow, the boundaries of events would have to be placed upon them by perception or thought, and there would be no real individuals.'[63]

No more pain? The Christian tradition has urged the idea of eternal suffering as strongly as the idea of eternal happiness. Gregory the Great spent some time in the fourth book of his *Dialogues* considering the ways in which the damned were going to be able to 'feel' the fires of hell once they had left their mortal bodies. No more desire? No more strong feeling? The ideal of tranquillity passed into the Christian tradition with the conviction that God himself is impassable. Tranquillity is neither passive nor colourless. It is characterized by a 'great joy', and by peace and harmony of spirit, says Seneca.[64]

Does getting what you want make you happy? It was a convention of the early modern novel that a marriage made a satisfactory ending. The story did not look beyond the happiness attained, the resolution of the problems which had made up the story and provided the necessary suspense about whether the couple would ever be united. More recent fiction tends to recognize that human happiness cannot be aspired to as a fixed achievement, that it is not a steady state. Is it, then, possible to see 'getting to heaven' as an end in itself, the finality, completion and perfecting of a life, which is at the same time not end but beginning?

That happiness is an appropriate ultimate goal for reasonable creatures was a well-developed theme in ancient philosophy before it became a desired thing in Christian eschatology. But happiness had already proved to be a complicated idea, and if we look at it now in the context of the unsatisfactorinesses of many of the options traditionally canvassed, it is easy to see some of the ways in which its stamp proved unhelpful to early Christian thinking about 'where' the individual was 'going'. In his book *On the Happy Life*, the late Roman philosopher Seneca warns that the path to happiness is not easily found, for it is not the one the mass of humanity takes. It is no good just following other people.[65] In 'On the Tranquillity of the Soul' (*De tranquillitate animi*), Seneca mentions the moments in a busy life when something upsetting happens and the disturbed administrator (the equivalent of the modern office worker) needs an inner place of quiet recreation (*otium*) to enable him to cope with what has happened.[66] Happiness is a thing learned inwardly, by 'building' the inner self. Moderation, explains Seneca, is not a mere middle position. It has a positive value. It is extreme fierce feeling that is a sign of weakness.[67] Then there is virtue, which some classical authors insist is important to the fullness of human happiness.[68] Seneca disagreed with Epicurus here. He points out that pleasure can be enjoyed by the wicked as well as by the good.[69] But he disputes whether the enjoyment of the wicked can amount to true happiness, *vera felicitas*, for that, he believes, rests in virtue: *in virtute posita est*.[70] The Stoic maintains that the happy or blessed life (*vita beata*) depends on the virtue of the mind or lack of it. Aristotle, on the other hand, while accepting that a miserable life was the result solely of wickedness, thought good health and wealth were capable of adding to happiness, and virtue alone was not enough for human fulfilment.

Iamblichus, another late Platonist who died about 325, exhorts the reader to adopt an essentially Pythagorean way of life, a life both intellectual and moral, by which the soul progresses little by little through all the forms of beauty, until it comes to know the highest good.[71] What we live by is what we become, is his message. So life is a 'journey' through time in the course of which we are to progress towards becoming something higher or better, or perhaps simply becoming what we ought to be, in rather the way Aristotle envisages an acorn becoming an oak tree, the acorn's natural teleology.

The views of Epicurus were popular in some quarters in the ancient world, but Cicero had his reservations. He questions whether Epicurus is right in saying that the happy life is found in the pursuit of pleasure and the avoidance of pain.[72] In reality, as Cicero was aware, Epicurus was not just a simple hedonist, and there are many ramifications of the idea that the man or woman who pursues happiness will find it in bodily health and a quiet mind, and will be left with nothing to desire if he or she has these. In a 'Letter to Menoeceus' Epicurus exhorts his correspondent to the pursuit of happiness and assures him that the man who practises the things which make him happy will be young when he is old and old when he is young, and will have nothing to fear.[73] The Epicurean ideal is to be free of longings, even the longing for happiness, for longing is incompatible with enjoyment of the very thing desired. Desire, Epicurus thought, is prompted only by the lack of happiness. Epicurus' principle is that this pursuit would not take as its objectives sensual indulgence, drinking and gluttony; instead it would require the steady application of thought to the process of choosing some things and avoiding others so as to preserve tranquillity.[74] This is a choice attended by moral constraints as well as by practical considerations. The unjust cannot be tranquil and will be disturbed. The just are the ones who are happy.[75]

We owe the survival of Epicurus' 'letter' to Diogenes Laertius, who, in his *Lives of the Philosophers*, imputes to Epicurus the distinction between two modes of happiness (*eudaimonia*). The first, the highest happiness, is enjoyed by the gods and it can never grow greater because it is already supreme. The second is capable of growing greater or less, and such is the happiness humans enjoy.[76] This view of things depends on Epicurus' opinion, expressed in the same letter, that with death all sentience ceases. There will, ultimately, be no more pain, and so there will, at last, be nothing to fear.[77]

Seneca claims that happiness is always unreliable: *Omnis instabilis et incerta felicitas*.[78] Cyprian speaks of one peaceful and reliable tranquillity, one solid and firm security, which is 'our peace',[79] yet the Christian theory of heavenly happiness has not always been sure that it will be a sharing with the angels of an eternal moderate calm joy. The desire of the Bride for the Bridegroom in the Song of Songs has been portrayed as the longing of the Soul for Christ, and also the longing of the Church, the Body of Christ, for its Head. Ambrose develops the theme of the soul (Isaac) longing for the kiss of the Word, which lights up the soul, not one kiss but many.[80] Apponius says that the daughters of Jerusalem are impatient in their waiting (*in hoc otio*[81] *impatientes*) and strongly desire the divine embrace.[82]

The possibility of the death of self is helpful in that it deals with many of these questions, which share that air of 'left-over business' which besets so many of the suggested possibilities for individual experience of heaven. Does the capacity for happiness lie within the person or does it depend to some degree on external circumstances?, asked Aulus Gellius.[83] One answer may be that the boundary between the external and the inward may not, eternally, lie quite where we thought.

8

Heavenly community?

Jesus' summary of the commandments or rules for living did not end with the first requirement to love God. He went on: 'The second [commandment] is like it. "Love your neighbour as yourself." Everything ... hangs on these two commandments' (Matthew 22.39). The fundamental concerns of Christianity, its very essence, as it was sketched at the beginning of this book, seem to include a concern for the well being of other people. Jesus' list of the basics makes self-love incomplete unless it involves 'loving' others. Yet if question marks hang over the eternal continuity of persons as we know them, there must be equally challenging questions about the continuity of other people, and that means asking what eternal future there can be for the societies and communities within which individuals 'love' one another.

Meeting old friends?

Heaven is not, traditionally, the place for a solitary. There has always been an expectation that there will be lots of company there. 'Aloneness is simply an aspect of temporal life. It is only in the field of time where separateness is possible. Such dualities as you and me, here and there, together and alone are temporal dualities,'[1] is a modern way of putting some very old questions. This takes us from the question of our own personal survival to the equally vexed question of the survival of other people. 'Shall I recognize anyone in the world to come?' is a question which makes sense only on the assumption that I and all my friends will continue as before.

For the Christian believer heaven has commonly been depicted as an enjoyment in which one will be oneself and other people will be themselves. 'We shall enjoy one another' in heaven, says Ailred of Rievaulx, writing of the pleasure people have in one another in this life as something which is to continue.[2] This is a hope hard to put aside without making a giant leap beyond the frame of reference of the known universe, for fear of an ultimate solitude in unfamiliar surroundings. Writers have reassured themselves and their readers as best they can:

> Death is nothing at all.
> I have only slipped away into the next room.
> I am I, and you are you.
> Whatever we were to each other, that we still are ...
> I am waiting for you,
> For an interval,
> Somewhere very near,
> Just around the corner.
> All is well.[3]

This is a comforting idea, that death is merely going through a door into another place where one's friends have gone already or will shortly join one, and the personal affection will continue, brighter, sweeter, but essentially the same in its individual preferences. The *wish* that human relationships formed in this life between individual selves should persist has fathered the conviction that they will. The depth of close relationships between individuals and their importance to those involved in them has made them hard to eliminate from the equation. People want to keep what has mattered a great deal to them.

Yet the Gospels record Jesus' assertion that in heaven there is no marriage or giving in marriage (Mark 12.25; Luke 20.35). This suggests that there may be no special friendships either. On that assumption, it has been the habit of orders of monks and nuns down the ages to discourage close friendships in case they became distractions from the soul's concentration on its primary relationship with God and its secondary obligation of a general loving 'neighbourliness'.

This is a hard doctrine and it runs counter to what has been seen age by age as natural feeling. It is not only the Christian tradition which has been as reluctant to part company with old friends as with the self. In the secular classical world of thought, Cicero describes personal grief for the loss of a particular friend. He describes how the remembrance of friends and the longing for their company survives death.[4] In the Old Testament David laments for Jonathan, and it seems no one but Jonathan could have caused that particular grief: 'Very dear to me you were, your love to me more wonderful than the love of a woman' (II Samuel 1.26).

Nevertheless, there is a trail of authority running alongside which expects a considerable degree of detachment and attention to the common good in the way people form and conduct their relationships. The classical world expected friends to assist one another to grow in virtue in a society of 'good citizens'. In his book *On Friendship* (ix.29–30), Cicero explains that true friendship is not a means by which a person with weaknesses makes good what he lacks. Rather, it is the self-reliant person and the one best fortified with wisdom and virtue, the person who believes he needs nothing and has all he possesses within himself, who is notable for seeking out and cherishing friendships. Cicero depicts such friendship as a process of mutual emulation. By familiar association with a close friend someone 'enjoys' his character, meets him in equal affection and the two become rivals in virtue, because they are good for one another (*On Friendship*, ix.32).

When Cicero taught that true friendships are eternal because they spring from nature,[5] he seems to have had in mind some common cause deeper than individual liking for the particularities of someone else. For him it was more a matter of having things in common than of liking one another. A similar detachment startling to modern perceptions is to be found in the medieval monastic world. It will be remembered how Anselm of Canterbury, writing to two young monks who had been his close friends at Bec and who had gone with his old teacher Lanfranc to live at Canterbury, says at the end of an intimate letter to each that it applies equally to the other, asking them to exchange their letters, so that each may read the one he has written to the other.[6]

By convention, even those who scarcely knew each other, or rarely saw each other, could agree to enter into a 'friendship' for their mutual spiritual benefit. In such a spirit it seems, Bernard and Hildebert, Archbishop of Tours, took a friendship oath.[7] It was all simply a version in miniature of the love of one's neighbour within one's love for God (Matthew 22.39; Mark 12.30–1; Luke 10.27). Ailred of Rievaulx envisages Christ as present at all meetings of Christian friends and as making a third in their relationship.[8]

Despite such attempts to lift it all on to a higher plane, the expectation of personal survival not only for oneself but for others, proved an immensely strong pastoral driving force in the Middle Ages, as the system of penance and indulgences developed, and with it the enticing

idea that surviving relatives could assist dead members of their fami-
lies to shorten their time in purgatory by making satisfactions on their
behalf, praying for the dead or arranging for the saying of 'masses for
the dead' or purchasing indulgences on behalf of other people – the
whole apparatus of organized vicarious sacrifice.

It is also natural enough, given the sense of unfinished business
and imperfect communication which is common to so much human
intercourse, that those cut off in the middle of an 'exchange' with
someone who has died should look for an opportunity to 'finish' it,
and 'put things right' if necessary. So strong an instinct is this that a
sense of 'failure to say goodbye' is known to impede grieving.

Many authoritative opinions, widely read within the Christian
tradition, have underpinned the Christian expectation that the individual would survive death in a recognizable way and people will be
able to recognize one another in the life to come. The *De senectute*
contains Cicero's confident assertion of the hope that he will meet
again after death those whose company he has most enjoyed during
his life. There is a significant emphasis on the companionableness of
that future.[9] Gregory the Great in his *Dialogues* (IV.34–6) confirms his
own view that the dead will recognize one another in the life to come,
on the evidence of the story of the rich man and Lazarus, for the rich
man clearly did recognize the beggar who had formerly lain at his gate
(Luke 16).[10] Dante has a theme of continuing longing for the presence of those loved on earth, who were dear to those now in heaven
before they themselves became 'eternal flames'.[11] The *Divina Commedia*
contains a series of hailings and greetings as he plays with the idea that
heaven will provide opportunities to meet famous people one would
have liked to know had one been born at another time or moved in
the right circles in one's life on earth.

In the heaven depicted in C.S. Lewis's *The Great Divorce*, the narrator and his fellow passengers are met by a bright crowd when they get
off the bus we saw them get on earlier, which has been involved in an
accident and now turns out to be taking them beyond death. 'Some of
the crowd were naked, some robed. But the naked ones did not seem
less adorned, and the robes did not disguise in those who wore them
the massive grandeur of muscle and the radiant smoothness of flesh.'
Those in the crowd are of no particular age, but each body seems
to 'express' childhood-to-maturity all at once, allowing the novelist to

deal neatly with a commonly expressed difficulty: will the resurrected body be young or old or middle-aged or somehow ageless?[12] Each of them has a particular passenger to meet, and there are surprises in the cries of recognition. The bright people and the newcomers have business to do with one another, mutual wrongs to put right, and the newcomers have to be educated in the ways of heaven.

Some of the new arrivals are determined at first to educate the denizens of heaven instead of learning from them: 'There were tub-thumping Ghosts who in thin, bat-like voices urged the blessed spirits to shake off their fetters, to escape from their imprisonment in happiness ... to seize heaven "for their own".' 'There were planning Ghosts who implored them to damn the river, cut down the trees, kill the animals, build a mountain railway.' 'There were materialistic Ghosts who informed the immortals that they were deluded: there was no life after death, and this whole country was a hallucination.'[13] But the debate is silenced by the encounter of each individual with one of those already dwelling in the life to come, who helps him see and understand until the newcomer ceases to be transparent (the narrator can see the grass through the soles of his feet when he arrives) and grows more and more solid and 'real', attaining that superior resurrected bodily being the bright crowd of welcomers all display.

The reason Jesus gave for there being no marriages in heaven is that in heaven human beings will be 'children of God' and 'like the angels' (Mark 12.25; Luke 20.35). This opens up the possibility that death may lead into another mode of being so fundamentally different that these comforting familiarities begin to look like unnecessary restrictions. Can a future be glimpsed in which not only 'self' but other 'selves' are revolutionized?

Heaven as an eternal conversation

The idea that heaven will involve an eternal exchange of ideas with God, already touched on, also hinted at a way of carrying on the enjoyable conversations of earthly life in which more than the individual could participate. The classical model of philosophical conversation was that of a group of mature like-minded friends getting together on someone's country estate to talk purposefully about great questions ('life, the universe and everything'). Cicero describes how eagerly the arrival of their friend Varro was greeted by his companions on one such occasion.[14] The idea was to get away from public life and its business and to consider things of enduring importance.

In late Roman times, friends liked if possible to gather to explore a subject over several days. In Macrobius' *Saturnalia* a group meets over the Roman holiday of the Saturnalia to 'spend the greater part of their time for the whole holiday together' in 'discussions' (*disputationes*). They continued even at mealtimes, but in a lighter vein.[15] There is a conscious comparison with Plato's *Symposium*,[16] itself a 'literary' dinner. The thing was not unlike a modern academic conference except that it was not confined to those with a specialist expert interest.

This model offered by a classical education fitted well enough with certain Old Testament passages. The seraphim in Isaiah 6.2 hover before God balancing on their six wings, and that was commonly interpreted as a shared and companionable eternal intellectual gazing. The Old Testament records that God told Moses to gather together 70 'elders' from Israel, so that he may allow them to participate in the 'spirit' he has bestowed on Moses himself (Numbers 11.16–30). They 'shared' a moment of prophetic ecstasy (Numbers 11.25). The theme persists into the New Testament. Again at Pentecost the disciples were assembled together and shared an experience of heightened spiritual communion (Acts 2). Such high moments as Pentecost were exceptional, but they describe a common and not a solitary experience. The theme of these Biblical texts is that the sharing takes each individual beyond what he or she could experience alone.

Augustine's first books, which derive from conversations he and his friends had at Cassiciacum on Lake Como near Milan while he was preparing for baptism, show that this kind of thing was found to be just as attractive for early Christians as it had been for secular classical people. They discussed such themes as Order and the Happy Life. Augustine's books on the subjects they talked about give the actual conversation they had in some detail (with no doubt such revisions as Augustine the former professor of rhetoric thought necessary). There is throughout an air of anticipating the conversations of heaven. The Christian writer Cassian (c.360–after 430) proposed a theory of human relationships in which the highest form resembles this conversational mode, with the relationships of working colleagues next and family relationships in their warmth and comparatively 'animal' emotional muddle lowest of all. He taught his monks that it was in the conduct of the Higher Conversation that they approached most closely to an anticipation of the life of heaven.

There was quite a literature of 'dialogue' in the centuries which followed. Anselm, in the late eleventh century, recording the thoughts generated in discussions with a group of the monks of Bec, is teacher to his admiring pupils rather than a mature adult with other mature adults, going together on a journey, but he is determined that his monks shall get some sense of what a philosophical conversation could be, and one historian remarked soon afterwards that Anselm had succeeded in turning even the dullest in these sessions into 'seeming philosophers'.[17]

Ailred of Rievaulx's twelfth-century *De spiritali amicitia* contains something which consciously anticipates the conversation of heaven. 'Here am I and here are you and Christ makes a third with us,' begins Ailred. Christ will not get in the way. Ailred invites his friend Ivo to 'open his heart' and 'drop whatever thoughts he likes into the ears of his friend'. 'And let us not be unappreciative of having time, place and leisure.'[18] This opening of hearts and minds, leaving no inner secret, with no inner life of the individual 'held back', takes the communication beyond the privacy which attaches to the unreadability of innermost thoughts and the defensiveness of much human exchange. It is possible because it is happening in the presence of God, Ailred suggests.

This suggests a way in which the encounter of individuals in heaven could be understood as an emptying out of the very individuality they 'recognize' in one another, into a talk in which there is no jostling for personal advantage. Augustine says he shared a vision with his mother at Ostia just before her death.[19] They were looking into a garden in a courtyard within the house where they were staying. This is a record of what appears to have been an unusual 'joint rapture'. It was peaceful in the courtyard, a place where they could rest after the fatigues of their journey, away from the crowds. They turned their thoughts away from the past and fixed them on what was before them (cf. Philippians 3.13) and thought about 'what it would be like in the eternal life to come'. They progressed in a shared journey of the imagination by making comparisons, even beyond that *iucunditas* which is more than the utmost *delectatio* of the bodily senses. Bit by bit (*gradatim*) they trod the very heaven (*ipsum caelum*) from which the moon and stars shine down upon the earth. Still they 'climbed, inwardly in their thoughts and in their talk', until they 'attained that region' where God feeds Israel 'with the bread of everlasting truth' and where dwells the living wisdom which creates all things, itself uncreated. There for an instant (*modice*) Augustine knew the *ictus cordis*, that experience of knowing God, of which those who have experienced that rapture speak.[20] It is his understanding that his mother knew it too. This is a rare example of an attempt to describe a specific instance of the way the 'personal' inward journey could become a shared experience.

Heaven as an eternal Church?

Would the Church be 'needed' after death, and if so what for? The concept of the 'Church' has been important to Christian belief from New Testament times and it remains the chief 'forum' in which the community of heaven is envisaged as continuing as an 'ecclesial community'. The Song of Songs was interpreted as authority for the idea that Christ was the Bridegroom and the Church was the Bride in an eternal union of Head and Body. Elsewhere in the Old Testament, Rebecca, the Church, comes to Isaac, who is taken to represent Christ, her beauty adorned with heavenly mysteries.[21]

Augustine was of the opinion that only God really knew whether someone was a member of the Church, for the true Church was invisible, a mystery, and only God knew who were his 'own'. He thought that being baptized into a visible community with a structure was not a guarantee that God regarded someone as a 'citizen' of the City of God. On the other hand, it was energetically argued that there was 'no salvation outside the Church', so cautious believers thought that being 'inside' the visible structure with its provisions to support the believer through the sacraments, to provide opportunities to take part in worship with others and so on, might turn out to be important.

The central question for the modern believer is whether 'entry to heaven' really does depend upon going to church or at least belonging to an 'ecclesial community'. The 'visible' Church's traditional roles became increasingly formal and institutional over the centuries, especially in the West. They came to embody power structures and 'requirements' (which dissidents such as Wyclif began to describe as 'impositions' a century or more before this became the battle cry of the reformers of the sixteenth century). This ecclesiastical machinery was mainly directed at 'getting people to heaven', and there emerged a conceptual distinction between the 'Church militant' whose business this was, and the 'Church triumphant', composed of those who had been successful and were saved and were consequently to spend eternity together in heaven. Put like that, the scheme seems crude, and as with the other debates we have been considering, it is important to try to get a sense of their complexity and the drivers which led to particular conclusions.

In human societies people depend on being able to make use of other people's contributions. No individual person can do all the things necessary to maintain himself. He cannot grow all the food and make all the goods he needs. Nor can one village be self-sufficient in that way.[22] This was already apparent to Aristotle, who wrote along these lines in his *Politics*. The same idea is found in the Bible's discussions of the different roles members of the faithful have in the 'body' of the Church (I Corinthians 12.15-31). The hand does not have the same purpose as the foot. Paul expressly says that it is no good one part of the 'body' envying another and trying to take over its function. Everyone cannot be a hand. The body needs only two hands. Similarly, everyone cannot be an apostle or a prophet or a teacher or a miracle worker, or a healer or an interpreter (I Corinthians 12.28-30, RSV). 'If all were a single member, where would the body be?' (I Corinthians 12.19, RSV).

God's arrangement of the parts, Paul says, is designed to ensure that there need be 'no dissension within the body' (I Corinthians 12.25, RSV). The body flourishes or suffers as one: 'If one member suffers, all suffer together with it; if one member is honoured, all rejoice together with it' (I Corinthians 12.26, RSV).

Paul was particularly anxious to encourage the congregation at Corinth to cultivate their skills of prophesying and interpreting rather than to indulge themselves in inspired 'speaking in tongues' to God, which seemed rather a selfish activity because only the speaker and God have any idea what is being said. The idea is, he says, to 'build up' other people and to do it in an orderly and balanced way. Individual activities should be adapted to this proper purpose.

> Love is patient; love is kind; love is not envious or boastful or arrogant or rude. It does not insist on its own way; it is not irritable or resentful; it does not rejoice in wrongdoing, but rejoices in the truth. It bears all things, believes all things, hopes all things, endures all things (I Corinthians 13.4-7, RSV).

Dante suggests that the way to approach this is to think in terms of a contributory interdependence. He too points out that the parts of a whole have different purposes. Thus the hand does not have the same purpose as the foot. In order to find out what something has as its purpose one must ask what sort of *operatio* is special to it (*Monarchia*, I.iii.3). One individual human being may have a different *operatio* from another and each a different operation from the human race as a whole.

This 'parts and wholes' model of the eternal structure of things is not the only possibility. In the theory of the Church which comes most naturally in the Orthodox Churches and which descended from the Greek-speaking Eastern half of the old Roman Empire, the natural image or model represents each local church as a microcosm in the macrocosm, complete but writ small. Western thinkers could also see the Church in this way. The *ecclesia primitiva* contained the full-grown Church of the present day in seed, argued Jean Gerson.[23] It is the same eternal Church from its first beginning to eternity. Paul's description of his 'body image' ends with an acknowledgement that the idea of parts and wholes is conceptually limited, and, by implication, the macrocosm–microcosm model too. There is, he says, 'a more excellent way', which involves an orderly 'loving' (I Corinthians 12.31–14.40).

An ecclesiology - or ecclesiologies - arose on these foundations, in which the activities of the Church in heaven have a significant place. The sixth-century North African bishop Primasius, writing on the Apocalypse,[24] takes the word 'paradise' simply to refer to the Church.[25] Within this theological framework the Church could be thought of as nothing less than the community of heaven. Christian theologians have almost universally expected to find the Church still there in heaven, and they interpreted the Bible accordingly. 'The Church is founded on the common life,' the twelfth-century Baldwin of Ford begins.[26] From its birth in the common life began the infancy of the Church.[27] His argument is that if the Apostles, men of such power, so distinguished, filled with such virtue, were prompted by the Holy Spirit to begin to live a common life, they were setting an example later generations would do well to follow.[28] Moreover, this common life echoes the life of heaven; it is ours by transference from the mode of life of the angels.[29]

The reason for thinking in this way could not be more fundamental, explains Baldwin. The divine life, the very life of God, is a companion-able unity, he argues. When he opens his sermon with, 'the Grace of our Lord Jesus Christ and the love of God and the communication of the Holy Spirit be always with us all', this is more than a convention.[30] He explains that the Trinity itself is a single 'life', one essence, and the fact that each Person has an individual *vita* does not make the life of the Trinity less a common single life. God is not *singularis* or *solitaris*.[31] God is companionship. For God is love, and love (noun) must love (verb). Love loves communion, and love would rather share with the beloved than possess alone anything which could be enough for both. Love wants its own good to be the beloved's good too.[32] The law of the common life is the unity of the Spirit in the love of God, the bond of peace in the mutual and continual love of the brethren, and the communion of everyone in the communication of all good things.[33]

Baldwin devotes the third part of his sermon to the question how far the individual continues to play a personal role in this mutual love. He explores the Pauline idea that even though many may form one body each member retains its distinct role and function.[34] Paul stresses that each has an individual gift, and the gifts are different (I Corinthians 7.7), points out Baldwin. How then can things be all in common if they are so clearly individual, he asks?

This takes us to the *nodus amoris*, the very crux of the definition of love, for, he says, individual particularity can contribute to the communion of all in such a way that it does not stand in its way at all, when what is special to each is put at the disposal of all.[35] This is his understanding of the meaning of Christ's summary of the command-ments. This is the way we are to love God wholeheartedly while loving our neighbours as ourselves.[36]

There is also a clear thread of expectation that worshipping will continue in heaven. As the eighteenth-century hymn has it:

> We'll crowd thy gates with thankful songs,
> High as the heavens our voices raise;
> And earth, with her ten thousand tongues,
> Shall fill thy courts with sounding praise.[37]

William Blake adds a note to the same effect from the same period. 'What, it will be Question'd, when the Sun rises, do you not see a round disk of fire somewhat like a Guinea? O no, no, I see an Innumerable company of the Heavenly host crying, "Holy, Holy, Holy is the Lord

God Almighty".'[38]

Worship (from 'worthship') implies honour, respect, adoration. The notion that it should be a shared activity has a strong tradition in Christianity. The call to companionable worship sounds down the ages, from New Testament times. 'Speaking one to another in psalms and hymns and spiritual songs, singing and making melody with your heart to the Lord' (Ephesians 5.19, RV). 'Teaching and admonishing one another with psalms and hymns and spiritual songs, singing with grace in your hearts onto God' (Colossians 3.16, RV). 'And they sing as it were a new song' (Revelation 14.3, RV).

Pliny the Younger (62–113), *Letters* X.96, refers to Christians singing songs to Christ as God. (Patristic authors may be referring to the singing of psalms rather than newly composed hymns?) Before feasts, sing hymns and do not get too drunk, recommends Clement of Alexandria (c.150–c.215).[39] Egeria, *Itinerarium* 24, describes how the monks and nuns come forth every morning at dawn, singing hymns, saying antiphons and praying, in a pilgrimage of procession round the holy places in Jerusalem. Augustine was moved to tears by the sweet sound of the heartfelt singing of hymns, and heightened feelings of devotion swelled in him.[40] By contrast, says Augustine, the Donatists sing new-fangled songs of human composition with which they intoxicate themselves while Catholics keep to traditional psalms and hymns.[41] Augustine defines hymns as praisings of God accompanied by singing, or songs praising God. If there is no singing it is not a hymn, he says.[42] This has all been expected to go on in heaven too, where the angels can join in with resurrected human beings:

> Monarch of all things,
> fit us for thy mansions;
> banish our weakness,
> health and wholeness sending;
> bring us to heaven,
> where thy saints united
> joy without ending,

exclaims a hymn of the tenth century.[43]

> I know not, O I know not
> what joys await us there,
> what radiancy of glory,
> what bliss beyond compare,

cries another author, a generation or two later. In fact the hymn writer thinks he does know, that the angels and the 'martyr throng' will all be there together, and there will go up:

> the shout of them that triumph,
> the song of them that feast.[44]

These were medieval conceits but the same assumptions are there in a hymn of about 1600, 'Jerusalem my happy home', whose third stanza runs:

> Apostles, martyrs, prophets, there
> around my Saviour stand;
> and all I love in Christ below
> will join the glorious band.[45]

The tradition is quite consistent about this eternal character of shared worship, and especially about the singing. Separate selves can of course 'lose themselves' in the excitement – of, say, a lynch mob – in that the members of a mob appear to lose those distinguishing features, those refinements of behaviour and controls, which would prevent their behaving individually as they are capable of behaving collectively. There remain important questions about the way in which groups of Christians from medieval sects and the Anabaptists of the sixteenth century to modern Pentecostal churches 'practise' the exciting of the congregation with singing and exhortation. Balancing is required. Nevertheless, the singing metaphor (for this does not have to be taken literally) is an agreeable image to end with, of a shared endeavour in which those who have been accustomed to human relationships characterized by individual encounters can see them swept up into a common action now addressed to God or entering some new and unimagined state of being.

John Donne suggested in the seventeenth century that the Church might be a help and support to the believer but God did what was necessary. Donne is discussing the passage in the Book of Revelation in which John sees an angel seal the servants of our God on their foreheads (Revelation 7.2–3). He says: 'All his saints being eternally knowne by him, shall be sealed by him, that is, so assured of his assistance, by a good using of those helps which he shall afford them, in the Christian Church, intended in this sealing on the forehead, that those afflictions shall never separate them from him, nor frustrate his determination, nor disappoint his gracious purpose upon them.'[46]

The modern believer may find that helpful or prefer to leave the question open. The foretastes of heaven that human beings sometimes believe they have had may not be a glimpse of a different kind of future but a way of 'being' now in anticipation of something unimaginably beyond the furthest reach of all the striving and exploring of 2,000 years. 'Things beyond our seeing, things beyond our hearing, things beyond our imagining' (I Corinthians 2.9 and Isaiah 64.4) offers a good deal to look forward to.

Conclusion

> The common cognomen of this world among the misguided and superstitious is 'a vale of tears' from which we are to be redeemed by a certain arbitrary interposition of God and taken to Heaven – What a little circumscribe[d] straitened notion![1]

When the young poet John Keats put this startling challenge into a family letter in the spring of 1819 what he said chimed with the ideas of other radical believers who have been met with in these pages, who were prepared to take the risk of setting aside much of the immensely complicated apparatus of requirements and entailments with which – in their view – the essence of Christianity had come to be cluttered and distorted. This book will have achieved part of its objective if it encourages the reader to take confidence from the history of Christian belief that he or she can think radically as well as rationally and still be a believer, that there is no need to labour under the burdensome complications with which the core message of Christian belief has become cluttered.

Belief can become anxiety-free, liberating, when it discards the clutter of added expectations. The sense of lightness, the practice of balancing options, adjusting perceptions, the emergence of a sure sense of the places where the core principles are to be found and how they fit together, can ease away the panicky sense of confusion for which modern believers may be forgiven when they confront the mountain ranges of the history of Christian belief.

This confidence about handling the basics, this sense of balance, and a resistance to being led by the mere emotional impact of extreme assertions, are more important than ever today. Everyone in the developed world is bombarded with messages 'hyping' products and tempting the consumer to buy them. A glittering sameness pervades shopping malls and the shopkeepers and manufacturers deliberately provide no guidance on the huge underlying questions about what they can satisfy in a human being, what growth in understanding is to be found in them. Sales are not going to be improved by getting shoppers to use their critical faculties. Modern evangelism itself can easily become a form of marketing, 'selling' a version of belief preferred by a particular group or community, perhaps with a hint of menace, if it is suggested that one version is the only 'saving truth'. Readers who can put what is said into the perspective of the centuries of debate will have some of the information they need to help them to weigh what they hear and decide.

Nor, it seems, is there any that need to give up on belief in the face of the claims of modern science – or any other challenge that claims the high ground of 'rationality'. Religious belief has been just as keen to claim reasonableness, and, as we saw at the beginning of this book, there turns out to be much more to 'reasonableness' than meets the eye. Claiming that a particular view is 'evidence-based' is a contemporary fashion, but it is not always accompanied by real frankness about the nature of the evidence and the manner in which it has been interpreted. An example is the scandal which broke surface in late 2005 about the way a pharmaceutical company was alleged to have controlled what was said in supposedly independent academic scientific publications. The research was supposed to be testing the effects of a drug treatment for the common bone disease osteoporosis. The academic 'author' was told that his research paper was going to be written by a ghost writer employed by the pharmaceutical company and that she was 'very familiar' with 'our key messages, in addition to being well clued up on competitor ... publications'. Despite strenuous attempts the academic was refused sight of the 'evidence', the full set of research data the company's author was claiming to rely on in his name. The company's statement to a newspaper admitted that 'it is standard industry practice to limit access to the raw data by external researchers' (*Observer*, 4 December 2005). The believer freed by a new awareness of the games which have been played with 'rational' proving over the centuries may not so easily be dazzled by the claims of a commercial science with vested interests in a product.

One of the clearest messages of the teaching of Jesus is that believing is meant to be simple. That is one of the most important practical implications of the story this book has been telling. Jesus said that the Kingdom of Heaven would be full of those who remained child-like (Matthew 18.3–4). Only 'one thing is needful' (Luke 10.42), he is reported as having said when he visited the sisters Martha and Mary and found Martha, overcome with housewifely anxieties, scolding Mary for her single-mindedness in simply sitting and listening to what Jesus was saying. What the elements of this simplicity included we can now only glimpse, but you may know someone who shines with it. It is something eminently 'recognizable'.

Nor is the life lived in accordance with the beliefs Jesus taught apparently intended to be burdensome. He spoke of an easy yoke and a light burden (Matthew 11.28). Living with this lightness and simplicity, say the Gospels, is just a matter of detaching oneself from those things which are distractions from the real business of life, step-ping away from the ensnarements of riches, even 'leaving' parents and home and children (Matthew 19.29; Mark 10.29; Luke 18.29), 'for the Kingdom of Heaven's sake'. There are indications in the Acts of the Apostles (for example Chapters 10–11) and in the Epistles of the New Testament that this sort of simplicity of life and attitude was encouraged among the first generation of believers. The memory of the confident freedom Jesus had offered was fresh and his return was expected at any moment.

Jesus said that things might most reliably be known for what they were by examining their fruits (Matthew 7.20). The opening out of belief into a general loving hopefulness seems, as far as it is now possi-ble to see, authentically Christlike. The believer who is honest with himself or herself in deciding what to believe, who tests it inwardly against a personal sense of 'rightness' and 'reasonableness' as well as outwardly as a practical way of living, is unlikely to go far wrong. And the future is wide open to unimaginably greater hope. Romans 8.28 speaks of the way everything can 'work together for good'.

This book has mainly been raising questions of the sort the modern believer who has persevered this far is likely to be asking by now. The answers will be personal to each reader, for everyone has special preoc-cupations in his or her own life which will focus the questioning on particular problems. Abort a baby when amniocentesis shows it is going to be disabled? Tackle a teenage gang which is threatening a schoolmate of another race when the likelihood is that the aggres-sion will be turned on you and your home will become the object of revenge attacks? Pick up a banknote someone has dropped in the street and keep it? Choose an applicant because a senior half-promised her the job, even though there are equally good and better candidates? On the face of it some of these ethical dilemmas are large, some small, but many medieval theorists about vices and virtues thought that what was at stake was always really the same thing, that there was no such thing as a minor ethical question. They would have encouraged the reader to use Christian freedom responsibly and in a principled and thoughtful way in the tiniest moments of decision.

Risk a friendship with uncomfortable home truths? Cast the 'beam of wood' out of your own eye before you criticize your friend for the speck of dust in his own, said Jesus (Matthew 7.5). Here, too, the general freeing-up to think 'outside the box' which is proposed in this book may be useful. The ego need not be the confining wall; it can have doors in it through which believers go out and talk - riskily - to other people about great matters and the way the small details of daily life relate to them, pooling their understandings, and accepting the discomforts of recognizing their own bad habits of thought and action. For the uncomfortable home truths may go both ways.

I do not think the answers readers of this book will find for themselves by applying its suggestions are likely to be so individual and idiosyncratic that the belief will cease to be recognizably Christian, in this deep sense of conforming with the first simplicity of Jesus' message. Something of the spirit of what was expected by Jesus is visible in the challenges of Matthew 5.17–48. There Jesus seems at first glance to be making things more difficult. His followers are to go beyond normal expectations: not even to think of wrongdoing, let alone commit it, to reconcile themselves straight away with those who get into quarrels and disputes with them, and not allow themselves the indulgence of keeping anyone as an enemy; they are to live plainly and straightforwardly in their thinking and speaking and regard no one as beyond their pale; there are to be no special terms for friends and favourites. But this is really no more than impressing on the disciples the importance of always trying to get to the heart of the matter, asking themselves 'what this is really about', forming the habit of looking at the context and meaning and implication of the way the matter in hand is being addressed.

Ideas and understandings are the less likely to stray from that centre if they are arrived at in a shared way with others similarly engaged. There can be many faces of the same truth, many ways of understanding and expressing it, and unanxious joint and common exploration may tend to show that they are really one.

The possibility of 'doing something' useful in the world lies open to everyone in this way and there is no reason why the spreading ripples should not reach far through time and spiritual space.

Notes

Preface

1. Fedor Dostoevsky, *The Idiot*, III, iv (Oxford World's Classics, 1992), p 399.

Chapter 1. What is reasonable?

1. Immanuel Kant, Preface to *Critique of Pure Reason*, trans J.M.D. Meiklejohn (London, 1964).
2. Paul Scade, letter to the *Independent*, 6 January 2005.
3. Thomas Aquinas, *Summa contra gentiles*, I, vii, ed P. Marc (Turin, 1961–67).
4. John Toland, *Christianity not Mysterious* (London, 1696; reprinted Routledge, 1995), p 29.
5. *Ibid.*
6. Thomas Browne, *Religio Medici*, ed. R.H.A. Robbins (Oxford, 1972), §56.
7. Owen Chadwick, *From Bossuet to Newman* (Cambridge, 1957, 2nd ed, 1987), p xix.
8. Augustine, *De fide rerum invisibilium*, CCSL 46 (Turnhout, 1969), p 1.
9. See Boethius, *De trinitate*, ed C. Moreschini (Leipzig, 2000), §2, pp 168–9 for the classic definition of *speculativa*.
10. Joseph Butler, *The Analogy of Religion, Natural and Revealed, to which are added two brief dissertations, 1. On personal identity. II On the nature of virtue* (Glasgow, 1817), p 314.
11. John Henry Newman, *Sermons Preached Before the University of Oxford*, introduction by M.K. Tillman (Notre Dame, 1996), pp 340–1.
12. Dorothy Sayers, *The Mind of the Maker* (1941), edited and introduced by Susan Howatch (Mowbray, 1994), p 23; cf. p 20.
13. Quoted in Noam Chomsky, *Hegemony or Survival: America's Quest for Global Dominance* (London/New York, 2004), p 17.
14. See the discussion in David J. DeLaura, *Hebrew and Hellene in Victorian England: Newman, Arnold and Pater* (University of Texas Press, Austin, 1969), p 34.
15. *The Tatler*, 15 August 1710, ed J.A. Bond (Oxford, 1987), III.114.

16. David Brown, letter to *The Times*, 18 August 2005.
17. PL 176.183.
18. Robert Grosseteste, *The Six Days of Creation*, I.ii.2, *Hexameron*, ed Richard C. Dales and Servus Gieben (London, 1982), p 68, and *The Six Days of Creation*, trans C.F.J. Martin (London, 1996).
19. Butler, *The Analogy of Religion, Natural and Revealed*, p 168.
20. Thomas S. Kuhn, *The Structure of Scientific Revolutions* (Chicago, 1962; 2nd ed, 1970). See also Wes Sharrock and Robert Read, *Kuhn, Philosopher of Scientific Revolution* (Cambridge, 2002).
21. John Wyndham, *The Trouble with Lichen* (London, 1960; reprinted, 1973), p 38.
22. Antony Flew, quoted in the *Sunday Times*, 19 December 2004.
23. For many centuries there was little questioning of the ancient tradition that Moses was the author of the first five books of the Old Testament (the Pentateuch), except for the last few verses describing his own death (which were said to have been contributed by his student Joshua), together with Balaam (Numbers 22-4) and the Book of Job. See Alexander Rofé, *Introduction to the Composition of the Pentateuch* (Sheffield, 1999), p 11, and the study as a whole for the probable real sequence of composition over 800 years of development.
24. Defined as 'the collection or list of books of the Bible accepted by the Christian Church as genuine and inspired' (*OED*).
25. On 'Wisdom' (*phronesis*), see in particular Wisdom 7-8; cf. Plato, *Phaedro* 250d, William Horbury, 'The Wisdom of Solomon', *The Oxford Bible Commentary*, ed John Barton and John Muddiman (Oxford, 2001), pp 650-67, Christopher Stead, *Philosophy in Christian Antiquity* (Cambridge, 1994), pp 18-21.
26. G.N. Stanton, *The Gospels of Jesus* (Oxford, 1989), *Evangelia Apocrypha*, ed C. Tischendorf (Leipzig, 1853), and see p 197 nn.7, 8.
27. Seneca, *De vita beata*, 1.1-4.
28. Gregory, *Moralia in Job*, II.iii.3, CCSL 143, pp 60-2.
29. *The Sermons of John Donne*, vol. X (1962), p 46.
30. On Joachim, see Marjorie Reeves, *The Influence of the Prophecy in the Later Middle Ages* (Oxford, 1969).
31. Andrew Marvell, *Preface to second edition of Paradise Lost*, 41-4, printed in John Leonard edition, p lvii.
32. William Blake, *The Marriage of Heaven and Hell*, in *The Complete Poems*, ed A. Ostriker (London, 2004).
33. T.S. Eliot, *The Love Song of J. Alfred Prufrock*.
34. J.N.D. Kelly, *Early Christian Creeds* (1950).
35. Vincent of Lérins, *Commonitorium*, CCSL 64, pp 125-231.
36. Owen Chadwick, *From Bossuet to Newman*, p xix.
37. G. Dix, *The Question of Anglican Orders* (1944).

38. *Ut verba caelestis oraculi restringam sub regulis donate*; Gregory the Great, *Moralia in Job*, ed M. Adriaen, *Letter to Leander*, CCSL 143 (1979), p 7.

39. See my *Augustine on Evil* (Cambridge, 1983).

40. Peter Abelard, *Sic et Non*, ed Blanche B. Boyer and Richard McKeon (Chicago, 1976–77), preface.

41. See E.R. Dodds, *Pagan and Christian in an Age of Anxiety* (Cambridge, 1990), p 23.

42. *Ibid.*, p 70.

43. The theories on which all this was based have their origins in Greek and Roman oratory, which understood the requirement that there be some similitude, some basis of comparison, to make the transfer of signification appropriate. The *Rhetorica ad herennium* (IV.xxxiv.35) describes transference of a word from the description of one thing so that it describes another: *Translatio est cum verbum in quamdam rem transferetur ex alia re*, a notion well established by Carolingian times.

44. Dorothy Sayers, *The Mind of the Maker*, p 20.

45. C.S. Lewis, *The Great Divorce* (London, 1945), p 74.

Chapter 2. Godness

1. Cicero, *Academica*, 1.xii.45.

2. Plato, *Republic*, Book VI, xix, 509b.

3. Cicero, *De natura deorum*, I.xiv.

4. *Ibid.*, I.xix–xx.

5. Boethius, *De trinitate*, IV, *Theological Tractates*, pp 17–18.

6. Anselm, *Proslogion*, XII, S 1.110.

7. PL 210.632.

8. On the later medieval complexities see for example, Richard Cross, *The Metaphysics of the Incarnation: Thomas Aquinas to Duns Scotus* (Oxford, 2002).

9. Anselm, *Proslogion*, Preface, S 1, p 93.

10. Anselm, *Monologion*, I–II, S 1.13–15.

11. Augustine, *Soliloquia*, I, 2, CSEL 89, pp 4–5.

12. Anselm, *Proslogion*, XVIII, S 1.114.

13. George Berkeley, *Principles of Human Knowledge*, ed Roger Woolhouse (London 1988), §30, p 63.

14. Dorothy Sayers, Letter to Herbert Kelly, 19 October 1937, in Barbara Reynolds (ed), *The Letters of Dorothy L. Sayers, Vol. 2, 1937–1943. From novelist to playwright* (London, 1997), p 54.

15. Anselm, *Proslogion*, VIII, S 1.106.

16. *Ibid.*, IX–XI, pp 106–10.

17. *Ibid.*, VII, S 1.105.

18. Peter Lombard, *Sententiae*, I, Dist. XLII, 184 (1). 'How can God be omnipotent when we can do many things he cannot do?' was a question which

continued to be asked. The same answer was forthcoming. He does not do those things which are not fitting for him. For example, he cannot sin. He cannot make a mistake. He cannot be unhappy. To do those things would be an impotence, not a power. Peter of Poitiers, *Sentences*, I, chapter 7.

19. John Scotus Eriugena, *De divina praedestinatione*, X, CCCM 50, p 66.

20. Anselm, *De concordia*, S III.246ff.

21. Lactantius, *De ira*, II.11, CSEL 27; cf. Plato, *Timaeus*, 28c and Cicero, *De natura deorum*, 3.22.56.

22. A.H. Armstrong, 'Plotinus' doctrine of the infinite and its significance for Christian thought', *Downside Review*, 73 (1954/5), pp 47–58, and *Plotinian and Christian Studies* (Variorum 1979), V.

23. Gregory P. Rocca, *Speaking the Incomprehensible God: Thomas Aquinas on the Interplay of Positive and Negative Theology* (Washington, 2004), pp 27–8.

24. 'No created intellect naturally possesses a quidditative knowledge of God's essence; and no created intellect can ever possess, in principle, a comprehensive knowledge of God's essence', Gregory P. Rocca, *Speaking the Incomprehensible God*, pp 27–8.

25. Acts 15 and the chapters leading up to it.

26. Lactantius, *De ira*, II.11 ff., CCSL; cf. Plato, *Timaeus*, 28c., Cicero, *De natura deorum*, 3.22.56.

27. *Deus non solum unus, immo et monas, id est unitas dicitur*, PL 210.623.

28. *Koran*, trans N.J. Dawood (Penguin, 1956; reprinted 2003), p 102.

29. *Ibid*.

30. Nisikânta Chattopâdhâya, *Buddhism and Christianity* (Freethought Publishing Company, London, 1882), p 4.

31. Peter Lombard, *Sententiae*, I, Dist. IV, 14 (2).

32. Augustine, *Retractiones*, I.iv, CCSL 57, p 13.

33. Augustine, *Soliloquia*, I,1, CSEL 89, p 3.

34. Anselm, *Monologion*, 67, S 1.78.

35. Hugh of St Victor, *La Contemplation et ses espèces*, ed R. Baron (Paris, 1955), pp 42–3.

36. Henry Chadwick, *East and West: The Making of a Rift in the Church* (Oxford, 2003), p 59ff.

37. Rowan Williams, 'Religious Lives', Romanes Lecture, Oxford, Thursday, 18 November 2004.

38. Peter Lombard, *Sententiae*, III, Dist. 1.1–2.

39. *Ibid.*, III, Dist. XV, 41.1.

Chapter 3. God's in his heaven; all's right with the world?

1. Plato, *Phaedo*, 65d–66a, 78c–79e, 65d, 75c, 75e, 100b, 1003e, 1004a–6d, gives examples of forms: justice, beauty, goodness, holiness, largeness, smallness, equality, health and strength, hotness, coldness, oddness and

evenness, life and death, indeed possibly all things which are opposites.

2. Addison, *Evidences*, p 324.

3. For example, Eusebius, *Historia ecclesiastica*, X.iv.70, ed G. Bardy, *Sources chrétiennes*, 55 (Paris, 1958), p 159.

4. Plotinus, *Ennead* 1. 6[1] 3. T.G. Sinnige, 'Plotinus on the Human Person and its Cosmic Identity', *Vigiliae christianae*, 56 (2002), pp 292-6 (p 293).

5. *Sed revocare gradum superasque evadere ad auras/hoc opus, hic labor est.* Virgil, *Aeneid*, VI, 126-8

6. Virgil, *Aeneid*, VI, 268-9.

7. Gary A. Anderson, 'The resurrection of Adam and Eve', in *'In dominico eloquio'*: *In Lordly Eloquence: Essays in Honour of Robert Louis Wilken*, ed Paul M. Blowers, Angela Russell Christman, David G. Hunter, Robin Darling Young (Eeerdmans, 2002), pp 3-34.

8. *Ibid.*

9. Jerome on Minor Prophets, in Jonah 1, CCSL 76, p 380.

10. Bernard of Clairvaux, *De consideratione*, *Opera Omnia*, ed J. Leclerq and H. Rochais (Rome, 1957-87), III, p 414.

11. John Milton, *Reason of Church-Government*, in Don M. Wolf (ed), *Complete Prose Works*, (New Haven and London, 1973), vol. I, chapter III, p 842.

12. Augustine, *Ennarrationes in psalmos*, 50.15, CCSL 38, p 610.

13. *Longe dissimiles Deo facti sunt et, iumentis comparati, descenderunt usque ad locum mortis. Sententiae*, Series 3.91, *Opera Omnia*, 6ii, p 139.

14. *Theologicae regulae*, *Regula*, 99, PL 210.673-4.

15. *Vel ascendendo in coelestium contemplationem: et talis excessus dicitur exstasis*, PL 210.673-4

16. John Gribbin, *Deep Simplicity: Chaos, Complexity and the Emergence of Life* (Allen Lane, London, 2004), pp 137-8.

17. John Donne, *Divine Poems*, *The Complete English Poems of John Donne*, ed C.A. Patrides (London, 1985), p 435.

18. Wordsworth, *The Prelude*, 1798-99, ed Stephen Parrish (Cornell, 1977), I, 67-81.

19. *Ibid.*, I, 119-28.

20. Wordsworth, 'Tintern Abbey'.

21. Stephen Younger, letter to *The Times*, 3 January 2005.

22. Cicero, *De natura deorum*, I.i.2, I.ii.3.

23. *Summa theologiae* I, q.2, a.3. (Thomas Aquinas, *Summa theologiae*, I.q.II, aa.1-3).

24. Ralph Glaber, *Historiarum libri quinque*, I.3, ed John France (Oxford, 1989), p 6.

25. Bernard of Clairvaux, *Sermons on the Song of Songs*, Sermon 28.IV.9-10, *Opera Omnia* III, pp 198-9. See also Gordon Rudy, *Mystical Language of Sensation in the Later Middle Ages* (Routledge, London, 2002), p 12.

26. Pascal, *Pensées*, trans J.M. Cohen (1961).
27. Benjamin Whichcote, *Select Sermons*, ed Anthony, 3rd Earl of Shaftsbury (1698), Part I, Sermon III, reprinted in C.A. Patrides, *The Cambridge Platonists* (London, 1969), p 47.
28. Ralph Cudworth, *The True Intellectual System of the Universe* (1678, repr. Stuttgart, 1964), I.iv.4, p 195.
29. 'The spacious firmament on high', Joseph Addison, in *Hymns Ancient and Modern* (Norwich, 2002), 103.
30. William Paley, *Natural Theology* (1802), chapter 1.
31. *Ibid.*
32. Jonathan Edwards, *A History of the Work of Redemption* (Philadelphia, 1773), pp 281–2.
33. Charles Darwin, *Autobiographies*, ed Michael Neve and Sharon Messenger (Penguin, 1986), pp 50–3.
34. Arthur Koestler, *The Act of Creation* (Hutchinson, 1964), p 449.
35. Robert Grosseteste, *Hexameron*, Particular Prima, XII, 1, ed Richard C. Dales and Servus Gieben (London, 1982), p 68, and *The Six Days of Creation*, trans C.F.J. Martin (London, 1996), p 66.
36. Grosseteste, *Hexameron*, Particular Prima, XVI, 1, pp 72–3, and *The Six Days of Creation*, trans C.F.J. Martin (London, 1996), p 73.
37. *Adversus hermogenem*, I.1, CCSL 1, p 397.
38. Augustine, *De Genesi ad litteram*, I.15, CSEL 28, p 21.
39. *Summa aurea*, ed J. Ribailler, *Spicilegium Bonaventurianum*, 16–20 (Paris, Grottaferrata, 1980–87), II.viii.ii, vol. II, p 175.
40. David Furley, *The Greek Cosmologists* (Cambridge, 1987), vol. I, p 3.
41. *Ibid.*, pp 1–2.
42. Lucretius, *De rerum natura*, the work of an admirer of Epicurus writing in Latin, is also of relevance. David Furley, *The Greek Cosmologists*, vol. I, p 3.
43. *Ibid.*, p 4.
44. Grosseteste, *Hexameron*, Particular Prima, XII, 4, p 68–9, and *The Six Days of Creation*, trans C.F.J. Martin (London, 1996), p 67.
45. Basil of Caesarea, *Hexameron*, 1.5, 1–3, ed A. de Mendieta and S.Y. Rudberg (Berlin, 1958).
46. Thomas of Chobham points to John 12.26: *volo ut uni ego sum, illic sit minister meus*, and to I Peter 2.9, *vos estis genus electum regale sacerdotium*. Thomas of Chobham, *Summa de commendatione virtutum et extirpatione vitiorum*, IV.1.3, ed F. Morenzoni, CCCM 82B (Turnhout, 1997), pp 131–6.
47. *De mundi aetatibus*, in Bede, *De temporibus liber*, XVI, ed C.W. Jones (Cambridge, Mass., 1943).
48. His *Epistola ad pleguinam* considers the various authorities and theories known to his generation. Bede, *Epistola ad pleguinam*.
49. Addison, *Evidences*, p 324.

50. Charles Darwin, *On the Origin of Species*, pp 183/117.
51. Colin Gunton, *Becoming and Being* (London, 2001, 2nd ed) is a useful introduction to the literature of this debate.
52. Cf. John B. Cobb Jnr and David Ray Griffin, *Process Theology: An Introductory Exposition* (Belfast, 1977), p 14.
53. Charles Hartshorne, *The Darkness and the Light* (New York, 1990), p 227.
54. John B. Cobb, Jnr and David Ray Griffin, *Process Theology*, p 16.
55. Roger Penrose (ed), *The Large, the Small and the Human Mind* (Cambridge 1997, 1999), p 93.
56. Stephen Hawking, in Penrose (ed), *The Large, the Small and the Human Mind*, p 169.
57. Roger Penrose, *The Emperor's New Mind* (Oxford, 1989), p 396.
58. *Ibid.*, pp 398–400.
59. James Gleick, *Chaos: Making a New Science* (Vintage, 1998), p 3.
60. *Ibid.*
61. Augustine, *De ordine*, I.i.1, CCSL 97 (1970), p 89.
62. *Ibid.*, I.iii.6, CCSL 97 (1970), pp 91–2.
63. C.A. Patrides, *The Cambridge Platonists*, p 35.
64. Gleick, *Chaos*, p 5.
65. For example, see L. Douglas Kiel, and Euel W. Elliot (eds), *Chaos Theory in the Social Sciences: Foundations and Applications* (Ann Arbor, 1996).
66. Roger Penrose, *Shadows of the Mind* (Vintage, 1995), pp 16–17.
67. *Ibid.*, p 411.
68. *Koran*, trans N.J. Dawood, p 101.
69. Plato, *Timaeus*, 31a.
70. Peter Lombard, *Sententiae*, II, Dist. 1 (1).
71. Philip Pullman, *Northern Lights* (London, 1995), p 397.

Chapter 4. A high-risk strategy?

1. P.D. James, *The Children of Men* (Faber, 1992), pp 89–90.
2. John Locke, *The Reasonableness of Christianity*, 1.
3. Augustine, *De Genesi ad litteram*, 1.1, *De civitate dei*, XII.15, *Confessiones*, XII.9.
4. *Iuxta Ysaiam seraphin die ac nocte conclamare non cessant: sanctus, sanctus, sanctus dominus deus sabbaoth*. Peter Abelard, *Theologia in scholarium*, Book I, CCCM 12, p 377.
5. William of St Thierry, *De contemplando deo*, VI, p 76.
6. Milton, *Paradise Lost*, I.157, I.187–8.
7. *Ibid.*, VIII.270–3.
8. Augustine, *De trinitate*, III.x.25, CCSL 50, pp 153–4.
9. Bede, *In principium Genesis*, IV.18, CSEL 118A, p 211.
10. Ambrose, *De Cain et Abel*, I.viii.30, CSEL 32, pp 364–5.
11. Cyprian, *Ad Quirinum*, III.ci line 2, CCSL 3, p 171.

12. Gregory, *Moralia in Job*, Preface, III.8, CCSL 143, p 14.
13. *Ibid.*, Preface, II.4–5, CCSL 143, pp 10–11.
14. *Ibid.*, Preface, III.7, CCSL 143, pp 12–13.
15. *Dixit ergo dominus ad Satan, ecce universa quae habet in manu tua sunt tantum in eum non extendas manum tuum.*
16. Gregory, *Moralia in Job*, II.xi.19, CCSL 143, p 71.
17. *Ibid.*, II.xii.20, CCSL 143, pp 72–3.
18. Salley Vickers, *Mr. Golightly's Holiday* (London, 2003), pp 328–9.
19. cf. I Samuel 15.17–18.
20. Nisikânta Chattopâdhâya, *Buddhism and Christianity*, p 4.
21. Peter Abelard, *Ethics*, ed D.E. Luscombe (Oxford, 1971), pp 24–5.
22. Speech of the Archangel Michael in Dorothy Sayers, *The Zeal of Thy House*, Part 4.
23. Dorothy Sayers, Letter to Herbert Kelly, 19 October 1937, in Reynolds (ed), *The Letters of Dorothy L. Sayers, Vol. 2* (1997), p 54, quoting a speech of the Archangel Michael in *The Zeal of Thy House*, Part 4.
24. Antony Flew, quoted in the *Sunday Times*, 19 December 2004.
25. In Coptic probably deriving from Syriac and Greek versions.
26. *A Manichean Psalm-Book*, in C.R.C. Allberry (ed), *Manichean Manuscripts in the Chester Beatty Collection* (Stuttgart, 1938), II, p 9.
27. John Painter, 'The Johannine Literature', in Stanley E. Porter (ed), *Handbook to Exegesis of the New Testament* (Brilolo, Leiden, 1997).
28. Tertullian, *Treatise on the Resurrection*, ed Ernest Evans (London, 1960), I, 17, p 45.
29. Basil, *Hexameron*, I. PG 29.21A–B. Gregory of Nyssa, *De homine opificio*, PG 44.213C. A.H. Armstrong, 'Plotinus' Doctrine of the infinite and its significance for Christian thought', *Downside Review*, 73 (1954/5), pp 47–58, and *Plotinian and Christian Studies* (Variorum 1979), V, p 55.
30. Origen, *De principiis*, III.iv.4, ed P. Koetschau (1913).
31. Isidore, *Sententiae*, 3, PL 83.673.
32. Ralph Cudworth, *The True Intellectual System of the Universe*, I.iv.4 (1678, repr. Stuttgart, 1964), p 195.
33. Rowan Williams, 'Religious Lives', Romanes Lecture, Oxford, Thursday, 18 November 2004.
34. Nisikânta Chattopâdhâya, *Buddhism and Christianity*, p 6.
35. See my *Augustine on Evil* (Cambridge, 1983).
36. Peter of Poitiers, *Sententiae*, II, chapter 11 and chapter 10.
37. See my *Augustine on Evil*.
38. William Paley, *Natural Theology*, chapter 1.
39. Butler, *The Analogy of Religion, II*, p 47.
40. *Ibid.*, p 48.
41. Cited in Bonamy Dobrée, *English Literature in the Early Eighteenth Century* (Oxford, 1959), p 262.

42. John Coventry, *Reconciliation* (London, 1985), p 97.

Chapter 5. Repair

1. Marriott Edgar and Charles Wolseley-Charles, 'Albert and the Lion', 1932.
2. Antony Flew, quoted in the *Sunday Times*, 19 December 2004.
3. *Glossa ordinaria* on Genesis 2.7.
4. Grosseteste, *Hexameron*, XI.xxx, ed Richard C. Dales and Servus Gieben (London, 1982), p 68, and *The Six Days of Creation*, trans C.F.J. Martin (London, 1996).
5. Gustav Aulén, *Christus Victor* (1930), trans A.G. Hebert (London, 1931).
6. Prudentius, *Opera*, CSEL 61.
7. Milton, *Paradise Lost*, III.210-13.
8. Spenser, 'An Hymn of Heavenly Love', in E. Greenlaw et al (eds), *The Works of Edmund Spenser, The Minor Poems, I* (Baltimore, 1943), p 217.
9. Robert J. Daly, *The Origins of the Christian Doctrine of Sacrifice* (Philadelphia, Fortress, 1978), p 3.
10. Francis X. Clooney, 'Sacrifice and its spiritualization in the Christian and Hindu traditions: a study in comparative theology', *Harvard Theological Review*, 78 (1985), pp 361-80 (pp 365-6).
11. S.W. Sykes (ed), *Sacrifice and Redemption*, Durham Essays in Theology (Cambridge, 1991), p 287.
12. Clooney, 'Sacrifice and its spiritualization', pp 361-80 (pp 365-6).
13. *Ibid.*, p 376.
14. *Ibid.*, pp 367-9.
15. Salley Vickers, *Mr. Golightly's Holiday*, pp 328-9.
16. Daly, *The Origins of the Christian Doctrine of Sacrifice*, pp 2-6.
17. Isaac Watts, based on Psalm 100, *Common Praise, Hymns Ancient and Modern* (Canterbury Press, 2002), p 387.
18. Stephen Sykes, *The Story of Atonement* (London, 1997), p xi.
19. Marilyn McCord Adams, inaugural lecture as Regius Professor of Divinity, University of Oxford, 8 November 2004.
20. Peter Lombard, *Sententiae*, III, Dist. XVI, 55.1-2.
21. Benjamin Whichcote, *Select Sermons*, ed Anthony, 3rd Earl of Shaftsbury (1698), Part I, Sermon III, reprinted in C.A. Patrides, *The Cambridge Platonists*, p 44-6.
22. *Three Byzantine Saints*, trans Elizabeth Dawes and Norman H. Baynes (Oxford, 1948).
23. See Thomas N. Tentler, *Sin and Confession on the Eve of the Reformation* (Princeton, 1977), p 273.
24. John Bunyan, *Grace Abounding to the Chief of Sinners*, ed R. Sharrock (Oxford, 1962), p 10.
25. Isaac Watts, version of Psalm 136, first line: 'Give to our God immortal

praise', stanza 3.

26. C.S. Lewis, *The Great Divorce*, p 8.

27. Locke, *The Reasonableness of Christianity*, 26, citing John 3.36.

28. Boethius, *De consolatione philosophiae*, I, Pr.VI.

29. *Ibid.*, II.

30. C. Mohrmann, *Études sur le Latin des chrétiens*, 4 vols. (Rome, 1958–77), vol. 3. on genus, pp 171–4 and the sense of a 'people' or Christian people.

31. See Desmond Henry, *The Logic of St. Anselm* (Oxford, 1967), on numerically definite reasoning.

32. John Dillenberger, *Martin Luther: Selections from His Writings* (New York, Anchor, 1961), p 11.

33. Locke, *The Reasonableness of Christianity*, 3–4.

34. Locke, opening to *The Reasonableness of Christianity*, ed. John C. Higgins-Biddle (Oxford, 1999).

35. *Ibid.*, 6.

36. *Ibid.*, 14.

37. Cf. Hebrews 3.1; Hebrews 10.19; I Peter 1.16.

38. The *Legenda Aurea* identifies four categories of undoubted saints: the Apostles, the martyrs, the confessors and the virgins. Jacobus de Voragine, *Legenda Aurea*, 162, trans W.G. Ryan (Princeton, 1993), 2 vols, vol. II, p 272, Latin text ed T. Graesse (1845).

39. A letter of Paulinus, which survives with the letters of Faustus of Riez (Epistola 4), hints that a person may well not be 'fit for heaven' when he dies, without necessarily being destined to spend eternity in hell. *Faustus of Riez* (Epistola 4), CSEL 21, ed Engelbrecht, pp 181–4. See also J. le Goff, *La naissance de purgatoire* (Paris, 1981), *The Birth of Purgatory*, trans A. Goldhammer (London, 1984).

40. Jacobus de Voragine. *Legenda Aurea*, 163, vol. II, pp 280–3, Latin text ed T. Graesse (1845). I Corinthians 3.12–17.

41. H. Hagendahl, *Latin Fathers and the Classics: A Study on the Apologists, Jerome and other Christian Writers* (Göteborg, 1958), pp 392–4.

42. *The Tatler*, ed Donald F. Bond (Oxford, 1987), p 86.

43. *De senectute*, xxiii.82.

44. Thomas à Kempis, *De imitatione christi, Liber internae consolationis*.

45. Ailred of Rievaulx, *De speculo caritatis*, I.xi.34, CCCM 1, p 26.

46. Gregory the Great, *Moralia in Job*, XIV.35 and XVII.32, CCSL 143A.

47. Ailred of Rievaulx, *De speculo caritatis*, 1.11.

48. *Summa Aurea*, Tractatus xviii.1, ed J. Ribailler, *Spicilegium Bonaventurianum* 16–20 (Paris, Grottaferrata, 1980–87), IV, p 491.

49. *Ibid.*, p 496.

50. Virgil, *Aeneid*, VI.565.

51. *Ibid.*, VI.679–84.

52. *Ibid.*, VI.610–11.

53. *De bono patientiae*, chapter 21, line 424.
54. In the *De tobia* (XVI.54, p 550, line 9).
55. Benjamin Whichcote, *Select Sermons*, Part I, Sermon III, reprinted in C.A. Patrides, *The Cambridge Platonists*, pp 44–6.
56. *Ibid.*
57. *Expositio totius mundi et gentium*, ed J. Rougé, *Sources chrétiennes*, 124 (Paris, 1966), of uncertain date, with most scholars favouring the mid-fourth century.
58. *Ibid.*, p 142.

Chapter 6. A nice place to be?

1. J.M. Neale, 'Jerusalem the golden', translating a hymn of Bernard of Cluny.
2. John Donne, *Deaths Duell: Sermons of John Donne*, ed Evelyn M. Simpson and George R. Potter (California, 1962), vol. X. Donne describes in order the deaths which take place in every human life, beginning with birth, which is an exit from the insensate 'death' of life in the womb, to putrefaction.
3. William Hazlitt's translation of Martin Luther, *Table Talk*, No. 797, introduction by Robert van de Weyer (London, 1995), pp 362–3. This Hazlitt was the son of the essayist.
4. Dorothy Sayers, letter to C.S. Lewis, 24 December 1945, in Reynolds (ed), *The Letters of Dorothy L. Sayers: A noble daring*, p 184.
5. C.S. Lewis, *The Great Divorce*, p 26.
6. Augustine, *De civitate dei*, XXII.29, CCSL 14 (1955), p 856.
7. Cyprian, *De mortalitate*, 2, CCSL 3A, pp 17–18.
8. Jerome, *Comm. in Isaiam*, VI.xiii.3, CCSL 73, p 226.21, also *Comm,. in prophetas minores*, on Joel. 2, CCSL 76, p 190.540.
9. Gregory the Great, *Moralia in Job*, CCSL 143, pp 83.77–8.
10. Bede, *De temporum ratione* 34, CCSL 123B (1977), p 388.
11. Cicero, *De senectute*, xiv.49.
12. Pliny, *Letters*, II.ii.2.
13. *Ibid.*, I.xxiv.4.
14. Virgil, *Aeneid*, VI.637–47.
15. 'Paradisus' appears in Pliny's *Natural History* (5.93) as the name of an actual town, but its metaphorical senses were chiefly shaped by the Vulgate.
16. Paradise is identified with heaven in other passages which do not make the link with the First Garden. *Paradisus* also appears in Ecclesiasticus (40.17), where the 'fear of God' (which means an awestruck respect for him) is described as a paradisal blessing. Jesus said to one of the robbers who were crucified beside him, 'today you will be with me in paradise' (Luke 23.43). In the Vulgate there is another reference to 'Paradise' in II Corinthians 12.4, at Paul's 'snatching up into heaven', where he heard

the secret words which could not be reported.

17. Bernard, *De diligentia dei*, 8.3, *Opera Omnia*, ed J. Leclerq and H. Rochais (Rome, 1957–87), III.126.3.

18. Augustine, *De civitate dei*, XIX.20, CCSL 14 (1955), p 87.1–15.

19. Hymn of C.A. Arlington (1872–1955).

20. McGrath, *A Brief History of Heaven* (Oxford, 2003), p 8.

21. The Temple was destroyed in AD70 by Titus, the Roman Emperor, who was putting down the Jewish revolt against occupying Roman forces.

22. John Bunyan, *The Pilgrim's Progress*, ed James Blanton Wharey (Oxford, 1967).

23. *Deaths Duell, Sermons of John Donne*, vol. X, p 238.

24. Augustine, *De civitate dei* XX.17, CCSL 14 (1955), p 727.

25. Gregory the Great, *In I Reg.* 2.10, CCSL 144, p 126.

26. Cicero, *De natura deorum*, ed H. Rackham (Loeb, 1933), I.xviii.

27. Cyprian, *De bono patientiae*, 5, ed C. Moreschini, CCSL 3A, p 121.

28. Augustine, *Letters*, 10, 2, ed A. Goldberg, CSEL 34.1 (1895–98), p 23.

29. R. Javelet, *Image et resemblance au douzième siècle* (Letouzey, Paris, 1967), 2 vols., I, pp 56–62 and pp 266–85, with a bibliography of studies on this theme.

30. *Sententiae*, Series 3.91, *Opera Omnia*, ed J. Leclerq and H. Rochais, viii, p 139.

31. Ailred of Rievaulx, *Sermo XXV*, 1, *In festivitate omnium sanctorum*, *Sermones*, ed G. Raciti, CCCM 2A (1989), pp 204ff.

32. Thomas of Chobham, *Sermones*, 2, CCSM 82A, p 20.

33. Elizabeth Salter, *Piers Plowman* (Oxford, 1962); cf. John A. Alford (ed), *A Companion to Piers Plowman* (California, 1988).

34. *The Letters of Dorothy Sayers*, p 182 (26 September 1944).

35. Penrose, *The Emperor's New Mind*, p 392.

36. [*Vulg. cellaria sua*] (Sg 1.4). Ambrose, *De Isaac vel anima*, 4.11, CSEL 32 (1896), p 650.

37. Ambrose, Exposition of Psalm 118, I.xvi., ed M. Petschenig, CSEL 62 (1999), p 16.

38. Bernard of Clairvaux, Sermons on the Song of Songs, 23.16, *Opera Omnia*, 1.149.26.

39. Augustine, *Confessiones*, XIII.viii.9, ed L. Verheijen, CCSL 27 (1981), p 246.

40. Cassiodorus, *In psalmos*, 30.21–2, CCSL 97, p 271.

41. The highest *aspectus* of the soul is the appetite for understanding what things are true and best, PL180.724.

42. Bonaventure, *Journey of the Mind to God*, Classics of Western Spirituality, Bonaventure, *Itinerarium*, I.2, M. Letterio (Milan, 2002), trans E. Cousins (Paulist Press, New York, 1978).

43. Bonaventure, *Itinerarium*, I.2.

44. This is of course *animus*, not *anima*, although there is a classical usage which makes *anima* the soul in the sense of a 'life-force' distinctive to the individual and persisting after death, that is not the central idea here.

45. *Manifestata divinae visionis gloria cognitione plena et perfecta*, Rupert of Deutz, *De sancta trinitate, De operibus spiritus sancti*, 42.ix.24, CCCM 24, p 2125.

46. *Ex occasione quipped ortus est diei natalis mei et tridui disputatione complete ... in quo libro constitit inter nos, qui simul quaerebamus, non esse beatam vitam nisi perfectam cognitionem dei*, Augustine, *Retractationes*, I.ii, discussing *De beata vita*, CCSL 57, p 11.

47. *Il 'Tractatus de Gratia' di Guglielmo d'Auvergne*, ed Guglielmo Cort (Rome, 1966), p 49.

48. *Festum sempiternum chorus angelorum, vultus praesens dei laetitia sine defectu*, Augustine, *Ennarrationes in psalmos*, 41, 9, CCSL 38, p 467.

49. Sydney Carter, in *Hymns Ancient and Modern*, 375.

50. Graham Ward, 'Postmodern theology', in David Ford (ed), *The Modern Theologians* (Blackwell, 1997), p 589.

51. Cf. Norman Pittenger, *Process-Thought and Christian Faith* (London, 1968), p 30.

52. A.N. Whitehead, *Process and Reality* (Cambridge, 1927–28), p 521.

53. T.S. Eliot, 'Mr Eliot's Sunday Morning Service', in *The Waste Land: The Complete Poems and Plays of T.S. Eliot* (1969, 2004), p 54.

Chapter 7. Is there a future for me?

1. *Sacramentarium Gelasianum*, XCI.1607 and 1612, ed L.C. Mohlberg, *Rerum Ecclesiasticarum Documenta, Fontes*, IV (Rome, 1960), pp 234–5.

2. *Paradisus enim significatur amoenissimus locus et felicissimae iucunditatis aeterna securitas*, Cassiodorus, *In psalmos* 138.12, CCSL 98, p 1247.

3. *The Tatler*, 30 March 1710, ed Donald F. Bond, vol. II.352.

4. Robert Dodaro, *Christ and the Just Society in the Age of Augustine* (Cambridge, 2004).

5. Cicero, *De amicitia*, VI.20 and VII.23.

6. Colin Morris, *The Discovery of the Individual, 1050–1200* (London, 1972), p 64.

7. Joseph Butler, *The Analogy of Religion, Natural and Revealed*, p 309.

8. *Ibid.*, pp 312–13.

9. Arthur Koestler, *The Ghost in the Machine* (London, 1967).

10. William Wordsworth, *Ode on Intimations of Immortality*, in John O. Hayden (ed), *The Poems* (Yale, 1981).

11. Ailred of Rievaulx, *De anima*, II.4–5, CCCM 1, pp 707–8.

12. Plato, *Phaedo*, 67e–68a.

13. Ambrose, *De excessu fratris, De obitu Theodosii, De obitu Valentiniani*, all edited in CSEL 73.

14. Jerome, *Letter* 39, CSEL 54, pp 293ff.

15. Jerome, *Letter* 75, CSEL 55, p 29, and compare Letters 66, 77, 108, 118, 127.
16. Gregory the Great, *Dialogues*, IV.v.1, ed A. de Vogüé and P. Antin, SC, 265 (1978-80), 2 vols., II.32.
17. Gregory the Great, *Dialogi*, IV.5, ed U. Moricca (Rome, 1924), pp 236-7.
18. *Ibid.*
19. See for example, John McManners, *Death and the Enlightenment* (Oxford, 1985), pp 234-69.
20. Grover Smith (ed), *Letters of Aldous Huxley* (Chatto and Windus, 1969), p 736.
21. Plotinus, *Ennead*, V.1[10] 1.1-5; see also T.G. Sinnige, 'Plotinus on the human person and its cosmic identity', *Vigiliae Christianae*, 56 (2002), pp 292-6 (p 294).
22. Cicero, *De senectute*, xxi.77.
23. C.A. Patrides (ed), *The Complete English Poems of John Donne* (London, 1985), p 437.
24. Ambrose, *Hexameron*, Dies 5, xxiii.79, CSEL 32, p 196, line 6.
25. Tertullian, *Treatise on the Resurrection*, I, ed Ernest Evans (London, 1960), p 5.
26. Augustine, *De trinitate*, II.xvii, CCSL 50. Similar remarks in the theological literature of the patristic and medieval period are legion.
27. Augustine, *De civitate dei*, XXII.29, CCSL 14 (1955), p 854.
28. Tertullian, *Treatise on the Resurrection*, I, 17, p 45.
29. Gregory the Great, *Moralia in Job*, XIV.57, CCSL 143A.
30. cf. Alan of Lille, *Contra hereticos*, I, PL 210.307-8.
31. Peter Abelard, *Collationes*, 161 ed John Marenbon and Giovanni Orlandi (Oxford, 2001), p 171.
32. William of St Thierry, *Expositio super epistolam ad Romanos*, VI.ix.26, on Romans 9.26, ed P. Verdeyen, CCCM 86 (Turnhout, 1989).
33. Gregory the Great, *Dialogues*, IV.26.3-4, ed A. de Vogüé and P. Antin, SC, 265 (1978-80), 2 vols., II. 82ff.
34. *Ibid.*
35. T.S. Eliot, 'Death by Water', in *The Complete Poems*, p 71.
36. William Harmless, *Desert Christians* (OUP, 2004).
37. Gregory, *Dialogues*, I, iiv.9, pp 46-7.
38. Harmless, *Desert Christians*.
39. Gregory, *Dialogues*, I, Prologue, 3-5, pp 10-13.
40. *Porro dum pergere in pace putabam, inopinate impulit inimicus et irruit in animum adhuc non in affluencia amoris occupatum ut everteretur; ac inde autumans auferre omne quod unquam operatus sum ad honorem Omnipotentis*, Richard Rolle, *Melos Amoris*, XXXI, ed E.J.F. Arnould (Oxford, 1957), p 93.25.
41. Lactantius, *Divinae institutiones*, VII.11, CSEL 19, p 615.

42. Bede, *Comm. in Lucam*, I.ii.24, CCSL 120, pp 64-5.
43. Anselm, *Proslogion* 25-6, S 1.118-19.
44. *Ibid.*, 25-6, S 1, pp 119-20.
45. Dante, *Paradiso*, Canto XXII.
46. Seneca, *De vita beata*, III.3-IV.4.
47. Juvenal, *Satura*, XI.27.
48. *Te consule. Dic tibi qui sis*, Juvenal, *Satura*, XI.33.
49. Abelard, *Ethics*, p xxxi, note 2 and *The Didascalicon of Hugh of St. Victor*, trans J. Taylor (Columbia, 1961), p 177 n.4; see also R. Javelet, *Image et resemblance au douzième siècle* (Letouzey, Paris, 1967), 2 vols., I.368-71 and II.278-81 on the literature and sources.
50. Leibniz, *De summa rerum*, §510, *Metaphysical Papers, 1675-76*, ed and trans G.H.R. Parkinson (Yale, 1992), p 60.
51. *Ibid.*, p 64.
52. See Andrew Brook, *Kant and the Mind* (Cambridge, 1994), p 235.
53. Leibniz, *De summa rerum*, §508, p 56.
54. G.W.F. Hegel, *The Phenomenology of Mind* (1807), trans J.B. Baillie, and Hegel's *Philosophy of Religion*, Part II, Sections I and II, and Part III.
55. Paul Crowther, *The Kantian Sublime* (Oxford, 1989), p 11.
56. Ludwig Wittgenstein, *The Blue and Brown Books* (Oxford, 1969), p 9.
57. Paul Johnston, *Wittgenstein: Rethinking the Inner* (London, 1993), p 171.
58. John MacMurray, *The Self as Agent* (London, 1957), p 11 and also pp 18-19 on the problem that mid-twentieth-century convention made it difficult to discuss 'natural theology' as distinct from a theology of religion.
59. *Ibid.*, p 24.
60. Nisikânta Chattopâdhâya, *Buddhism and Christianity*, p 13.
61. *Ibid.*, p 24.
62. *Ibid.*, p 6.
63. John B. Cobb, Jnr and David Ray Griffin, *Process Theology: An Introductory Exposition*, p 15.
64. Seneca, *De vita beata*, III.4.
65. *Ibid.*, 1.1-4.
66. Seneca, *De tranquillitate animi*, I.11; Seneca, *De otio*, I.4.
67. Seneca, *De vita beata*, III.4.
68. Aulus Gellius, *Noctes Atticae*, XIII.xvii.
69. Seneca, *De vita beata*, VIII.1.
70. *Ibid.*, I.1.
71. Iamblichus, *Protreptiche*, 1, ed E. de Places (Les Belles Lettres, 1989), pp 40-1.
72. Cicero, *De finibus bonorum et malorum*, I.V.13ff.
73. Diogenes Laertius, *Lives of the Philosophers*, X.122.
74. *Ibid.*, X.122 and 131.
75. *Ibid.*, X.144.

76. *Ibid.*, X.121.
77. *Ibid.*, X.122.
78. Seneca, *Controversiae*, I.1.3.
79. Seneca, *De tranquillitate animi*, II, 3; cf. Cyprian, *Ad donatum*, 14, CCSL 3A, p 11.
80. *Et haec anima oscula verbi multa desiderat, ut inluminetur divinae cognitionis lumine*, Ambrose, *De Isaac vel anima*, 3.8, CSEL 32 (1896), p 647.
81. On *otium* see pp 171 and 174.
82. Apponius, *In cantica canticorum*, Book 11, CCSL 19, p 266.
83. Aulus Gellius, *Noctes Atticae*, XVIII, 1.

Chapter 8. Heavenly community?

1. Stephen Sayers, 'The paradox of being', *Friends Quarterly* (July 2004), pp 118–24.
2. Ailred of Rievaulx, *Compendium speculi caritatis* 36, CCCM 1, pp 213–15.
3. Henry Scott Holland, *Death is Nothing At All* (London, 1987).
4. Cicero, *De amicitia*, ii.10 and vii.23.
5. *Ibid.*, ix.32.
6. Anselm, *Letters* 4, 5, S III.
7. Bernard of Clairvaux, *Letters* 122, 123, *Opera Omnia*, ed Leclerq and Rochais, VII.302–4.
8. Ailred of Rievaulx, *De spiritali amicitia*, I, CCCM 1, p 289.
9. Cicero, *De senectute*, xxiii.83–4.
10. Gregory the Great, *Dialogues*, IV.1.1, ed A. de Vogüé and P. Antin, SC, 265 (1978–80), 2 vols., II. 112ff.
11. Dante, *Paradiso*, Canto XIV.
12. C.S. Lewis, *The Great Divorce*, p 29.
13. *Ibid.*, pp 70–1.
14. See my *Academics and the Real World* (Buckingham, 2002), Part I.
15. Macrobius, *Saturnalia*, ed J. Willis (Leipzig, 1963), I.i.2.
16. *Ibid.*, I.i.3.
17. Orderic Vitalis, *Historia ecclesiastica*, IV, ed Marjorie Chibnall (Oxford, 1973), 8 vols., II, p 296.
18. Ailred of Rievaulx, *De spiritali amicitia*, I.1, CCCM 1, p 288.
19. Augustine, *Confessiones*, IX.x.23ff., CCSL 27.
20. *Ibid.*, IX.x.24, CCSL 27.
21. Ambrose, *De Isaac vel anima*, 3.7, CSEL 32 (1896), p 647.
22. Dante, *Monarchia*, I.iii.2–3, ed and trans P. Shaw (Cambridge, 1995).
23. Louis B. Pascoe, *Jean Gerson: Principles of Church Reform* (Leiden, 1973), p 27.
24. In terms heavily indebted to Tyconius and Augustine.
25. Primasius, *In apocalypsim*, I.2, CCSL 92, p 25.
26. Baldwin of Ford, Cistercian monk, friend of John of Salisbury and eventu-

ally Archbishop of Canterbury (*d.* 1190). He took as his subject in Sermon 15 the institution of the common life (*institutio vite communis*), and he develops in parallel the implications for the Church and for the monastic community.

27. Baldwin of Ford, *Sermones*, CCCM 99, p 230.
28. *Ibid.*
29. *Ibid.*
30. *Ibid.*, p 229.
31. *Ibid.*, p 230.
32. *Ibid.*, p 231.
33. *Ibid.*, p 243.
34. *Ibid.*
35. *Ibid.*, p 246.
36. *Ibid.*, p 244.
37. Isaac Watts, based on Psalm 100, *Common Praise, Hymns Ancient and Modern*, p 387.
38. William Blake, *A Vision of the Last Judgement*, in A. Ostriker (ed), *The Complete Poems* (London, 2004).
39. Clement of Alexandria, *Paedogogus*, II.iv, *Opera*, ed Otto Stählin (Berlin, 1936–70).
40. Augustine, *Confessiones*, IX.6 and 7, CCSL 27, pp 141–2.
41. Augustine, *Letter*, 55.28, PL 33.220–1.
42. Augustine, *Ennarrationes in psalmos*, CCSL 39, p 986.
43. Tenth century, trans Percy Dearmer, *Common Praise, Hymns Ancient and Modern*, p 3.
44. Bernard of Cluny, trans J.M. Neale, *Common Praise, Hymns Ancient and Modern*, p 482.
45. *Common Praise, Hymns Ancient and Modern*, p 481.
46. Preached on All Saints Day (1623?), *Sermons of John Donne*, ed Evelyn M. Simpson and George R. Potter, vol. X (California, 1962), p 43.

Conclusion

1. John Keats, Letter 123, to George and Georgiana Keats (14 February–3 May 1819), in Maurice Buxton Forman (ed), *Letters*, (Oxford, 1953), p 334.

Dates of authors mentioned

The Oxford Dictionary of the Christian Church, ed F.L. Cross and E.A. Livingstone (Oxford, 1957 and later editions to date) is an indispensable reference work for dates and outline biographies and bibliographies.

Abelard, Peter (1079–1142/3)
Addison, Joseph (1672–1719)
Ailred of Rievaulx (1110–67)
Alan of Lille (*d.*1202)
Ambrose of Milan (*c.*339–97)
Anaxagoras (*c.*500BC)
Anselm of Canterbury (1033–1109)
Anselm of Havelberg (mid-twelfth century)
Aquinas, Thomas (*c.*1225–74)
Aristotle (384–322BC)
Arlington, C.A. (1872–1955)
Augustine of Hippo (354–430)
Baldwin of Ford (*d.*1190)
Basil of Caesarea (*c.*330–79)
Bede (*c.*673–735)
Berkeley, George (1685–1753)
Bernard of Clairvaux (1090–1153)
Bernard of Cluny (*c.*1100–*c.*1150)
Biddle, John (1615–62)
Blake, William (1757–1827)
Boethius (*c.*480–*c.*534)
Bonaventure (*c.*1217–74)
Bossuet, Jacques Bénigne (1627–1704)
Browne, Thomas (1605–82)
Bunyan, John (1628–88)
Butler, Joseph (1692–1752)
Calvin, John (1509–64)
Cassian (*c.*360–after 430)
Cassiodorus (485/90–*c.*580)

Cicero, Marcus Tullius (106–43BC)
Clement of Alexandria (c.150–c.215)
Constantine the Great (d.337)
Cooper, A.A., Third Earl of Shaftesbury (1671–1713)
Crispin, Gilbert (c.1055–1117)
Cudworth, Ralph (1617–88)
Cyprian (d.258)
Dante Alighieri (1265–1321)
Darwin, Charles (1809–82)
Democritus (460–370BC)
Descartes, René (1596–1650)
Diogenes Laertius (third century BC)
Donne, John (1571/2–1631)
Dostoevsky, Fedor (1821–81)
Dryden, John (1631–1700)
Edwards, Jonathan (1703–58)
Eliot, Thomas Stearns (1888–1965)
Epicurus (341–270BC)
Eriugena, John Scotus (c.810–77)
Euclid (325–265BC)
Eusebius of Caesarea (c.260–c.340)
Faustus of Riez (d.c.490)
Gregory the Great (c.540–604)
Grosseteste, Robert (c.1170–1253)
Hegel, Georg Wilhelm Friedrich (1770–1831)
Heraclitus (c.500BC)
Herbert, George (1593–1633)
Hobbes, Thomas (1588–1679)
Hugh of St Victor (c.1096–1141)
Huxley, Aldous (1894–1963)
Iamblichus (d.c.325)
Irenaeus (c.130–c.200)
Isidore (c.560–636)
Jerome (c.342–420)
Joachim of Fiore (c.1135–1202)
Kant, Immanuel (1724–1804)
Keats, John (1795–1821)
Kempis, Thomas à (c.1380–1471)
Lactantius (c.250–c.325)
Langland, William (c.1330–c.1400)
Leibniz, Gottfried Wilhelm (1646–1716)
Lewis, C.S. (1898–1963)
Locke, John (1632–1704)

Lombard, Peter (c.1100–60)
Luther, Martin (1483–1546)
Marvell, Andrew (1621–78)
Milton, John (1608–74)
Newman, John Henry (1801–90)
Newton, Isaac (1642–1727)
Origen (c.185–c.254)
Paley, William (1743–1805)
Pascal, Blaise (1623–62)
Philo of Alexandria (c.20BC–c.50AD)
Plato (427–347BC)
Pliny the Younger (62–113)
Plotinus (c.205–270)
Primasius (6th century)
Prudentius (348–c.410).
Ps-Dionysius 'the Areopagite' (5th century)
Pythagoras (fl.530BC)
Rupert of Deutz (c.1075–1129/30)
Russell, Bertrand (1872–1970)
Sayers, Dorothy L. (1893–1957)
Seneca (c.4BC–c.64AD)
Socinus (1525–62, uncle, and 1539–1604, nephew)
Spenser, Edmund (1552–99)
Spinoza, Benedict de (1632–77)
Tertullian (c.160–c.225)
Toland, John (1670–1722)
Traherne, Thomas (c.1636–74)
Vincent of Lérins (before 450)
Virgil (70–19BC)
Watts, Isaac (1674–1748)
Whichcote, Benjamin (1609–83)
William of Auvergne (d.1249)
William of St Thierry (1075/80–1148)
Wittgenstein, Ludwig (1889–1951)
Wordsworth, William (1770–1850)
Wyclif, John (c.1330–1384)

Glossary

Baptism. The unrepeatable 'sacrament' of formal admission to membership of the Church, in which the person being baptized declares his or her faith by saying a version of the Creed; if it is a baby, the parents and godparents make the declaration. Water is sprinkled on the person being baptized, or there may be complete immersion in water. From early times, baptism has been carried out 'in the name of the Father, the Son and the Holy Spirit'.

Bible. A collection of writings gradually accepted by the Church as especially authoritative, including the Jewish Scriptures of the Old Testament and a New Testament of four Gospels (or lives of Jesus), the Acts of the Apostles (a history of the first Christian generation), a series of letters written by the Apostles to the young Churches and a vision of what would happen at the end of the world.

Chaos theory. The scientific hypothesis that all events are causally linked in complex ways so that outcomes always have antecedents.

Church. The Christian community, visible and invisible, local and universal, which developed a complex institutional structure in the medieval centuries.

Creed. Formal statement of belief agreed by the Church, either for use in worship or as the declaration of a universal Council.

Crucifixion. The death of Jesus on the Cross, which Christians believe transformed the future for the human race.

Deism. The belief that God is a power that set the universe in motion but takes little interest in it thereafter.

Eucharist. Celebration by Christians of a 'memorial' of the occasion when Jesus shared the Last Supper with his disciples before his arrest and crucifixion and handed them the bread and wine saying, 'This is my body which is given for you' and 'This is my blood which is shed for you'. This 'sacrament' became the subject of intense debate during the Reformation about whether it was a sacrifice in its own right and could in any way add to the effect of Christ's crucifixion.

Fathers. Christian writers in both Greek and Latin up to about the seventh century who came to be held in special respect as having laid the authoritative foundations of Christian theology.

Fundamentalism. Acceptance of the literal truth of the Bible (or the holy book of another world religion) accompanied by a tendency to adhere to conservative views on socio-moral issues.

Holy Communion *see* Eucharist.

Incarnation. The Son of God's 'becoming man'. Exactly what this involved was the subject of debate in the first Christian centuries until it was generally accepted that he remained one Person but has two 'natures', divine and human.

Interfaith dialogue. Mutually respectful discussion between believers in different world religions with the objective of arriving at a better understanding of one another's faiths. This has largely replaced the missionary work of earlier centuries, which sought to convert non-Christians to the Christian faith.

Lord's Supper *see* Eucharist.

Mass *see* Eucharist.

Mediation. The belief that God became man in Jesus to reconcile humanity to himself.

Natural theology. The system of inference which arrives at an idea of God from observation of the world and the use of reason.

Original sin. The belief developed mainly in Western Christendom in the early centuries that the first sin committed by Adam and Eve contaminated all their progeny, so that all human beings are now born in 'original sin' and even a new-born baby is a sinner in the sight of God.

Patristics *see* Fathers.

Penance. The belief that sinners who become sorry for what they have done must make up for it by doing set tasks imposed by the Church, in order to wipe the record clean.

Person. In the doctrine of the Trinity, Father, Son and Holy Spirit are believed to be distinct Persons in one God, each having aspects which are not shared with the others. For example, the Father is not a Son.

Platonism. An enduring philosophical system based on the teaching of the Greek philosopher Plato, who published the dialogues of his master Socrates. Plato believed that abstract goods such as 'beauty' and 'truth' are absolutes and more real than any particular exemplification in the physical world. Platonism developed links with Stoicism and some of the teachings of Aristotle and emerged into a Neoplatonism which was profoundly influential on the formation of the theology of early Christianity.

Predestination. The belief that God destines his creatures to go to heaven or hell, and that the individual believer cannot alter his or her destiny.

Process theology. A twentieth-century theory that the universe is in a process of change and that God himself is dynamic, not static, and can change with it.

Providence. The belief that a power in the universe is ultimately in charge of the way it will work out.

Purgatory. The place where for a time believers who had died with penances uncompleted could discharge the remainder of their debt and fit themselves for heaven. Purgatory was largely a creation of the twelfth century.

Redemption. The belief that the death of Jesus paid for the sins of humanity and that he 'bought back' the human race for God.

Reformation. The period mainly in the sixteenth century when several 'reformers' challenged the need for the institutional structures of the Church as they had developed in the late Middle Ages.

Resurrection. Revival after death, usually believed to include the body as well as the soul.

Revelation. The idea that God teaches his creatures about himself both by making the world full of clues and also by direct inspiration of the human authors of the books of the Bible.

Sacrament. An action of and within the Church which gives visible expression to a spiritual mystery.

Saints. Those made 'holy' by their belief, especially the exceptionally 'good' who were 'canonized', or placed on an approved list from the Middle Ages.

Sin. Deliberate disobedience, knowingly going against God's will.

Stoicism. A philosophical system popular in the ancient world which taught calm acceptance of whatever happens.

Theism. The belief that there is a personal God who takes an interest in the world and cares about individuals.

Theology. The study of God and the universe.

Trinity. The belief that the one God is also three Persons, Father, Son and Holy Spirit.

Unitarianism. The belief that God is one and not three Persons; *see also* Trinity.

Bibliography

Sources

The works of classical authors, both Greek and Roman, had a significant influence on the formation of early Christian ideas. They are available in numerous editions and translations. Only the section reference is given in this book. Readers without Greek or Latin may find useful the Loeb series of editions of these authors (Heinemann and Harvard University Press), with English and the original language on facing pages. Most of the Latin early Christian and patristic texts and the medieval texts in Latin modern editions are available in the *Corpus Christianorum* series (CCSL and CCCM), or in the *Corpus Scriptorum Ecclesiasticorum Latinorum* (CSEL). English translations are available for some of these works.

Abelard, Peter, *Opera*, CCCM 11, 12, 13
—, *Ethics*, ed D.E. Luscombe (Oxford, 1971)
—, *Sic et non*, ed Blanche B. Boyer and Richard McKeon (Chicago, 1976-77)
—, *Collationes*, 161, ed John Marenbon and Giovanni Orlandi (Oxford, 2001)
Addison, Joseph, *Evidences of the Christian Religion* (Oxford, 1809)
Ailred of Rievaulx, *Opera*, CCCM 1 and 2
Alan of Lille, *Opera*, PL 210
—, *Theologicae regulae*, Regula, 99, PL 210.673-4
Ambrose, *Opera*, CSEL 32, 62, 64, 73, 79, 82, and bilingual edition in progress (Milan, 1977-)
Anonymous, *Expositio totius mundi et gentium*, ed J. Rougé, *Sources chrétiennes*, 124 (Paris, 1966)
Anselm, *Opera Omnia*, ed F.S. Schmitt (Rome/Edinburgh, 1938-68), 6 vols
Apponius, *In cantica canticorum*, CCSL 19
Aquinas, Thomas, *Commentary on the Pauline Epistles*, ed P. Raphael (Rome, 1953)
—, *Summa contra gentiles*, ed P. Marc (Turin, 1961-67)
—, *Summa theologiae* (Rome, 1962)

Augustine, Opera, CSEL 12, 25, 28, 33, 34, 36, 40, 41, 43, 44, 51, 52, 52, 57, 58, 60, 84, 85, 88-92, and CCSL 14, 27, 29, 30-50

Basil of Caesarea, Hexameron, 1.5, 1-3, ed A. de Mendieta and S.Y. Rudberg (Berlin, 1958)

Baldwin of Ford, Sermones, CCCM 99

Bede, Opera, CCSL 118-23.

—, Opera de temporibus, ed C.W. Jones (Cambridge, Mass., 1943)

Bernard of Clairvaux, Opera Omnia, ed J. Leclerq and H. Rochais (Rome, 1957-87)

Bernard of Cluny, in J.M. Neale (trans), Common Praise, Hymns Ancient and Modern (Canterbury Press, 2002)

Blake, William, The Marriage of Heaven and Hell, ed G. Keynes (Oxford, 1985)

—, The Complete Poems, ed A. Ostriker (London, 2004)

Boethius, Theological tractates and de consolatione philosophiae, ed and trans S.J. Tester and E.K. Rand (new edition, London, 1973)

Bonaventure, Itinerarium, I.2, ed M. Letterio (Milan, 2002), trans E. Cousins, Classics of Western Spirituality (Paulist Press, New York, 1978)

—, The Soul's Journey into God, Classics of Western Spirituality (Paulist Press, New York, 1978)

Browne, Thomas, Religio Medici (London, Everyman, 1906), and ed R.H.A. Robbins (Oxford, 1972)

Bunyan, John, Grace Abounding to the Chief of Sinners, ed R. Sharrock (Oxford, 1962)

—, The Pilgrim's Progress, ed James Blanton Wharey (Oxford, 1967)

Butler, Joseph, The Analogy of Religion, Natural and Revealed, to which are added two brief dissertations, 1. On personal identity. II On the nature of virtue (Glasgow, 1817)

Cassiodorus, Opera, CCSL 97-8

Clement of Alexandria, Opera, ed Otto Stählin (Berlin, 1936-70)

Common Praise, Hymns Ancient and Modern (Canterbury Press, 2002)

Cudworth, Ralph, The True Intellectual System of the Universe (1678, reprinted Stuttgart, 1964)

Cyprian, Opera, CCSL 3

Dante, Divina Commedia, trans A. Mandelbaum (London, 1995)

—, Monarchia, ed and trans P. Shaw (Cambridge, 1995)

Darwin, Charles, Autobiographies, ed Michael Neve and Sharon Messenger (Penguin, 1986)

—, On the Origin of Species (6th edition, London, 1994)

Donne, John, Sermons of John Donne, ed Evelyn M. Simpson and George R. Potter (California, 1962)

—, The Complete English Poems of John Donne, ed C.A. Patrides (London, 1985)

Dostoevsky, Fedor, *The Idiot* (Oxford World's Classics, 1992)

Edwards, Jonathan, *A History of the Work of Redemption* (Philadelphia, 1773)

Eliot, T.S., *Collected Poems* (London, 2002)

Eriugena, John Scotus, *Opera*, CCCM 31, 50

Eusebius, *Historia ecclesiastica*, ed G. Bardy, *Sources chrétiennes*, 55 (Paris, 1958)

Faustus of Riez, *Opera*, CSEL 21.

Glaber, Ralph, *Historiarum libri quinque*, I.3, ed John France (Oxford, 1989)

Gospel of Nicodemus, *New Testament Apocrypha*, ed W. Schneemelcher (Louisville, 1992), I

Gregory of Nyssa, PG 44

Gregory the Great, *Opera*, CCSL 140-144

——, *Dialogues*, ed A. de Vogüé and P. Antin, SC, 265 (1978-80), 2 vols

Grosseteste, Robert, *The Six Days of Creation*, trans C.F.J. Martin (London, 1996)

——, *Hexameron*, ed Richard C. Dales and Servus Gieben (London, 1982)

Hegel, G.W.F., *The Phenomenology of Mind* (1807), trans J.B. Baillie (London, 1931)

Hobbes, Thomas, *Leviathan*, ed J.C.A. Gaskin (Oxford, 1998)

Holland, Henry Scott, *Death is Nothing at All* (London, 1987)

Hugh of St Victor, *La Contemplation et ses espèces*, ed R. Baron (Paris, 1955)

——, *The Didascalicon of Hugh of St. Victor*, trans J. Taylor (Columbia, 1961)

Huxley, Aldous, *Letters of Aldous Huxley*, ed Grover Smith (Chatto and Windus, 1969)

——, *The Doors of Perception*, ed J.G. Ballard and David Bradshaw (London, 2004)

Iamblichus, *Protreptiche*, 1, ed E. de Places (Les Belles Lettres, 1989)

Isidore, *Sententiae*, PL 83

Jacobus de Voragine, *Legenda Aurea*, Latin text ed T. Graesse (1845), trans W.G. Ryan (Princeton, 1993), 2 vols

Jerome, *Opera*, CCSL 72-80

Julian of Eclanum, *Expositio libri Job*, 1.6, ed L. de Coninck and M.J. d'Hont, CCSL 88 (1977)

Kant, Immanuel, *Critique of Pure Reason*, trans J.M.D. Meiklejohn (London, 1964)

Keats, John, *Letters*, ed Maurice Buxton Forman (Oxford, 1953)

Kempis, Thomas à, *Opera*, ed M.J. Pohl (1902-22), 7 vols

Koestler, Arthur, *The Act of Creation* (Hutchinson, 1964)

Koran, trans N.J. Dawood (Penguin, 1956, reprinted 2003)

Lactantius, *Opera*, CSEL 19, 27

Langland, William, *Piers Plowman*, ed Elizabeth Salter (Oxford, 1962)

Lawrence, Brother, *The Practice of the Presence of God* (Grand Rapids, Spire Books, 2003)

Leibniz, G.W., *De summa rerum, Metaphysical Papers (1675–76)*, ed and trans G.H.R. Parkinson (Yale, 1992)

Lewis, C.S, *The Great Divorce* (London, 1945)

Locke, John, *Discourse on Miracles* (Edinburgh, 1743)

—, *The Reasonableness of Christianity*, ed John C. Higgins-Biddle (Oxford, 1999)

Lombard, Peter, *Sententiae*, Spicilegium Bonaventurianum (Grottaferrata, 1971–81), 4 vols

Luther, Martin, *Martin Luther: Selections from His Writings*, ed John Dillenberger (New York, Anchor, 1961)

—, *Table Talk*, trans William Hazlitt, introduction by Robert van de Weyer (London, 1995)

Macrobius, *Saturnalia*, ed J. Willis (Leipzig, 1963)

A *Manichean Psalm-Book*, ed C.R.C. Allberry, *Manichean Manuscripts in the Chester Beatty Collection*, II (Stuttgart, 1938)

Marvell, Andrew, Preface to second edition of *Paradise Lost*, 41–4, printed in John Leonard edition

Maximus Confessor, *Ad thalassium*, SG 7

Milton, John, *Complete Prose Works*, ed Don M. Wolf (New Haven and London, 1973)

—, *De doctrina christiana*, ed Maurice Kelley, *Complete Prose Works* (New Haven and London, 1973)

—, *Paradise Lost*, ed Philip Pullman (Oxford, 2005)

Neale, J.M. (trans), *Hymns of the Eastern Church* (2nd ed, London, 1863)

Newman, John Henry, *Essay on the Development of Christian Doctrine* (1845)

—, *Sermons Preached Before the University of Oxford*, introduction by M.K. Tillman (Notre Dane, 1996)

Origen, *De principiis*, ed P. Koetschau (1913)

Paley, William, *Natural Theology* (1802)

Pascal, *Pensées*, trans J.M. Cohen (1961)

Peter of Poitiers, *Sententie*, ed Philip S. Moore, Joseph N. Garvin and Marthe Dulong (Notre Dame, Indiana, 1943, 1950), 2 vols

Primasius, *Opera*, CCSL 91–2

Prudentius, *Opera*, CSEL 61

Rolle, Richard, *Melos amoris*, XXXI, ed E.J.F. Arnould (Oxford, 1957)

Rupert of Deutz, *Opera*, CCCM 7, 21–4, 26

Sacramentarium gelasianum, ed L.C. Mohlberg, Rerum Ecclesiasticarum Documenta, Fontes, IV (Rome, 1960)

Sayers, Dorothy L., *The Mind of the Maker* (1941), ed and introd Susan Howatch (Mowbray, 1994)

—, *The Letters of Dorothy L. Sayers*, ed Barbara Reynolds (London, 1997), vol. 2

Summa Aurea, ed J. Ribailler, Spicilegium Bonaventurianum 16–20 (Paris,

Grottaferrata, 1980–87)

The Tatler, 15 August 1710, ed J.A. Bond (Oxford, 1987)

Tertullian, *Treatise on the Resurrection*, I, ed Ernest Evans (London, 1960)

Thomas of Chobham, *Sermones*, 2, CCSM 82

—, *Summa de commendatione virtutum et extirpatione vitiorum*, IV.1.3, ed F. Morenzoni, CCCM 82B (Turnhout, 1997)

Three Byzantine Saints, trans Elizabeth Dawes and Norman H. Baynes (Oxford, 1948)

Toland, John, *Christianity not Mysterious* (London, 1696, reprinted Routledge, 1995) with Peter Browne, 'A letter in answer to Christianity not Mysterious' and an introduction by John Vladimir Price

Traherne, Thomas, *Centuries of Meditations*, ed H.M. Margoliouth (Oxford, 1958), 2 vols

Vickers, Salley, *Mr. Golightly's Holiday* (London, 2003)

Vincent of Lérins, *Commonitorium*, CCSL 64

Virgil, *Aeneid*, ed R.A.B. Mynors (Oxford, 1969)

Whichcote, Benjamin, *Select Sermons*, ed Anthony, 3rd Earl of Shaftsbury (1698), Part I, Sermon III, reprinted in C.A. Patrides, *The Cambridge Platonists* (London, 1969)

William of Auvergne, *Il 'Tractatus de Gratia' di Guglielmo d'Auvergne*, ed Guglielmo Cort (Rome, 1966)

—, *Summa Aurea*, ed J. Ribailler, Spicilegium Bonaventurianum 16–20 (Paris, Grottaferrata, 1980–87)

William of St Thierry, *Expositio super Epistolam ad Romanos*, ed P. Verdeyen, CCCM 86

—, *Oeuvres*, ed M.M. Davey, *Études de philosophie médiévale*, 29 (1940–49), 2 vols

Williams, Charles, *The Place of the Lion* (London, 1933)

Wittgenstein, Ludwig, *The Blue and Brown Books* (Oxford, 1969)

Wordsworth, William, 'Ode on Intimations of Immortality', *Oxford Book of English Verse*

—, *The Prelude*, 1798–1799, ed Stephen Parrish (Cornell, 1977)

—, *The Poems*, ed John O. Hayden (Yale, 1981)

Wyndham, John, *The Trouble with Lichen* (London, 1960, reprinted 1973)

Secondary sources

Adams, Marilyn McCord, Inaugural lecture as Regius Professor of Divinity, University of Oxford, 8 November, 2004

Alford, John A. (ed), *A Companion to Piers Plowman* (California, 1988)

Anderson, Gary A., 'The resurrection of Adam and Eve', 'In dominico eloquio', in Paul M. Blowers, Angela Russell Christman, David G. Hunter, Robin Darling Young (eds), *Lordly Eloquence: Essays in Honour of Robert Louis Wilken* (Eeerdmans, 2002), pp 3–34

Armstrong, A.H., 'Plotinus' doctrine of the infinite and its significance for Christian thought', *Downside Review*, 73 (1954/55), pp 47–58, and *Plotinian and Christian Studies* (Variorum 1979), V, p 55

Aulén, Gustav, *Christus victor* (1930), trans A.G. Hebert (London, 1931)

d'Avray, D.L, *Death and the Prince: Memorial Preaching before 1350* (Oxford, 1994)

Bodkin, Maud, *Archetypal Patterns in Poetry* (1934, reprinted Oxford, 1963, 1965)

Brent, Allen, *The Imperial Cult and the Development of Church Order, Supplements to Vigiliae Christianae* (Brill, Leiden, 1999)

Chadwick, Henry, *East and West: The Making of a Rift in the Church* (Oxford, 2003)

Chadwick, Owen, *From Bossuet to Newman* (Cambridge, 1957; 2nd edition 1987)

Chattopâdhâya, Nisikânta, *Buddhism and Christianity* (Freethought Publishing Company, London, 1882)

Chomsky, Noam, *Hegemony or Survival: America's Quest for Global Dominance* (London/New York, 2004)

Clooney, Francis X., 'Sacrifice and its spiritualization in the Christian and Hindu traditions: a study in comparative theology', *Harvard Theological Review*, 78 (1985), pp 361–80

Cobb, John B., Jnr and Griffin, David Ray, *Process Theology: An Introductory Exposition* (Belfast, 1977)

Coventry, John, *Reconciliation* (London, 1985)

Cross, Richard, *The Metaphysics of the Incarnation: Thomas Aquinas to Duns Scotus* (Oxford, 2002)

Crowther, Paul, *The Kantian Sublime* (Oxford, 1989)

Daly, Robert J., *The Origins of the Christian Doctrine of Sacrifice* (Philadelphia, Fortress, 1978)

DeLaura, David J., *Hebrew and Hellene in Victorian England: Newman, Arnold and Pater* (University of Texas Press, Austin, 1969)

Dix, G., *The Question of Anglican Orders* (1944)

Dobrée, Bonamy, *English Literature in the Early Eighteenth Century* (Oxford, 1959)

Dodaro, Robert, *Christ and the Just Society in the Age of Augustine* (Cambridge, 2004)

Dodds, E.R., *Pagan and Christian in an Age of Anxiety* (Cambridge, 1990)

Evans, G.R., *Augustine on Evil* (Cambridge, 1983)

—, *Academics and the Real World* (Buckingham, 2002)

Furley, David, *The Greek Cosmologists* (Cambridge, 1987)

Gleick, James, *Chaos: Making a New Science* (Vintage, 1998)

Goff, J. le, *La Naissance de purgatoire* (Paris, 1981), *The Birth of Purgatory*, trans A. Goldhammer (London, 1984)

Gribbin, John, *Deep Simplicity: Chaos, Complexity and the Emergence of Life* (Allen Lane, London, 2004)

Gunton, Colin, *Becoming and Being* (London, 2001, 2nd edition)

Hagendahl, H., *Latin Fathers and the Classics: A Study on the Apologists, Jerome and other Christian Writers* (Göteborg, 1958)

Harmless, William, *Desert Christians* (OUP, 2004)

Hartshorne, Charles, *The Darkness and the Light* (New York, 1990)

Henry, Desmond, *The Logic of St Anselm* (Oxford, 1967)

Horbury, William, 'The Wisdom of Solomon', in John Barton and John Muddiman (eds), *The Oxford Bible Commentary* (Oxford, 2001), pp 650-67

Javelet, R., *Image et resemblance au douzième siècle* (Letouzey, Paris, 1967), 2 vols

Johnston, Paul, *Wittgenstein: Rethinking the Inner* (London, 1993)

Kelly, J.N.D., *Early Christian Creeds* (1950)

Kiel, L. Douglas and Elliot, Euel W. (eds), *Chaos Theory in the Social Sciences: Foundations and Applications* (Ann Arbor, 1996)

Koestler, Arthur, *The Ghost in the Machine* (London, 1967)

Kuhn, Thomas S., *The Structure of Scientific Revolutions* (Chicago, 1962; 2nd edition 1970).

Logan, A.H.B., *Gnostic Truth and Christian Heresy: A Study in the History of Gnosticism* (Edinburgh, 1996)

McGrath, A.A., *Brief History of Heaven* (Oxford, 2003)

McManners, John, *Death and the Enlightenment* (Oxford, 1985)

MacMurray, John, *The Self as Agent* (London, 1957)

March, Phyllis, *Visionary Women: Ecstatic Prophecy in Seventeenth-Century England* (Berkeley, 1992)

Martin, Cohen, *Wittgenstein's Beetle* (Oxford, Blackwell, 2005)

Mohrmann, C., *Études sur le Latin des chrétiens*, 4 vols (Rome, 1958-77)

Morris, Colin, *The Discovery of the Individual, 1050-1200* (London, 1972)

Music, David W., *Hymnology: A Collection of Source Readings*, Studies in Liturgical Musicology, 4 (Scarecrow Press, London, 1996)

Painter, John, 'The Johannine literature', in Stanley E. Porter (ed), *Handbook to Exegesis of the New Testament* (Brilolo, Leiden, 1997)

Pascoe, Louis B., *Jean Gerson: Principles of Church Reform* (Leiden, 1973)

Patrides, C.A., *The Cambridge Platonists* (London, 1969)

Penrose, Roger, *The Emperor's New Mind* (Oxford, 1989)

—, *Shadows of the Mind* (Vintage, 1995)

— (ed), *The Large, the Small and the Human Mind* (Cambridge, 1997, 1999)

Pittenger, Norman, *Process-Thought and Christian Faith* (London, 1968)

Porter, Roy, *Flesh in the Age of Reason* (Penguin, 2003)

Reeves, Marjorie, *The Influence of the Prophecy in the Later Middle Ages* (Oxford, 1969)

Reynolds, Barbara (ed), *The Letters of Dorothy L. Sayers*, 4 vols (London, 1997)

Rocca, Gregory P., *Speaking the Incomprehensible God: Thomas Aquinas on the Interplay of Positive and Negative Theology* (Washington, 2004)

Rofé, Alexander, *Introduction to the Composition of the Pentateuch* (Sheffield, 1999)

Rudy, Gordon, *Mystical Language of Sensation in the Later Middle Ages* (Routledge, London, 2002)

Sayers, Dorothy L., 'The Beatrician vision in Dante and other poets', *Nottingham Medieval Studies*, 2 (1958), pp 3-23

Sayers, Stephen, 'The paradox of being', *Friends Quarterly* (July 2004), pp 118-24

Sharrock, Wes and Read, Robert, *Kuhn, Philosopher of Scientific Revolution* (Cambridge, 2002)

Sinnige, T.G., 'Plotinus on the human person and its cosmic identity', *Vigiliae Christianae*, 56 (2002), pp 292-6

Stanton, G.N., *The Gospels of Jesus* (Oxford, 1989)

Stead, Christopher, *Philosophy in Christian Antiquity* (Cambridge, 1994)

Swinburne, Richard, 'Could there be more than one God,' in *Faith and Philosophy*, 5 (1988), pp 225-41

Sykes, S.W., *The Story of Atonement* (London, 1997)

— (ed), *Sacrifice and Redemption*, Durham Essays in Theology (Cambridge, 1991)

Tentler, Thomas N., *Sin and Confession on the Eve of the Reformation* (Princeton, 1977)

Tischendorf, C. (ed), *Evangelia Apocrypha* (Leipzig, 1853)

Ward, Graham, 'Postmodern theology', in David Ford (ed), *The Modern Theologians* (Blackwell, 1997)

Weisheipl, J. A., *Friar Thomas d'Aquino* (New York/Oxford, 1974-75)

Whitehead, A.N., *Process and Reality* (Cambridge, 1927-28)

Williams, Rowan, 'Religious Lives', Romanes Lecture, Oxford, Thursday, 18 November 2004

Yates, Frances, *The Art of Memory* (London, 1969)

Index

225